The Top Gear Years

Jeremy Clarkson began his writing career on the Rotherham Advertiser. Since then he has written for the *Sun*, the *Sunday Times*, the *Rochdale Observer*, the *Wolverhampton Express & Star*, all of the Associated Kent Newspapers and *Lincolnshire Life*. Today he is the tallest person working in British television.

The Top Gear Years

JEREMY CLARKSON

MICHAEL JOSEPH
an imprint of
PENGUIN BOOKS

MICHAEL JOSEPH

Published by the Penguin Group
Penguin Books Ltd, 80 Strand, London WC2R 0RL, England
Penguin Group (USA) Inc., 375 Hudson Street, New York, New York 10014, USA
Penguin Group (Canada), 90 Eglinton Avenue East, Suite 700, Toronto, Ontario, Canada M4P 2YR
(a division of Pearson Penguin Canada Inc.)
Penguin Ireland, 25 St Stephen's Green, Dublin 2, Ireland (a division of Penguin Books Ltd)
Penguin Group (Australia), 707 Collins Street, Melbourne, Victoria 3008, Australia
(a division of Pearson Australia Group Pty Ltd)
Penguin Books India Pvt Ltd, 11 Community Centre, Panchsheel Park, New Delhi – 110 017, India
Penguin Group (NZ), 67 Apollo Drive, Rosedale, Auckland 0632, New Zealand
(a division of Pearson New Zealand Ltd)
Penguin Books (South Africa) (Pty) Ltd, Block D, Rosebank Office Park,
181 Jan Smuts Avenue, Parktown North, Gauteng 2193, South Africa

Penguin Books Ltd, Registered Offices: 80 Strand, London WC2R 0RL, England

www.penguin.com

First published 2012
001

Copyright © Jeremy Clarkson, 2012

Set in 13.5/16 pt Garamond MT Std
Typeset by Jouve (UK), Milton Keynes
Printed in Great Britain by Clays Ltd, St Ives plc

A CIP catalogue record for this book is available from the British Library

HARDBACK ISBN: 978–0–718–17685–3
OM PAPERBACK ISBN: 978–0–718–17686–0

www.greenpenguin.co.uk

ALWAYS LEARNING   **PEARSON**

For my friends

The contents of this book first appeared in Jeremy Clarkson's *Top Gear* magazine column between 1993 and 2011.

Clarkson on:

Introduction

One day, I may write an autobiography. But this isn't it. This is a collection of columns I've written since I was asked to spend a life on television, gurning and driving a bit too quickly round corners.

Some of them were written many years ago and reflected a view I held at the time. I might not necessarily hold it now because I am older and wiser. So if you disagree with what I've said, don't worry. There's every chance I disagree with myself.

Jeremy Clarkson, 2012

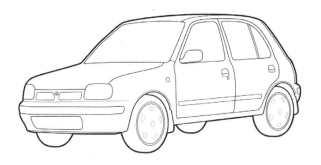

CAR OF THE YEAR: NISSAN MICRA

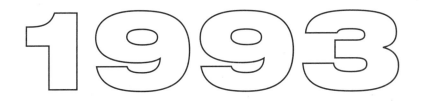

TOP 5 BESTSELLING SINGLES
SONG TITLE – ARTIST

1 I'd do anything for love (But I won't do that) – Meat Loaf
2 (I can't help) Falling in love with you – UB40
3 All that she wants – Ace of Base
4 No Limit – 2 Unlimited
5 Dreams – Gabrielle

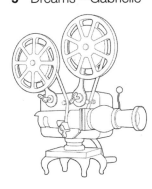

TOP 5 BOX OFFICE MOVIES

1 Jurassic Park
2 Mrs. Doubtfire
3 The Fugitive
4 The Firm
5 Sleepless in Seattle

Statistics

Several statistics can make you raise an eyebrow. When Krakatoa exploded, for instance, they heard it 13,000 miles away in the Falkland Islands. To move its own length, a modern Royal Navy destroyer uses a ton of fuel. And then there's the most startling of them all. In 100 years, cars have killed more people than every single battle that's ever been waged.

Cars are irresponsible, environmentally unsuitable, noisy and dangerous. Cars are as daft as unprotected sex, but who really wants to wear a condom? And that's why upwards of six million people regularly watch *Top Gear* on BBC2. That's also why there are 130 different publications about cars and none at all about washing machines.

In this country the driving licence is treated as a right rather than a privilege and then, when we have our pink slip, it is another right to have a car. That's why there are 22 million of them roaming the roads, killing trees, people and anything else they happen to drive past or over.

Now, with the exception of all those people on the A1 last night and anyone with an old Nissan Micra, everyone who uses a car has to have some sort of interest in it. Not necessarily in what makes it go, but in things like how much it costs to run, how fast it will go, where the nearest dealer is, how they can stop people stealing it, how to find cheap insurance and, most important, whether they can pull birds in it.

What we want to do in *Top Gear* magazine is cater for all

those interests (though we can't do much if you're a pimply seventeen-year-old and want to pull Sharon Stone).

We want to talk to the guy in the anorak and the grey shoes who's a little worried about the price of an overrider on his Maxi and we shall be addressing the old boy with the medals and the handlebar moustache who has owned an Alvis from new. People in overalls who can recite chassis numbers like I can old Monty Python sketches won't be left out either. We'll have something for the racegoer, the spotty youth who salivates over photographs of Lamborghinis, the worried father who wants to buy his eighteen-year-old daughter a used Metro and the spoiled little rich kid who can't decide whether his next car should be an Integrale or a Cosworth. It should be a Cosworth, actually.

We're going to try and be funny, which will be difficult for Quentin, and we're going to try and be serious, which is downright impossible for me.

Which is why each month this column is going to talk very little about cars and quite a lot about the evils of socialism, smoking and why it's good for you, and cricket and why it's boring. You thought I was opinionated on TV. You ain't seen nothing yet.

Occasionally, of course, there will be references to the machines you have seen me hurl all over your living room, but these will be short, to the point and free from techno-speak, for two reasons: first, I don't really know anything about engines and, second, you don't either.

You want a taster? This morning I took a 330bhp Citroën ZX Rallye Raid car round a special off-road track. It was like driving a bucking bronco through a tumble drier and the five-point seat belt hurt my testicles. After two miles I wondered about the people who drive such a car flat out across the Sahara.

And I reckoned they were probably the only people in the world who are silly enough to read this column.

As for the rest of you, I should read Quentin's. He's much better looking and he uses words like vituperative and emetic, which means he's cleverer, too.

October 1993

Norfolk

In a previous life I spent a couple of years selling Paddington Bears to toy and gift shops all over Britain. Commercial travelling was a career that didn't really suit – because I had to wear one – but I have ended up with an intimate knowledge of Britain's highways and byways.

I know how to get from Cropredy to Burghwallis and from London Apprentice to Marchington Woodlands. I know where you can park in Basingstoke and that you can't in Oxford. However, I have absolutely no recollection of Norfolk. I must have been there because I can picture, absolutely, the shops I used to call on in, er, one town in this flat and featureless county. And there's another thing, I can't remember the name of one town.

The other day I had to go to a wedding in one little town in Norfolk. It's not near anywhere you've heard of, there are no motorways that go anywhere near it, and God help you if you run out of petrol.

For 30 miles, the Cosworth ran on fumes until I encountered what would have passed for a garage forty years ago. The man referred to unleaded petrol as 'that newfangled stuff' and then, when I presented him with a credit card, looked like I'd given him a piece of myrrh.

Nevertheless, he tottered off into his shed and put it in the till, thus providing that no part of the twentieth century has caught up with Norfolk yet.

This is not surprising because it's nearly impossible to get there. From London, you have to go through places such as Hornsey and Tottenham before you find the M11, which sets off in the right direction, but then, perhaps sensibly, veers off to Cambridge. And from everywhere else you need a Camel Trophy Land Rover.

Then, when you get there and you're sitting around in the hotel lobby waiting for the local man to stop being a window cleaner, gynaecologist and town crier and be a receptionist for a while, you pick up a copy of *Norfolk Life*. It is the world's smallest magazine.

In the bar that night, when we said we had been to a wedding in Thorndon, everyone stopped talking. A dart hit the ceiling and the man behind the counter dropped a glass. 'No one,' he said, 'has been to Thorndon since it burned down forty years back.' Then he went off, muttering about the 'widow woman'.

Moving about Norfolk, however, can be fun. I am used to having people point as I go by. Most shout, 'Hey, look, it's a Cosworth!' but in Norfolk they shout, 'Hey, look, it's a car!'

Everywhere else people want to know how fast it goes, but in Norfolk they asked how good it was at ploughing. The spoiler fascinated them because they reckoned it might be some sort of crop sprayer.

I'm sure witchcraft has something to do with it. The government should stop promoting the Broads as a tourist attraction and they should advise visitors that 'here be witches'.

They spend millions telling us that it is foolish to smoke, but not a penny telling us not to go to Norfolk – unless you like orgies and the ritual slaying of farmyard animals.

The next time some friends get married in Norfolk, I'll send a telegram. Except, it won't get there because they haven't heard of the telephone yet. Or paper. Or ink.

December 1993

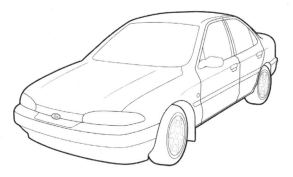

CAR OF THE YEAR: FORD MONDEO

1994

TOP 5 BESTSELLING SINGLES
SONG TITLE – ARTIST

1 Love Is All Around – Wet Wet Wet
2 Saturday Night – Whigfield
3 Baby Come Back – Pato Banton
4 Stay Another Day – East 17
5 I Swear – All 4 One

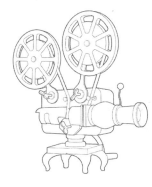

TOP 5 BOX OFFICE MOVIES

1 Forrest Gump
2 The Lion King
3 True Lies
4 The Santa Clause
5 The Flintstones

Babies

So there I was, standing around in the crush bar at Pebble Mill, when my wife telephoned to say that she was pregnant. Initially, I was pleased because it meant all my bits work properly, but then I was hit by wave after wave of problems. So great is the list that after six cups of hot sweet tea and some Marlboro, I began to wish that the bits had been surgically removed at birth, like we should do with stupid people.

It isn't so much that I will now have to wait until 2110 before I get a decent night's sleep, or even that every penny I earn will be gobbled up by the perverts and beardies who run whatever public school we choose. (And that's only if we have any money left after the unavoidably massive investment in Pampers, Fisher Price and a pouting sixteen-year-old Swedish au pair has bled our bank account dry.)

Already, we are arguing about names. I like the idea of Boadicea if it's a girl or Rumpelstiltskin if it isn't, but this has gone down about as well as the idea of a sixteen-year-old blonde locked up in the house with me all day.

I keep trying to point out that I'll be far too tired for any horizontal jogging with the staff after I've been up all night long wiping vomit and faeces off the walls. But despite my protests I have been told, quite firmly in fact, that the nanny will be a moose, or there will be no nanny at all.

The rows, however, are not the worst aspect of babydom. Nor do we mind very much that the days when we can simply disappear off to California are over. Sure, we could take the child, too, but I really do believe that no one should ever be allowed to take a baby on a long-haul flight.

Airlines ban smoking because it inconveniences other passengers, yet children are allowed to howl all the way from Cornwall to Nova Scotia.

Babies should be carried in soundproof boxes stowed safely in the hold, and as I don't want my baby in a box, it won't be going on an aeroplane. And that means we won't either.

We won't be much fun at dinner parties. Like every other couple that has ever spawned a child, we will be able to talk of nothing else, which will make us dull and tedious. I may even start wearing corduroy.

Certainly, I shall need to go to church and renounce the devil. But all this, we can live with.

What sends Mrs Clarkson scuttling for the Gordon's and the coathangers is the mere mention of the 'V' word.

What we find difficult is the thought of a Volvo. The Cosworth we have as a second car only has two doors and will be no good as a pram, despite the large handle on the back. And anyway, thieves keep breaking into it, so it will have to go.

My Jaguar has enough doors and space to be a sort of wheeled playroom, but I will ruin its caddish image by fitting baby seats, so we need something else.

And if we're going to be dull and tedious, and wear corduroy, and have no money, and if we're going to carry on living in south-west London, and if we're going to conform on every other front, too, then it will have to be a Volvo, with a 'Baby on Board' sticker and maybe even an animal of some sort on the bonnet.

Got to go now. I can hear the unmistakable sound of boiling water being poured into an already hot bath.

March 1994

Motoring journalism

Such has been the volume of letters from small boys recently that I'm thinking of changing the name of my house to Neverland. It seems everyone under the age of fourteen would hack off parts of their bodies to have my job.

Two things, though. First, I haven't finished with it yet. And second, while I do spend a lot of time driving Ferraris and Aston Martins, I spend even more time explaining to people how they can, too. And this is how.

First of all, get back to basics. It doesn't matter if you have nine illegitimate children or sleep with your sister, but you must be able to spell. Sadly, most people who write to us can't. Without wanting to be racist, a grasp of the local dialect comes in handy, too. I know they let you learn all sorts of exotic languages these days, but most of Britain's motoring magazines, except *Max Power*, are written in English. So do a GCSE in it at least.

When you finally extricate yourself from education, your best bet is to try for a job on a local newspaper. The three or so years you spend on a local rag will give you a grasp of wedding fashion, pony clubs, vegetable contests and – most important of all – the ability to tell a story.

As a qualified journalist, you may then go for a job on a national newspaper. But, almost without exception, they use motoring features from freelancers who have been in the business for an aeon. So if you still want to write about cars, your best bet is one of the 130 motoring magazines. Make your letter short, to the point and obsequious. And don't give up.

Write stories about your car and send them in. If they're good, we'll use them. Then we might ask for another, or even give you a trial. But be warned, we're the biggest and we only have a full-time writing staff of five, including the editor. There are more astronauts than motoring magazine journalists.

And I'll let you into a little secret. We never talk about cars in the pub at lunchtime. We don't care what sort of car we drive home in at night. We like cars, but we don't wear anoraks. If you do have an anorak, try *Autocar*.

Those who float, like cream, to the top of this profession are wordsmiths – people who can turn their hands as easily to a Lamborghini as to a parish council meeting. Our features editor, for instance, failed his test four times and drove a Datsun Sunny for years. When he started, he knew less about cars than Barbara Cartland knows about shot-blasting. It doesn't matter if you can tell a Lantra from a Corolla, or if you can strip an MG to its component parts in seven seconds, or if you can reel off every Ferrari's 0–60 time from memory. If you can't write, you can't come in.

Unless, of course, you are a girl with the morals of a rabbit and are able to send us the sort of cheque that would make Littlewoods blanch. In which case, you start on Monday.

April 1994

Michael Schumacher

Michael Schumacher is a German. Which means that he should, by rights, be fat, loud, vulgar and in possession of some ridiculous clothes to go with his absurd facial hair.

Yet his torso is the shape of Dairylea cheese, and his face is unburdened with any form of topiary. At post-race press conferences, he is intelligent and modest when he wins, and quick to congratulate when he doesn't.

So when I met him at Silverstone this month I was rather disappointed to note that he was surly, impatient and about as communicative as that Red Indian chappie in *One Flew Over the Cuckoo's Nest*. I have had more inspiring conversations with my pot plants. And they're dead.

I told him my wife hoped he would be world champion, and he gave me a look that made me think I'd inadvertently said, 'You are the most disgusting human being I have ever had the misfortune to encounter.'

Later I tried again, asking him what he thought of the Mustang. Which, judging by his reaction, translates into German as 'I know that you like little boys and I'm going to tell your team manager unless you give me some money'. Had he driven a Mustang before, I asked, fully expecting another withering glance from the driver's seat. 'Yes,' came the reply. 'Where?' I asked, not realizing that 'where' in German means 'I hope you fall into a combine harvester, you maggot-faced creep'.

So I gave up with the conversation and settled back to

watch the fastest man in Formula One deal with the slowest sports car in the world.

On lap one there were other cars on the track so we pottered round. Then on lap two, instead of giving me the ride of my life, Mr Schumacher chose to demonstrate the driving positions.

On lap three, we were following *Top Gear*'s camera car, so I asked if we could see some wild and leery tailslides. We did, but sadly each one ended up with a spin. I couldn't help wondering if these gyrations might have been avoided if Mr Schumacher had kept both hands on the wheel. But who am I to question the ability of the greatest driver Germany has ever produced?

The new Mustang's body is not particularly pretty or brutal, but it is big and eyecatching. Everyone turns to look and everyone knew what it was, even though this was the first in Britain.

To drive, it's American and rather good in a cheesy grin, firm handshake, hi, howya doin' sort of way. It's a big, open, honest sort of car that, despite the air conditioning, cruise control, power seats, power windows, power roof and five-litre V8 engine, costs just $22,000 in the USA.

It's not very fast – ask it to go beyond 130 and it gives you a look of pure incredulity – and it treats corners with the same disdain I reserve for vegetarians.

It will do everything in its power to go straight on, but there's never a moment when you think it might go round a bend, so there are no surprises. You know where you are with this car.

It also makes a good noise, unless you take it past 3,500rpm when it sounds strangled. But hey, have you ever heard Stallone hit a high C?

No, the Mustang is muscle-bound, dim-witted and slow, but it's a good guy to have around town at night, looking mean and threatening.

It's the automotive equivalent of Carlsberg Special, which is probably the reason why Mr Schumacher was so underwhelmed. He, after all, is sponsored by Mild Seven which are the most limp and pathetic cigarettes I have ever encountered. They have about as much to do with hairy-armed Mustangs as fish.

And apart from muttering about how the Mustang had plenty of grip and wasn't bad for an American car, he told me nothing about what it was like to drive. So I set off on my own, and fell head over heels in love.

September 1994

Iceland

Greetings from Iceland, the land of fire and ice. It's 11 o'clock at night, and outside the sun is beating down on the roofscape of the world's most northerly capital city.

I'm drinking a glass of scotch which cost twelve quid and I've just finished reading the wedding vows I took to see if there's a get-out clause – the women here are just unbelievable. It said in *The Times* last week that they're good enough to give any one of the top supermodels a complex, but this is a terrible understatement. If Elle Macpherson turned up here, people would be sick all over her.

I interviewed Miss World last night and I panted from start to finish. After five minutes, my knees had all the rigidity of custard – and she's the second ugliest girl here, after Björk.

The producer had only been here five minutes when a young woman, right under her mother's nose, asked if he'd had an Icelandic girl yet. She then went on to explain why it would be a fine idea. Maybe he'd like to try out her mother!

TV soundmen are normally shy and mysterious, and our man Murray is no different, but as he strolled the streets of Reykjavik at 4 a.m., waving his Dougal around, he was Mel Gibson in a diamond jumper, Tom Cruise in Rohans. Young girls wanted to have his babies.

The countryside is beautiful and quiet, geological lunacy from start to finish, and the roads are even more spectacular than the women. Road One is a 1,500 kilometre ribbon of asphalt that circumnavigates the entire island, cutting a tortured, sinewy path through the lava fields and the volcanoes and the vast fields of ash. It may have a 90kph limit, but on most stretches, that's fast enough. And just in case you were wondering, there is no Road Two.

Of all the cities I've ever been to, Reykjavik is by far the most alive. During the summer, the entire population of 120,000 goes out for a party every Friday and Saturday night. It is held on the streets, in the clubs and in people's houses, and it goes on until work resumes on Monday morning. You can get very drunk over here.

But the thing is, no-one drinks and drives. Yes, it's against the law and yes, the penalties are severe, but that is irrelevant. No one drives while drunk in Iceland because there's a strong possibility that you'll know the person you've just run over. And if you don't know them, you'll definitely know someone who does.

Feeling duty-bound to go to the funeral of someone you've killed is a sure-fire way of ensuring you take every precaution to make sure you don't kill them in the first place.

The trouble is, of course, that it would never work here. We all live in suburbs and the only time we see our neighbours is when their curtains twitch a bit. Anyone who attempts to open a restaurant or a bar in a suburb can be assured that when they sell it, ten years later, it will be as-new because suburban types feel that if they go out, it has to be in the bright lights of the big city.

And therein lies our problem. We can't afford to use taxis, the buses are full of the working classes and Jimmy Knapp has finished off what Lord Beeching started with the railways.

The car is our only realistic means of transport, especially for single young women who are fearful of what might happen in a dark bus shelter at 3 o'clock in the morning. The last reported sex crime in Iceland, by the way, was in 1962. But you can't take the car because you can't have a very good time if you can't drink. And you can't drink because you're not allowed to drink and drive.

So people either stay in at night with their lamb chops and their TV guides, or else they get into their cars and drive around drunk. And neither option makes Britain a particularly spectacular place to live.

But look, there's a way round the problem. If the best that your village can manage is a trivial pursuit quiz every Thursday down at the local, and every girl in the place looks like a tractor, don't feel you have to move to some dreadful, characterless suburb just so you can be five miles from some God-awful town centre.

There is an alternative. All you have to do is develop a fondness for eating whales and move to Iceland. And if you find our sound man up there, tell him to come home.

November 1994

Bob Seger

Last night, in one of the world's five great cities, I shared an alligator with Bob Seger.

Ever since that long hot summer of 1976, when I ricocheted around Staffordshire desperately trying to shake off those awkward teenage blues, I have worshipped the ground on which old Bob has walked.

I know that it's desperately trainspotterish to have heroes, but here we have a man whose lyrics are pure poetry, whose melodies are a match for anything dreamed up by Elgar or Chopin and whose live act is, quite simply, the best in the world.

After a gig at the Hammersmith Odeon in London in 1977, the manager wrote to *Melody Maker* to say that in all his years, he had never seen a better concert. I was there and it was even better than that.

And there I was, eighteen years later, in a restaurant in downtown Detroit, sharing a piece of battered alligator with the man himself. My tongue wasn't just tied, it looked like a corkscrew. I wanted to talk music, but Bob's a chatterbox with the laugh of a cement mixer, and he wanted to talk cars. He was born in Detroit and, apart from a brief spell in LA, which he hated, he's lived there all his life.

He argued, quite forcefully, that if you're a Detroiter, you are bound to be part man and part V8. The only jobs are in car factories, all your neighbours work there, and the only way to escape the production line is music. It's no coincidence that Motown began in the Motor City.

The buses move around empty, as does the hopeless monorail. The train station is derelict. Everyone drives a car in Detroit because cars are everyone's soul. And Bob Seger is no exception.

A point that's hammered home by the GMC Typhoon in which the great man had arrived. He has a brace of Suzuki motorcycles on which he tears around the States, getting inspiration for songs like 'Roll Me Away', but for family trips to Safeway he uses the 285bhp, four-wheel-drive truck – you may remember that we took its pickup sister, the Syclone, to a drag race on *Top Gear* last year.

Bob's mate, Dennis Quaid, has one too apparently, which made me itch to ask what Meg Ryan was like – they're married to one another – but Bob was off again, telling us between mouthfuls of reptile how things used to be in Detroit, how he used to go and race tuned-up muscle cars between the lights, how a side exhaust gave an extra 15bhp and how they posted lookouts for the cops.

This was heaven. The man I've most wanted to meet for nearly twenty years is a car freak, but the best was still to come. When we'd finished dinner, he sat back and pulled a pack of Marlboro from his pocket. He smokes, too! And so, he added, does Whitney Houston. By this stage, I had regressed to the point where I could easily have been mistaken for a four-year-old boy – I may have even wet myself slightly – but the full flood was saved until later that night.

Do they, I enquired gingerly, still race their cars on the streets. 'Oh sure,' came the reply. 'Most Friday and Saturday nights up on Woodward you can find some races going down.'

And this, I'm happy to tell you, was not just some rock-star-close-to-your-roots-SOB. Because they do.

Big money changes hands as a hundred or more guys turn up in Chargers and Road Runners and God knows what else. And then, from midnight until dawn, they simply line up at the lights, wait for the green and go. We watched it all, and happily, from your point of view, we filmed it too for a new series called *Motorworld*.

We learned, too, that in days gone by, the big three American car manufacturers used to take their new, hot cars to these races to see how quick they were. And that, even today, engineers may sneak a new development engine out of the factory and down to Woodward to see if it can cut the mustard.

And all this is set to a backdrop of Martha Reeves, Marvin Gaye, Smokey Robinson, Don Henley, Ted Nugent and Bob Seger – plus the thousand or so other stars that were born and raised in the Motor City.

And we have Longbridge and Take That. Which makes me want to throw up.

December 1994

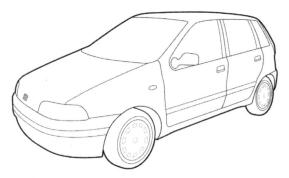

CAR OF THE YEAR: FIAT PUNTO

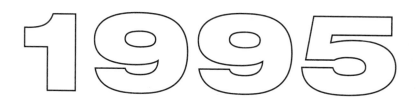

TOP 5 BESTSELLING SINGLES
SONG TITLE – ARTIST

1 Unchained Melody/ White Cliffs of Dover – Robson and Jerome
2 Gangsta's Paradise – Coolio featuring LV
3 I Believe – Robson and Jerome
4 Back For Good - Take That
5 Think Twice – Celine Dion

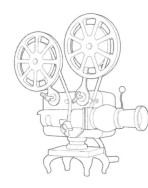

TOP 5 BOX OFFICE MOVIES

1 Toy Story
2 Batman Forever
3 Apollo 13
4 Pocahontas
5 Ace Ventura: When Nature Calls

Books

Quentin Willson has read a great many books and is prone to inserting large and complicated pieces of Shakespeare into normal conversation. My wife's bedside book table, on the other hand, is filled entirely with those orange-spined Penguin Classics, all of which are about women in bee-keeper hats who walk around fields full of poppies, doing nothing. These make for good bedtime reading, only on the basis that you need to go to sleep. 'A Saturday afternoon in November was approaching the time of twilight and the vast, unenclozzzzzzz . . .'

With Quentin's books, I'd have to spend the whole time buried in a dictionary, finding out what all the words meant. The guy reads Chaucer for fun, for Chrissakes!

All my books have either a submarine or a jet fighter on the front and they're full of goodies who seem like they're going to lose but who, on the last page, do in fact win. I like plots, and Hardy wouldn't recognize a plot if one jumped out of a hedge and ate his foot. A book is no good, as far as I'm concerned, unless I just cannot put it down. I missed a plane once – on purpose – because I was still sitting at home finishing *Red Storm Rising*. If Princess Diana had walked into my bedroom naked as a jaybird just as I was three quarters of the way through *The Devil's Advocate*, I wouldn't have looked up long enough even to tell her to get lost. My wife, however, has just taken two years – yes, years – to read *Wild Swans*, which is about a woman in China who has a daughter who goes to live somewhere else.

But I have just read a book which has no plot, no F-16 on the cover, no goodies, no baddies, and I absolutely loved it. Which is a bit of a worry. It's called *Rivethead* and it's by an American person called Ben Hamper who, in the review section, describes it as 'an enormously enjoyable read. I laughed. I cried. I learned. I got naked and performed cartwheels for my repulsed neighbours'. My kinda guy.

Basically, *Rivethead* is the story of one man; a man who gets up every morning and goes to work at the General Motors truck and bus plant in Flint, Michigan. Really, it should have an orange spine, but mercifully it doesn't. Because if it did, I never would have heard about GM's answer to the Japanese threat. You see, when American cars were being sold with tuna sandwiches under the driver's seat and coke bottles rattling in the doors, GM decided it must impress on its workforce the need for better standards. The workforce, largely, was a doped-up bunch of ne'er-do-wells who thought only of their weekly pay cheques and how much beer they could cram in at lunchtime, which is why GM's decision to have a man dress up as a cat and prowl the aisles, spurring people on, is a trifle odd. That they called him Howie Makem is stranger still.

Equally peculiar was the later scheme, which involved the erection of several sizeable electronic noticeboards all over the plant. These kept people informed of sales, production figures and such, but could also be used for messages. One day it would say, 'Quality is the backbone of good workmanship', and on another, 'Safety is safe', but Hamper saves his vitriol for the day when he looked up from underneath a suburban pickup to see the sign, 'Squeezing rivets is fun!'

He goes on to wonder whether, in the local sewage works, there are boards telling the guys that 'Shovelling turds is fun'. And asks why, if the 'demented pimps' who had dreamed up this message thought riveting was so much fun, they weren't all down on the line every lunchtime, having the time of their lives.

Hamper also lays into the likes of Springsteen and John Cougar Mellonfarm, asking what they know about the daily grind. He says they should be forced to write about things they understand, like cocaine orgies, beluga caviar and tax shelters.

I made an exception and read this book because I am interested in the car industry, but I can recommend it to you even if you have never been in a car plant, and don't ever intend to.

I tried to get Quentin to read it, but as the first word is 'dead' and not 'sibilance', he said he couldn't be bothered . . . and asked how Janet and John were these days.

January 1995

Rallying

This is what it said on the first page of my joining pack for the world's weirdest motorsport event: 'Rallying has never featured very significantly in the lives of blind people.'

No, and neither will it. Men can't have babies. Fish can't design submarines. BBC producers can't make up their minds. And blind people don't make very good rally drivers.

However, they can navigate. More than that, in the last six years there have been twenty-five rallies in India where the co-drivers have had more in common with a bat than Tony Mason.

Now, to be perfectly honest, I'm not talking about the sort of rally where the car's wheels only ever touch the ground in service halts. No, this sort is best desbribed as a treasure hunt.

Even so, disappointingly, there are rules, the worst of which is that all cars must be fitted with seat belts. This meant that when I took part there were only sixty-six competitors, which isn't good enough in a country with nine million blind people.

But hey, I'm used to rules and the best way round them is to indulge in a bit of Boss Hoggery. I figured that if I nicked the notes from the navigator, he'd never know and we'd win. But the organisers had that one covered; all the directions were in Braille, a language which means as much to me as Swahili or German. Like everyone else, we had to use the force. But unlike everyone else, we went wrong at the very first turn.

Let me explain. The Braille was in English and this was not a language that featured on my co-driver's CV. So he spelled out each instruction, letter by agonizingly slow letter.

Thus we left the base and headed off towards the centre of Madras in our Maruti Gypsy, with Mr Padmanabhan muttering t-y-r-d-i-n-a-k-l-m-t-e-y-r-l-e-f-f. Which, if you have a pen and a piece of paper and a fortnight, you could work out meant turn left in a kilometer.

Trouble was it took me nearly five miles to figure it out, by which time we were completely and hopelessly lost. Not only do I not speak Braille but my Tamil's not that good either. And there I was, with a blind man, in a city I've never been to before (and never want to go to again incidentally), on the same land mass, worryingly, as Portugal and Yemen. Things could go wrong here.

We'd be drifting down a road and, all of a sudden, Mr Padmanabhan would look up from his notes to ask, 'What is l-k-j-r-i-j-l-s-s-s-a-e-q-j-t?' And to be honest, there isn't really much of an answer.

But somehow, and I guess quite by chance, we did happen upon a checkpoint. Relieved, I wound down the window and asked just how far behind we were. But here's a funny thing; they said we were the first to come through, which was strange as we'd been the last to leave.

However, it all became crystal clear when they told us that we were at checkpoint six and that we had somehow missed one to five. I knew damn well how we'd missed them. We'd been in Tibet.

Nevertheless, we ploughed on until suddenly I was told to

stop. 'We are now at checkpoint seven,' he said. But we weren't. We were in the middle of an industrial estate, and it's hard to point out to a blind man that he's gone wrong. Again.

'I'm sorry,' I said, 'but we're not.'

'Yes we are,' he insisted. And to avoid hurting his feelings, I had to leap out of the car to get my card stamped by a non-existent official at a checkpoint that wasn't there.

'Told you so,' he said when I got back in the car.

Back at base, the event over, we learned that we'd been scrubbed from the running order altogether, on the basis that we'd only found one of the checkpoints. They all figured we'd given up and gone home. We didn't even get any lunch, which was no bad thing because it seemed to consist of still-born blackbirds which had been trodden on then coated with curry powder, bay leaves and ginger.

Oh how we all laughed as the navigators tried to pick bits of beak out of their teeth. And oh how they all laughed as they reminisced about how hopeless all their drivers were.

We must see this sport in Britain. All you Round Table, Rotarian types, stop pushing beds up the high street, jack in the three-legged pub crawls and give the RNIB a call. And then call me to say where and when.

February 1995

The MGF

At a major league party, there are certain rules you won't find in any book on etiquette. And the most important one is this: when called upon to move into the dining room for dinner, never arrive at the table first because you will have no control over who sits next to you.

And don't get there last either, because when there's only one space left, you can be assured that the people on either side of it will be ghastly.

Unless you pay attention to these simple rules you could find yourself sandwiched between a footballer and a vegetarian. Or a homosexual and a lay preacher. Or a caravanner and a socialist. There are any number of shiversome combinations, but the absolute worst is finding yourself between two members of the MG Owners' Club.

For a kick-off they will have beards, bits of which will fall in your soup. And because they like fresh air, they are likely to be vegetarians. This means you'll be told, at length, about the plight of dewy-eyed veal calves and baby foxes with pointy ears and snuggly tails . . . and chicken feathers stuck to their rabid fangs. By the time their nut cutlet is served, the subject will have turned to their horrid cars.

Now, you and I know the old MG was a gutless bucket of rust that leaked every time it rained, broke down every time it was cold and overheated every time the sun put his hat on. It turned with the agility of a charging rhino, stopped with the panache of a supertanker and drank leaded fuel as though it had a Chevy V8 under the bonnet.

However, our bearded friends don't see it quite like this. These people actually enjoy the frequent breakdowns because it gives them an excuse to get under the damn thing.

And then, in the pub that night, they can talk liberally about exactly what went wrong and precisely how they fixed it. To you and I a track rod end is very probably the dullest thing in the world, but to MG Man it is a steel deity, an almost religious icon, an automotive Fabergé egg.

MG man can talk about a track rod end for two hours without repetition or hesitation. And the only reason he stops after two hours is because you've shot him. MG fanatics are the people that give all car enthusiasts a bad name. These days you only need mention that you like cars – meaning that you'd buy a Ferrari if you won the lottery – and the person you're talking to will run away screaming.

They'll recall a conversation they once had about track rod ends and will assume that you're about to do the same, that you are a member of CAMRA and that you only drink beer if it has some mud in it.

For this reason, I am concerned about the new MG. If you can be labelled an anorak for simply liking cars, can you begin to imagine how you will be spurned if you walk into the pub brandishing an MG key ring?

Other people at the bar will conclude that you have a Seventies Midget in the car park and that you're about to regale them with the interesting tale of how you adjusted the timing that morning. They will all feign illness or urgent appointments so they can get out.

Except, of course, for the landlord, who'll be stuck. His only escape is suicide. He may even impale himself on his hand pump levers and die horribly without even realizing that, in fact, you have a new MG.

I don't doubt that this is a wonderful car, what with its clever engine, cleverly arranged between the axles. It is lovely to look at, too, and those white dials make what's an ordinary interior look a bit special.

I feel sure that the hood won't leak and that, mechanically, the MGF will be as bulletproof as your fridge. And though no journalist has driven it yet – contrary to what many would have you believe – I don't doubt that it will handle tidily and be fast.

And it's British, which automatically makes it better than the Barchetta and the Speeder and the MX-5 and the SLK and the Z3 and all the other roadsters that are due to be launched in the coming months.

The trouble is, though, that if you do buy one of the new foreign convertibles, you will be perceived as someone whose feet are loose and whose fancy is free. But if you go, instead, for anything with an MG badge on the bonnet, people will think you are a git.

May 1995

The Ford GT40

Back in 1962, Enzo Ferrari was trying to sell his company and Henry Ford was in the frame to buy it. The talks were going well and a deal was only days away when the old man decided that his pride and joy would wither and die under the weight of Ford's global bureaucracy.

Mr Ford was livid and told his Brylcreemed designers to build a car that would make mincemeat out of the Ferraris at Le Mans. He was going to teach that Eye-tie Dago a lesson he wouldn't forget.

The bunch of fives came in the shape of the GT40 which, in various guises, won the 24-Hours four times.

Now, ever since I was old enough to run round in small circles, clutching at my private parts, I have been a huge fan of Ferrari and especially the 250 LM. But here was a Ford that was beating it.

The GT40 became my favourite car and I would plead with my dad to buy a Cortina to replace the last one he'd crashed. Ford need the money, I'd argue, to build more GT40s.

I had three Dinky Toy GT40s and my bedroom wall was plastered with pictures of them. I even sat in one once, when I was eight or so, and decided there and then it would be the car I'd have one day.

Like the Lamborghini Miura, which was also built to spite Enzo Ferrari, it came from a time when car design was at its peak. Look at a McLaren or a Diablo today and tell me they have the sheer sexiness of a Sixties supercar.

There have been loads of good-looking cars since, but none has had quite such dramatic lines as the GT40 – I'm talking about the racers, not the elongated and muted Mark 3 car.

I was at the Goodwood Festival of Speed earlier in the summer and, though there were many stunning cars squealing up that hill, I maintain that the GT40 was best. Yes indeed, the best-looking car of all time.

And fast, too. 0–60mph took 5.4 seconds and you could get the needle round to the 170mph quadrant on the M1, should you choose. There were no speed limits then, because homosexuality hadn't been invented.

It was also a proper engine. I've always subscribed to the view that there ain't no substitute for cubes and here was a car with 7,000 of them in a rumbling V8 package.

And there it was, in the grounds of the Elms Hotel in Abberley, fuelled and ready. The keys were in my hand, the sun was shining, the temptation to run round in circles was large. I was going to realize a thirty-year-old dream and actually drive a GT40; and I didn't really care that it was a 300bhp, 4.7-litre, Mustang-engined road car with a boot.

Ford had only made seven of the things before the American magazine *Road & Track* said it was a badly made crock of donkey dung and the plug was pulled. And I, the man who loves the GT40 the most, was going to use it to tear up some tarmac.

Actually, I wasn't. For the first time in ten years of road-testing cars, I had to admit, after desperate struggling, that I am just too tall. And no, it wasn't a Mansell whinge about being uncomfortable. I was simply unable to get my knees under the dash, my head under the roof or my feet anywhere near the pedals.

If you'd put a pint in front of John McCarthy when he stepped off that plane from Beirut and then peed in it when he was about to take a swig, he would have been less disappointed.

But now I'm glad. Yes, I'm happy that Ford made the car only suitable for hamsters and other small rodents. I'm happy that my trip to Worcester was a waste of time and that I had to rewrite the item I'd written for the programme. I'm delighted that I shall go to my grave never having driven a GT40, because the dream will never be tarnished with a dose of reality.

Vanessa Redgrave was my childhood film star idol and now I've learned she is the sort of woman who probably doesn't shave her armpits. Then there was the Ferrari Daytona, another car I'd wanted to drive since I was old enough to use crockery, but which actually feels like it should sport a Seddon Atkinson badge.

So, if you're a child longing for the day when you can get behind the wheel of a McLaren or a Diablo, may I suggest you stand in a bucket of Fison's Make it Grow. Because by the time you're old enough they will have been made to feel old and awful by the hatchback you use every day.

September 1995

Big Foot

After a million or so years doing nothing, man really seemed to be coming along in the last hundred or so. He motorized his wheels, sprouted wings, went to the moon and, best of all, he invented the fax. But in the last twenty years it all seems to have stopped. Where's the follow-up to Concorde? When are we off to Mars? What comes after rock 'n' roll?

I blame miniaturization. Clever people have stopped inventing things and started making what we've already got, only smaller. When I had a hi-fi system in the Seventies, it was a massive, teak thing with an arm like something from the Tyneside docks. But today, you need tweezers to hit the buttons and Jodrell Bank to see the read-outs.

Then there are cameras. I saw a guy in the States last month with a device that was actually lighter than air. Had he dropped it, it would have floated, which is perhaps a good thing, but honestly, you can't beat my Nikon, which needs its own team of baggage handlers at the airport.

And then there's Kate Moss.

Well look. I like big breasts, a big amount of food on my plate and I'd much rather watch *Terminator 2* at the cinema than on video. I also like big cars, a point rammed home this month when I drove Big Foot.

First of all, its nine-litre V8 gets through alcohol at the rate of five gallons for every 300 yards. This is good stuff. This is 29 gallons to the mile and that makes it by far the least economical vehicle in the world.

It's fast, too. No one has ever done any performance tests, but having done a full-bore, full-power standing start, I can report that we are talking 0–60 in about four seconds.

This is impressive in any car, but it's especially noteworthy in something that has tyres that are over six feet tall. To get in, you climb up through the chassis, emerging into the cockpit through a trapdoor in the perspex floor. Everything about the pickup truck body perched up there on the top is fake. It's just a plastic facsimile of a real Ford F-150 – not even the doors open.

There's just one, centrally mounted seat with a full, five-point racing harness and about 2,500 dials in front. There are warning lights too, each of which was carefully identified by my tutor before I was allowed to set off. But I didn't listen to a word he said.

Nor did I pay attention when he talked me though the gearbox. It's an auto but, though there's no clutch, you do have to pull the lever back each time you want to shift up. And that was the problem: pull is the wrong word. You are supposed to wrench it back, as I was soon to discover.

With the lecture over and my neck brace in place, the instructor was disappearing through the trapdoor when he turned and said, 'Have you ever driven a fast car before?' I told him I'd driven a Diablo and he left, wearing a peculiar smile on his face.

To fire that mid-mounted towerblock of an engine, you just hit a big rubber knob and then thank God you're wearing a helmet. It's loud, like a hovering Harrier, and when you hit the throttle it sends your vision all wobbly.

About one second into what felt like an interstellar voyage, various dials and the noise suggested a gear change might not be such a bad idea, so I eased the lever back. Nothing happened. The revs kept on building, so I tried again. Nothing, except this time, a selection of warning lights came on.

By now I was in a temper, so I yanked the lever back and the truck just seemed to explode forward. This could catch a Diablo and run over it.

And even though it was on wet grass, it seemed to 'dig and grip' pretty well. I never did find out how well, though, because by then I was struggling for third and may have hit first instead. I was in Vermont, but people in Gibraltar heard the bang.

They gave me another five minutes before the people from Ford hit their remote shut down button and the engine died. I was going to give them hell, but decided to run away instead when I noticed the rev counter telltale said I'd taken the £100,000, nine-litre motor to 10,000rpm.

I didn't stop running until I was in Chicago, where I decided that Big Feet (is that the plural?) are wasted at exhibitions, jumping over saloon cars. We should use them for trips into town. I'm about to move to Chipping Norton where, I'm sure, it'll go down a storm.

November 1995

Texas

Look, when you go to pick your car up from a service and it isn't ready, accept it, in the same way you expect pain at the dentist.

And thank your lucky stars you don't live in Lubbock, Texas.

Most years I go to America six or seven times and, usually, I have a good time. But this is because I often end up in San Francisco, which is one of the world's three greatest cities, or Detroit, which is heaven, or Colorado, where the skiing is fine and the views are pointy.

Key West was good too, even though most of the men have an odd habit of holding hands and Michael Barrymore was staying in our hotel. I like New England as well, and for sheer geological lunacy Utah gets quite close to Iceland.

But Lubbock was my first experience of the 'real' America. Stuck in the middle of Texas, it is basically a collection of grain towers sticking out of a trailer park. As far as claims to fame go, it is Buddy Holly's birthplace, and that's it.

However, it was in Lubbock that I met Bill Clement, the bolshiest car dealer ever to call a customer shit-head. Above the door to his premises, which are on Martin Luther King – or 'Kink' as he puts it – Boulevard, there is a sign saying who is not allowed in. It's too long to list here, but basically, it includes everyone from wives and girlfriends to preachers, politicians and smokers. Bleeding hearts, collegiates and long hairs are also not welcome. And to make sure you stay outside the barbed wire fence, the gate is padlocked with a device that would foil even Q.

If you shout for attention or, worse, blow your horn, Bill will open his office window and empty a .44 into your chest. I'm not kidding. In Texas, you are allowed to shoot anyone who commits criminal mischief on your property in the hours of darkness.

The last person who tried to break into Bill's garage was a young black guy from 'N*****-town'. 'He got an overdose of lead that night,' said Bill proudly.

You sort of know what you're in for because on the door to his office, there's a sticker that says, 'Speak English Or Get The F*** Out'. Plus, there's a WWII German army helmet on the coffee table and a list of 'N****** Names' on the wall. Bill was wary of the 'Limey crapass motherf*****' who'd come for a chat until he discovered the cameraman was South African. Then everything was fine, and he gave us a lecture about the Merlin engine and how the Spitfire was the best ever plane.

He also discovered we'd come in a Chevrolet people carrier, which was a good thing because if it had been a Ford, he'd have shot us. Bill would rather push a Chevy than drive a Ford. No one who has even even thought about renting a Ford is allowed within a mile of Bill's place.

Bill's desk is the front half of a '57 Chevy. His yard plays host to over 200 old ones and his museum has seventeen fully restored SS models. 'They weren't too popular with non-Third Reich enthusiasts,' he said.

In his workshop, Bill is helped by Bob, who bought a pair of jeans thirteen years ago, before he became fat. Rather than throw away the jeans, Bob now does them up underneath his arse. When he bent over it was quite a sight.

Bill's sartorial elegance wasn't up to much either. His jeans were four inches too short, his stomach four inches too fat and his hair was four inches too short. I didn't much care for his Buddy Holly specs or the laser straight parting in his hair. And when he dismissed the Rolling Stones as Pewkie Dolls, I nearly hit him.

He saved himself from a punch in the mouth, though, when he expressed an interest in the Aston Martin Vantage engine. He bounced up and down at that ridiculous desk when I said it was a V8 with two superchargers, and squeaked with excitement when I said it developed 550ft-lbs of torque. But then he went purple with rage when I explained it had 5.4 litres – no metric measurements allowed in Bill's place – and finally exploded when I said Aston Martin is owned by Ford.

Bill hated Fords almost as much as I hated him, but he did have one redeeming feature. His T-shirt. Which said, and I quote, 'If you haven't seen God . . . it's because you're not going fast enough'.

December 1995

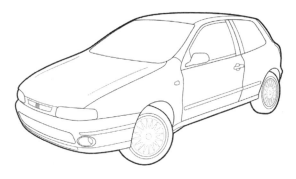

CAR OF THE YEAR: FIAT BRAVO/BRAVA

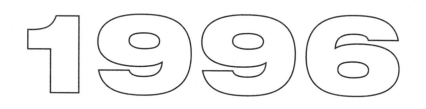

TOP 5 BESTSELLING SINGLES
SONG TITLE – ARTIST

1 Killing Me Softly - The Fugees
2 Wannabe – Spice Girls
3 Spaceman – Babylon Zoo
4 Say You'll Be There – Spice Girls
5 Return of the Mack – Mark Morrison

TOP 5 BOX OFFICE MOVIES

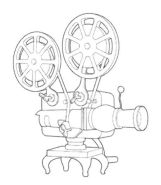

1 Independence Day
2 Twister
3 Mission: Impossible
4 Jerry Maguire
5 Ransom

The Jaguar XJ220

One hour ago, I was nudging 200mph on a desert highway in a Jaguar XJ220. It felt good, but it wasn't quite as good as the view in my rear-view mirror, because behind me was a Porsche 959 and a Ferrari F40. And in front was an F50.

We weren't exactly racing, but it was impossible to come out of a roundabout without mashing the Jag's heavy-duty throttle into its equally heavy-duty carpet and feeling those turbos start to sing their alto tunes.

It was the first time I'd driven the big Brit bruiser and though it was ponderous compared to the Italian duo, it was a lot better than I thought it would be. However, despite giving the fat cat some serious stick, I was left feeling a bit empty. Here I was in one of the most exciting cars ever made, and I was bored. You see, I've now driven the ultimate machine, a world championship winner that's hurled along by 1,800 horsepower.

I'm talking about a powerboat – the Victory Team's all-conquering Class One 43-footer with its brace of big block Chevy units, tuned to rip the ocean apart with 1,500ft-lbs of torque. There are only two seats. On the left was Saeed Al Tayer, who would operate the throttles and the four gears. I was in the right pod, with the wheel. The cockpit glass is taken from an American F-16 fighter and the dash has all the hallmarks of a jet too, but there's a steering wheel, a racing seat and a five-point harness, so it feels kind of like a car as well.

The points of the twin hulls stretched into the middle distance, obliterating the view. This was a problem because Saeed had just fired up the £600,000 beast and it was my job to get it out of the marina.

'You must be pretty nervous,' I said over the intercom as we headed into the open sea. 'Oh no,' came the reply. 'I've never done the throttleman's job before.' With that, he pushed them all the way to the stops.

The gear changes are ponderously slow, but the GPS speedometer's relentless churning defied belief. Thirty seconds from the line and we were doing 100mph. Then we went past 120, 125 and 130. At 132mph, you could hear us in Barnstaple, but that was all the small propellers would give. With the big racers on, they've had this baby up to 144mph. 132 feels fast enough, though, especially when you look out of the side of the canopy at the water just four feet below. It has a solid, concretey sort of appearance. I was mesmerized and didn't hear the rescue helicopter's pilot begging us to slow down. Seems his Jet Ranger couldn't keep up.

Now, so far we'd been on a flat sea, going in a straight line, but with Iranian waters ahead, Saeed asked me to make a wide right turn. And that was like nothing I have ever felt. Damon Hill tried this boat and said it was like a 300mph forklift truck, but that's cobblers because the response was immediate – one twitch of the wheel and those twin points were turning, with no roll. And, even though Victory weighs four tons, I could feel the hull on my side gripping the water. This was like a racing car. 'Yes,' said Saeed, 'and it will spin like a racing car too, so not so much lock next time.'

The deck of the boat is essentially an aeroplane wing, designed to hoist the hulls out of the water and reduce friction. So, as we cruised past the ton once again only the bottom third of the props were in the water. Everything else was airborne. This makes the ride almost Jaguaresque, but it's not always so. A modern day powerboat is expected to race through 40-knot winds in six-foot seas if need be, and they must be able to average 100mph in the process.

If you've never seen this spectacle, I urge you to catch a race one day soon. The boats skip from wave to wave, with the throttleman desperately trying to make sure he has full power when he's in the sea, and not much when he's twelve feet above it. To land with props spinning at Mach 2 would rip the shafts apart.

Race tracks are designed to aid the passage of racing cars, but the sea is designed to create weather, and as a home for sharks. If you get it wrong in a race car, Murray Walker will have something to talk about. But if you get it wrong in a Class One boat, you will only need a coffin big enough for your ear, toe or whatever tiny bit they happen to find. It is the ultimate thrill.

February 1996

The FSO Polonez

I don't doubt that you go a bit red round the gills every morning when you find that Postman Pat has filled your hall with junk mail. You don't want to win a tumble dryer, you don't need an Amex card and you'd rather buy *Razzle* than *Reader's Digest*.

But consider for a moment what life would be like if you actually had to read everything that came through your door. Imagine if you were forced to open bank statements and bills, rather than simply feed them to the waste disposal unit.

Well that's what happens at Telly Towers every morning. I have to scoop up the debris that Pat has fed to my doormat, and read it.

I'm talking about press releases from the world's car companies – tomes that redefine the concept of dull. They are more boring than a Jane Austen novel, more shiversomely tedious than a parish council meeting.

Just last week, Nissan changed the radiator grille or something on the Micra and poor Pat gave himself a hernia lugging the press pack up my drive. Seventeen pages in, I'd already worked out that the whole thing could have been done in one sentence: 'We've changed the Micra a bit.'

But today, in amongst the encyclopaedic volume on the Corsa's new engine and a gushing diatribe about the new Hyundai Lantra Estate, was something that stopped me dead.

FSO is not dead. The Polish car company has managed to

survive the transition from Communism to Lech and back to Communism again. And more than that, the cars are still being imported to Britain. Oh no.

I still maintain that the Nissan Sunny was the worst car of all time. It had absolutely no redeeming features; nothing that you couldn't find better and cheaper elsewhere. But the worst car in the world to actually drive was the FSO Polonez.

Its did have a redeeming feature: it was cheap. But it had to be, because it was a car that wasn't really a car at all. It was a box under which the careless car buyer would discover a Forties tractor.

The styling was enough to put most people off, but it only had to compete with the Wartburg and the Trabant, neither of which will ever feature in a book called *Beautiful Cars* by Jeremy Clarkson.

You cannot begin to imagine how bad the ride was on this truly awful car, and just as you were marvelling at its ability to bounce so high off the ground, you'd find its steering didn't really work because the front wheels had been concreted on.

If Karl Benz had invented its engine, he'd have given up with the whole concept of internal combustion. The noise frightened birds and the fuel consumption read like the spec sheet from an InterCity 125.

The last time I actually went in a Polonez was last year. It was a minicab and it broke down in Heathrow's tunnel. Then I had an argument with the fat driver when I point blank refused to pay.

But since that long, fume-filled walk to the terminal, I've not heard anything about this wart on the bottom of motoring. Until now. It seems FSO has a new car called the Caro which has met with some success in Britain. Four hundred and eighty were sold here last year, but I can only assume that the owners limit forays onto the road to the hours of darkness. I've certainly never seen one.

I'm sure though that it's a pretty hateful machine, but there's no denying one thing. At £4,527, it is cheap.

Also, it can be ordered with a 1.9-litre Citroën diesel engine and it will eventually get ZF power steering and Lucas brake systems. It may then become a half-decent car, but I'm also sure its price will rise.

They'll end up with a half-decent car at an indecent price. Except they won't, because this press release says that Daewoo has taken a 10 per cent stake in FSO and that in the next five or six years, the Korean company's share will rise to 70 per cent.

The idea is simple. Daewoo will ship bits of old Astras and Cavaliers from Korea to Poland, where they will be nailed together to form a vague but inexpensive interpretation of what motoring should be all about in the next millennium.

We know all about that already, of course, because Vauxhall has shown us. No more fast cars. Birds in the trees and the good people of the world transported to and from work in Vectras. God Help Us.

March 1996

Environmentalists

Throughout history, there's been a selection of anti-establishment figures whose dreams of creating a new world order have shone like the most brilliant stars in the firmament, and then burnt out and died. The world has been to the outermost reaches of extremism throughout the nineteenth century – from Fascism to Communism – and it has survived. When the Wall fell down we all breathed a sigh of relief, but there will always be anti-establishmentism, hell bent on suppressing free thought and democracy. Idealists will never go away; they'll just surface again with a new corporate identity.

Now they're back under the environmentalist banner. Only this time, in their quest to bring down commercialism and give power to the people, they really do seem to have hit a raw nerve. 'If we carry on like this, the planet will die. In five minutes of geological time, we have turned paradise into a rubbish dump.'

Horse shit. They're not the slightest bit bothered about the environment; it's just a weapon that allows them to attack a system that no idealist has ever accepted: democracy.

But they've had a huge effect. Fearful of creeping sympathy for the so-called Greens, stupid, short-sighted governments all over the world have imposed Draconian environmental laws on what they see as easy meat – the internal combustion engine.

And the car firms are being equally wet. Why don't they

just go along to Downing Street and explain that cars put a massive £18 billion a year into the British exchequer? Instead, we get that idiotic Mercedes ad where some poppies burst into life when an E-Class slides by.

Let me fill you in on a few facts. The London Marathon generates more carbon dioxide than every grand prix in the whole Formula One calendar. A house produces more so-called global warming gases than your car. And, according to a Friends of the Earth advisor I spoke to, 97 per cent of the world's carbon dioxide is generated by nature. And even if man's 3 per cent contribution isn't simply absorbed by the oceans, the resultant heat rise will create more dynamic weather, more snowfall over land and therefore lower sea levels!

Cars do not cause asthma. Cars do not shit in the streets and cause typhoid. And, since the catalytic converter came along, every single noxious exhaust emission has been slashed. Lead is down two-thirds. Sulphur is down tenfold.

But still the eco-twats tell us to leave our cars at home and take the bus. Why? Because that'll slow the economy down to the same pace as the snails who are holding up the New-bury bypass. If they had their way, they would have us all up in trees, eating lentils and not washing our hair. They must do because their views are so completely at odds with what's realistic.

Whenever I suffer from asthma or acne, I take drugs to cure the problem. When I'm cold, I put the heating on. When I go out, I take the Jag. When I'm hungry, I have a Big Mac. And when I'm on edge I have a Marlboro.

These things make life fun and easy. They provide jobs, generate wealth. They keep society moving down its chosen path.

Take them away and we'd have to think again. We'd have to invent a system where money played no part, so that there was nothing to be gained from making something which *may* damage the environment.

There is no way that such a system could be implemented by a committee, so the responsibility would have to be shouldered by one man. Elections would be a casualty too.

And he couldn't go about it in a parochial way. There's not much point cleaning up Britain if the French are still filling the Pacific with plutonium. So, this one man would have to be a global dictator. A god.

If the environmentalists ever realize their dreams, you can kiss goodbye to free thought and say hello to the Gestapo or the KGB or whatever they decide to call their secret police.

In fact, environmentalism is every bit as dangerous as Communism or Fascism.

But we need not worry. Extremism will always be defeated by common sense. One day, in the Greenpeace bunker, there'll be the welcome sound of a Luger going off.

May 1996

The Skyline

The Japanese car makers should take a long hard look at Linford Christie and Barbara Cartland. One does not attempt to win 100-metre races and the other does not try to look like a big, pink crow.

They should say to themselves, 'All the best-looking cars in the world are European or American and if we try to copy them, we end up with hopeless facsimiles like the Supra.'

And they should go further: 'Boys, we do not understand "soul", so let's not try to replicate it.'

'Soul' is what you get when you've won the Formula One World Championship and Le Mans ninety-nine times. You can't design 'soul' or 'character'. You earn it.

Cars are like friends. I have many, many acquaintances, but friends are people whom I've known for years and years. 'Soulful' friendships are forged when you've been drunk together, arrested together.

That said, there are shortcuts. I'd be pretty matey with someone who gave me a million pounds. And I wouldn't slam the phone down if Princess Diana rang, feeling a bit horny.

The Nissan Skyline GT-R is just such a shortcut. Nissan accepted they could never match European finesse and style, so decided to go where Europe can't follow – into the auto cyber zone where silicone is God and Mr Pininfarina is the doormat.

It worked. The Skyline is not a facsimile of something

European. It is as Japanese as my Nintendo Game Boy, only more fun.

I was smitten by the old model, but now there is a new version which, after a week-long orgy of big numbers and lurid tailslides, has left me in no doubt. Forget the Ferrari 355. Forget the Lotus Elise.

For people who want their car to be the last word in ball-breaking ability and to hell with style and comfort, the Skyline is Mr Emperor Penguin. King of the hill. The biggest cheese in Stiltonshire.

Whether its ability is down to the four-wheel-drive system or the four-wheel steering or the peculiar diffs and electronic whizz bangs, I don't know and I don't care.

The Skyline goes around corners faster than anything else. And when it does get a bit skew-whiff, it's a doddle to rein in again.

Unfortunately, the price tag has gone right above the Skyline; from £25,000 for the old model to a stratospheric £50,000 for this one.

But the biggest problem is not the price, it's bloody Nissan GB. As before, they won't import the Skyline officially, saying it would cost a million quid to make it Euro legal, but adding that if a hundred people show real interest, they may take the plunge.

A miserable hundred people. For heaven's sake, thousands spend a fortune every year on golfing trousers and thousands more spend every surplus penny in their bank account on model aeroplanes.

Surely, there are a paltry hundred people out there who would make the very sensible decision to buy a Skyline instead of a Porsche, or an M3 or even a Ferrari.

I fully understand that the Nissan badge is a turn-off but

the Volvo badge wasn't something you shouted about until the T5 came along.

Once a few people have a Skyline and word gets out, you will be seen as a wise and thoughtful person with immense driving skill. Women, almost certainly, will want to spend the night with you.

At the same time, your customers will see you as a restrained person with no need for frills. They will double their orders, enabling you to spend even more money with Andy Middlehurst, taking the motor up to perhaps 420bhp. Including the cost of replacement turbos – the ceramic ones can't cope – this will set you back £3,200 – beer money in Porsche land.

As far as reliability is concerned, I understand that there are no real problems. The Marquis of Blandford says that his old model with 390bhp never went wrong in 40,000 miles.

He pointed out that there is no other comparable car that can handle the snow in Verbier, a family and the need to maintain a low profile. All that and a top speed of 180mph.

I know I go on about this car, but every time I drive it I can't wait to get to a computer to write about it. Wordsworth was moved by flowers, I get all foamy about the Nissan.

October 1996

The Corvette

So, underachiever, how do you feel today? Let me guess; you got up, went to work, flirted with the secretaries, came home and watched telly. Now, *Newsnight* is on and you're reading this, yawning and wondering why you've got nipples.

It's OK, I do pretty much the same sort of thing most days and that's why I know Hoot Gibson will gall you as much as he galled me.

Here is an all-American dude with Paul Newman eyes who learned his art in Vietnam, flying F-4 Phantoms and shooting down MiGs which may, or may not, have been piloted by top flight Russians.

He was so adept at blowing things out of the sky, they sent him to the Top Gun Academy, where he became a better instructor than Kelly McGillis. And after that he found himself stationed at Pax River, flying all the new, experimental fast jets.

When his Navy flying career was over, instead of a desk, the services gave him a space shuttle – something he's used to visit space on no fewer than five occasions.

So what does Mr All American Hero choose to drive when he's back on Texan earth, and restricted to 55mph? A Viper? A Jag? A Bimmer?

Er, no. Mr Gibson has a Toyota Camry, finished in aubergine with a matching interior. I pointed out that this was a terrible car and he agreed, but said it was, at least, reliable – 'something that's important to me'.

OK, I can understand that, but in *The Right Stuff* – the best book in the world, incidentally – Tom Wolfe says all the early test pilots and astronauts hurtled into town in Corvettes – the first American sportscar.

Why, I suggested, do you not have one of those? 'Because', he said, 'it's a piece of junk.'

Whoa there, boy. Mr Pumping Pecs calling his auto equivalent 'junk'? This needed exploring and so, two days later, in Nevada, I hired myself an egg-yellow convertible with a slushmatic box.

I slithered elegantly into the vibrantly shiny cockpit, the 5.7-litre V8 burbled into life and the sleek nose edged its way onto Las Vegas Boulevard. I felt good. The Corvette is dangerously handsome and my views on US V8s are well documented. The steering was quick, the stereo was sound and I began to suspect Hoot should stick to sounding off about planes.

But then I ran over a piece of chewing gum. Jesus H. Christ, did you know the 'Vette has no suspension travel at all? The wheels are connected directly to your buttocks.

I suspected there was something wrong with it and then, that night, it broke down altogether. But the red replacement was just as bad.

OK, I'll let you in on a secret. The Corvette is a slow motor car that doesn't handle at all.

Because there's no suspension to absorb the roll, the car just slides, which must be why it has traction control. But this comes in so viciously and so early that I decided to turn it off and . . . whoops eek and wahay, guys and gals, we're going backwards. It was fun right up to the moment when I saw the guard rail approaching.

Here's another secret. Anti-lock brakes don't work when

you're going sideways. But it was OK – I ground to a halt with a good five inches to spare. I was doing that post-trauma bit where you breathe out and lower your shoulders by five yards when an officer of the law arrived.

The guy knew his cars and pretty quickly conversation turned to the Corvette that had nearly killed me.

'You know the big problem with the 'Vette?' he said. 'It's the worst goddamn car in the whole world.'

He hadn't actually seen my spin, but said he wouldn't even think of writing out a ticket for speeding because he knows just how easy it is to lose control of Detroit's biggest balls-up.

'Goddamn 'Vette spins so easy, you can park one outside a store and when you come out, it'll be facing the other way,' he added.

As he climbed back into his cruiser, he gave me some advice. 'Tonight, leave the roof down and the keys in. With luck, someone'll steal it.'

I've always liked the Corvette and even once toyed with the idea of buying one. But I'm better now.

It's simple, really. The Americans are good at space shuttles. And we're good at cars.

December 1996

CAR OF THE YEAR: RENAULT MÉGANE SCÉNIC

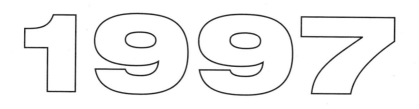

TOP 5 BESTSELLING SINGLES
SONG TITLE – ARTIST

1 Candle in the Wind 1997 – Elton John
2 Barbie Girl – Aqua
3 I'll Be Missing You – Puff Daddy and
   Faith Evans
4 Perfect Day – Various Artists
5 Teletubbies Say Eh – Oh – Teletubbies

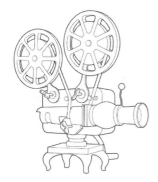

TOP 5 BOX OFFICE MOVIES

1 Titanic
2 Men in Black
3 The Lost World: Jurassic Park
4 Liar Liar
5 Air Force One

The Rover 200

I'm sorry about this but I rarely concern myself with the plight of elderly drivers. In fact, they annoy me. As many of you will have gathered by now, I have moved to the countryside – which is all very lovely and autumnal and so on.

But, frankly, too many of the drivers round here wear hats. Nissan Sunnys kangaroo out of side turnings and trundle along at 40, irrespective of road conditions, weather or the 20-mile tailback they've created.

Mind you, I was delighted yesterday when a car that had held me up for 15 miles trundled into a village, still doing 40, and was zapped by a Gatso.

When I finally got past, I noticed the driver was several hundred years old. I knew this because his suit was finished in a colour that wasn't brown, or green or grey, but a peculiar blend of all three. It was, for want of a better word, 'old' colour.

Anyway, I hope they take his licence away and confiscate his car because it is antisocial to drive at 40 on the open road and stupid to drive at 40 in villages. I think it would be a good idea, too, if he were forced to write to his local newspaper, saying that, behind the wheel, old people are not as good as young people.

Car manufacturers have certainly realized this. Ponder this. What is the single biggest advance in car safety in living memory?

Seat belts? Crumple zones? Anti-lock brakes? Nope. Airbags? Heavens, no. Anti-submarining seats? No.

I'll tell you. The biggest advance in car safety is . . . the Rover 200.

Here's the thing. Take yourself back to the Eighties and already BMW, Audi, SEAT, VW, Porsche, Daihatsu and pretty well every car maker under the sun were targeting young people with their designs and their advertising.

But, still, a handful of manufacturers were out there, plodding away with their wheeled tartan rugs. Volvo for instance. No one under seventy-eight would buy a 300, or a 200 or, especially, a 700. But then came the 850, and then the T5. In a flash, Volvo was in the BTCC, and T5s were on the TV driving over gorges and racing through hurricanes. Volvo was out at the disco with a sock in its underpants, chatting up teenagers.

Nissan, too, was trying the same trick. Having made a great deal of money selling crap cars to the over-eighties, they launched the Micra at a younger audience. Unshaven stunt men were taking it to work.

There was a clear message here for the older buyer: 'Got a pension book? Stuff off.'

Old people were being squeezed left and right. But, just as there's always one pub in town that will serve the under-eighteens, there's always one car maker who'll welcome the over-eighties.

Step forward Rover, with your traditional values and your chrome kick plates. Modern though the 600 may be, it still has that look of classic, understated, elegance. And why change the 800 when it's so right for the retired GP from Carlisle?

But then, without so much as a by your leave, along comes

the 200, led into battle by a 135mph VTi flying machine. As pretty as Renault's Mégane Coupé, and fun to hustle as well, it was very obviously quite wrong for the whist-drive brigade.

For heaven's sake; most that I've seen are in vibrant purple, which doesn't go with 'old' colour at all.

And it was advertised by a git in a Paul Smith suit who lives in a warehouse and has a fit bird. The only concession to traditional values came right at the end of the ad when he tucked into a biscuit.

The ad cost £750,000, much of which went to Sting, who did the soundtrack. But old people don't know who Sting is. I'm talking about people so old they think The Police are who you talk to when you forget to slow down in villages.

The message, however, is most certainly not in a bottle. Rover has gone the way of SEAT and Nissan and Volvo and all the others.

Since the 200 came along, old people have lost the last pub in town. They're going to have to make do with the cars they have now. Which, in the not-too-distant future, will break down and disintegrate.

They will then have to use the bus and Britain's reputation as a safe country to drive in will be enhanced.

The Rover 200 is, without doubt, the greatest contribution to road safety since Sir Robert Mark.

January 1997

Airboats

Yesterday, I cheated death when my 100mph airboat capsized in an alligator-infested swamp. It may be *Sun*speak, but it's true.

For years, I've argued that boats are far more dangerous and exciting than cars. Formula One inshore racers accelerate faster than even the fastest GP bike and their offshore Class One cousins can hit 145mph these days.

Few competitions bother to book return air flights to a powerboat race because, on average, two people can expect to finish each season smelling much, much worse than they did at the beginning.

You see, a race track is designed with safety in mind. Bumps are ironed out, Armco barriers are set back from the racing line and huge swathes of the infield are filled with gravel to help slow cars that have gone out of control.

There are no such luxuries on the water. You can go round the Old Hairpin at Donington a thousand times and become inch-perfect but, at sea, the surface is always different.

Down the main straight at Silverstone, I could beat Damon Hill if I had a faster car, but in a boat, how fast you go in a straight line is all down to buttock-clenching bravery.

Rarely does the sea allow you to reach the boat's preposterous top speed, so you choose a safe speed and watch your mirrors to see what everyone else is doing. If the boat behind is catching up, you ease the throttles forward a tad.

The ride gets rougher, the boat is airborne for longer, it smashes down harder.

And still the guy behind is catching up. It's suicidal to go faster, but you're a racer, so you do. And then the onus is on the other guy's anus. How much can he pucker it up?

It's a giant game of aquatic chicken and you can forget all about marshals and gravel traps if it goes wrong. Chances are, if the boat flips, you will be dazed, confused and underwater. If you still have a head, you'll lose it.

Now, I've driven the world championship-winning Class One boat, and last month I had a go in its inshore Formula One equivalent – but neither get close to the ultimate waterborne transport, the airboat.

Basically, you have a tray, which can be up to 18 feet long. And at the back, there's an engine driving a propeller.

If your engine is powerful enough – and one bloke I found was using a turbo seven-litre motor from a Cadillac – you can drive your boat on dry land. Indeed, we filmed him doing just this for my series, *Extreme Machines*, which goes out in a year's time.

Then we piled all our gear – worth about £100,000 – into another airboat and set off to see some Florida rednecks race. We never got there.

When the pilot turned on the power, the back end settled down, water poured into the hull and it was *Herald of Free Enterprise* time.

To make matters worse, passengers sit four feet off the deck, so they don't block airflow to the prop. This means the centre of gravity is in the clouds somewhere, so we were upside down in the time it took the director to say, 'Fu—'

So there I was, fully clothed, wearing a crash helmet, in

15 feet of water. And our kit was at the bottom, being eaten by snakes and alligators.

But I got back in again because an airboat is huge fun. The acceleration is vivid – like, say, a VR6 – but the steering is not. You push a lever and the rudders swing, causing you to turn . . . at some point in the future.

And here's another difference between cars and boats. Racing cars have carbon-fibre brake discs; air boats have nothing. Come off the power and you start to slow down a bit – but with no prop action, there's no draught to turn the rudders.

Umpteen times, I found myself with the rudders hard over but the boat surging forwards. In the nick of time, I'd remember to hit the gas and, whoa, the boat would spin on its axis and hurtle the other way. Even if you get it right, there's always a delay between steering and turn, and all corners are done in a huge powerslide.

You'd call it oversteer in a car, and people like Tiff and Nik Berg would get all excited. But they've never done it in a boat, at 70mph, on water, with a hazy Florida sun making the lilies bright orange.

When it comes to excitement, cars are good, bikes are better – but the airboat is the king of the hill.

February 1997

Motorbikes

If you're one of our more level-headed readers, you might think that when it comes to no-go areas of office conversation, cars top the list here at *Top Gear* magazine.

I mean, for sixteen hours a day, these guys drive cars, and in the remaining eight, write about them. The last thing they want to do over a beer or in sub-zero fag breaks is discuss the merits of a Proton over an Escort.

Well I'm going to tell you a little secret. They don't talk about cars very much, but it has nothing to do with overkill. They don't talk about cars because they are too busy talking about bloody motorbikes.

The editor rides bikes. The assistant editor rides bikes. The art director rides bikes. So does the art editor – and she's a girl. I've just been to Barbados with the road test editor and he sat on the beach every day reading *Bike* magazine.

I've given up calling in because if I do, I always forget the rules and mention the 'c' word. I mean, it is a car magazine; maybe the people who work on it would be interested to hear that I've just driven a turbo-charged Ferrari F50.

So I'll say, 'Hey everyone, I drove a turbocharged F50 yesterday,' and, guess what . . . nothing happens. So I'll tell them again, and if I'm very lucky, one will stick his head up and mumble something about it not being as fast as the Triumph T595.

Then they're off. 'Yeah, but the chassis on a Blade is better.'

'Oh sure, but I prefer the 43mm Showa usd teles on a 916.'

And me, I'm the pork chop in a synagogue.

I've given up arguing. Yes, yes, yes, bikes are cheaper than cars, more fun and, providing you never encounter a corner, they're faster too.

I've tried pointing out that round a track, where there are bends, a car will set faster lap times; but a deathly hush descends over the office as everyone sets to work with slide rules and calculators. Three minutes later, the managing editor will announce that, at Thruxton, his calculations have shown a T595 would, in fact, be faster than an F50.

Well, I can now shut them up for good because I've just flown an F-15E, and no bike on Earth even gets close. Oh, and you'll note I said 'flown' and not 'flown in'. Even though I've never even held the stick in a Cessna, the US Air Force let me take the controls of a plane that cost $50 million and, in ninety minutes, used $7,000 worth of fuel.

You might guess that once you're airborne there is no real sensation of speed, but this is simply not the case, a point the pilot was keen to prove. So, at 1,000 feet he hit everything to slow the plane down to something like 150mph.

And then, after asking me if I was ready, he lit the afterburners. And let me tell you this, Mr Sheene and Mr Fogarty: you know nothing. I wasn't timing it, but I would guess that in ten seconds we were nudging 700mph.

And then, just to show what an F-15 is all about, he stuck the plane on its tail and did a vertical climb from 1,000 to 18,000 feet in exactly eleven seconds.

You've all been in lifts that make you feel funny if they're fast, but just think what it feels like to do a 17,000-foot vertical climb in the time it takes a Mondeo to get from 0–60.

There was no let up, either, because having shown me how fast an F-15 accelerates, I was then introduced to its manoeuvrability. Put it like this, in a gentle Sunday afternoon turn it'll dole out 10g, and I don't know of any bike that can do that.

And nor can a bike post a 1,000lb bomb through your letterbox. What's more, in a battle between a MiG-29 and a Ducati 916, the Italian motorcycle would lose. Whereas no-one has ever shot an F-15 down. Ever.

But the best bit was when the pilot said 'you have the plane'. I did a roll and a loop, flew in tight formation with another F-15, went for a peek at BMW's new factory, flew over Kitty Hawk and got within a fraction of going supersonic. It can do Mach 2, but only over water, and my ejection training hadn't covered survival in such conditions.

I really didn't mind, though. I honestly believe I've now experienced the ultimate; from this point on, everything will be a little bit tame.

As I see it, a bike only has one advantage over a fighter-bomber. On a bike you don't get sick. In the plane, you do. Twice.

April 1997

Jaguar's birthday

Later this summer, Ferrari is celebrating its fiftieth birthday in Rome with a party that will make Elton's half-century look like an old people's whist drive.

They say that Rome will be brought to a standstill by 10,000 Ferraris and that even the Pope will be there. The Pope, for Christ's sake. The Pope is going to a car firm's birthday party.

Check out *Q* magazine's gig guide and I doubt you'll find a single rock 'n' roller on stage that night. Eric Clapton, Chris Rea, Jay Kay and Rod Stewart have each bought a 550, and the word is they'll all be in Rome, talking Armani and quad-cam motors.

Me though, I'm not going. I have decided that I shall be at the Coventry British Legion that night, where Jaguar is celebrating, not its fiftieth, but its seventy-fifth anniversary.

That's not fair. The ball, in fact, is being held at the Brown Lane factory and 1,000 people will be there including er . . . David Platt . . . possibly. The Queen – our equivalent of the Pope – is sadly unavailable because she's opening a computer park in Telford that day. Or is it a dog food factory in Cwmbran?

Honestly, it's pathetic and it isn't Jaguar's fault. In fact, they've done bloody well to scrape up 1,000 people who are prepared to get out there and celebrate the birth of what we're told is a bunch of wires, some Zyklon B and a slab or two of metal.

It's amazing. Since British Aerospace handed Rover over

to the Germans, I've had hundreds of letters from retired majors in Bognor Regis saying that it's all deplorable, hardly worth fighting the war . . . etc . . . etc . . .

But people in the UK are told cars are dirty and that we're no good at making anything, and we shrug and accept it. We accept almost anything.

Some years ago, the EC, as it was called at the time, decided that all beaches must achieve a certain standard of cleanliness, which was not one of their more idiotic ideas.

Naturally, the British delegation dispatched beardy types in parkas to our sandier bits where, to their horror, none met the new requirements. Cue the *Daily Mail* with all sorts of headlines deriding Britain as the dirty man of Europe.

But, according to my sources, this isn't an entirely fair picture because the other countries had simply gone home and done . . . precisely nothing. No beardy types had been sent out to check; they just said, 'Our beaches are all clean.'

So hey, it turns out that the unspoiled wilderness in northern Scotland is filthy while that turd-infested expanse of litter-strewn shingle called Greece is dew fresh.

Continental types treat rules with exactly the right amount of disdain. Because Italy has had so many rulers this millennium and so many governments since the war, they've learned to treat authority as though it's something they've trodden in.

What's the point of obeying one new rule when next week, Hannibal is coming over the mountains with an elephant and an entirely new set?

Over there, you can run around waving your arms in the air, telling anyone who'll listen that Ferrari is a symbol of the unacceptable face of capitalism, and that cars are killing children. No one will give a damn.

The same happens in France. When the government tried to impose new taxes on truckers they didn't have a puny strike. No. They blockaded motorways and stood around smoking Gitanes until sense prevailed.

Even the Belgians are out and about throwing rocks as I write because Renault is closing a factory down.

But here, apart from a bunch of long-haired ne'er-do-wells with suspicious stains on their trousers, no one ever complains.

This is why, in Italy, the whole country will be out on the streets celebrating Ferraris, while in Britain, Jaguar's birthday will be marked by one person in every 56,000.

We shouldn't expect more really, because if you went into the street and put up bunting, a council official would tell you to take it down again.

And if you held a street party, number 54 would ring the police who'd ask you to turn it down a bit.

The only consolation is that things are worse in America, I'm told that in Los Angeles nowadays, it is illegal to consume alcohol after 2 a.m. – even in your home. I bet GM's big birthday party will be a real wow.

June 1997

Nelson Mandela

You know how Greenpeace is prone to charging around the sea in small boats, trying to stop perfectly harmless oil rigs from being sunk. Well once – just once – they came up with a cunning plan.

They argued that the earth is 46 million years old, a number that's hard to handle. So they asked us to think of it as being forty-six years old – middle-aged in other words.

A leaflet explained that almost nothing is known about the first forty-two years and that dinosaurs didn't appear until just last year. Mammals came along eight months ago and it wasn't until the middle of last week that apes began to walk on their hind legs.

This was an amazing read, but it was all complete mumbo jumbo because their claim that the earth is 46 million years old simply isn't true. It's actually 4,600 million years old, which makes their idea even more mind boggling. The last ice age didn't happen at the weekend. It happened half an hour ago!

However, I don't want to get into an environmental debate here. What I want to talk about, in fact, is the puniness of Nelson Mandela.

If you divide time by a thousand million to make the planet forty-six years old, it means that seventy years passes in four-hundredths of a second. So, as far as the earth is concerned, Nelson is simply not relevant at all. And nor was Hitler. And nor was Jimi Hendrix. Truth is, in four-hundredths of a second, absolutely nothing you do or say will make the slightest bit of difference.

For 4,600 million years, you weren't born and you'll be dead for even longer, so it's therefore vital that you explode out of the womb like your hair is on fire. In real time, you've only got 600,000 hours and then you'll wind up on the wrong side of the flowerbed.

So what's the best course of action? Well, you could watch *Pride and Prejudice*, which manages to make an hour seem like a day, but prolonging a boring life is worse than not starting it in the first place. That's why you must also not drive one of the new Toyota Corollas.

Certainly, it is not exciting to behold. Yes, it has a bobby-dazzler of a radiator grille and the sort of eyes that only exist deep in the ocean, where light is at a premium.

But from this point backwards, there is a styling vacuum, whether you're talking about the saloon, the estate, the lift-back or the hatch. However, this time round there is a sporty figurehead - the G6. (I always thought it was G7, but perhaps Japan got lobbed out for making dull cars.) Anyway, this has some definite sporting overtones, in the shape of alloy wheels, red instrumentation and a leather steering wheel. There is a nifty little six-speed gearbox too, which beeps when you put it into reverse.

Excited? Thinking of getting one? Well whoa there, because it's powered by a 1,300cc engine, the smallest of all the new Corolla's power plants. This means old people in their not-at-all-sporty 1.6-litre liftback will be able to blow you away at the lights.

Toyota argue that by putting a small engine in the G6, they've kept insurance costs down. But that's like choosing a mild curry in case your arse hurts in the morning. Life's too short to be bothered about insurance premiums. Or a fiery ringpiece.

The G6 Corolla amazed me, time and again. No matter what I threw in its direction, it behaved like a school swat and refused to join in the fun.

The engine is actually quite sweet and the gear change utterly delightful, but to take it through the gears is about as rewarding as eating flour.

One night, I sneaked it into a stubble field, knowing that any form of motorized transport is a laugh when there's 100 acres and a surface slippery enough to be an East End geezer. I did some handbrake turns and generally looned about and came home suffering from acute stupefaction. Honestly, I'd have been better off reading a book with an orange spine.

The G6 is, far and away, the most idiotic way of blowing £14,000. This is a car for people who see life as a chore to be undertaken, rather than as an experience to be milked. It is for a cardigan-wearing, non-smoking gardening fanatic who thinks 'E' is a vowel. It is for people who think that living to be seventy-five, rather than seventy, *really* matters. It is, therefore, not for you, and it sure as hell is not for me.

September 1997

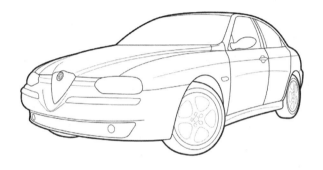

CAR OF THE YEAR: ALFA ROMEO 156

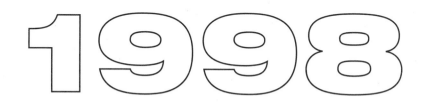

TOP 5 BESTSELLING SINGLES
SONG TITLE – ARTIST

1. Believe – Cher
2. My Heart Will Go On – Celine Dion
3. It's Like That – Run DMC vs. Jason Nevins
4. No Matter What – Boyzone
5. C'est La Vie – B*Witched

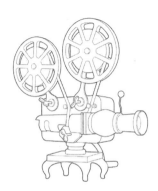

TOP 5 BOX OFFICE MOVIES

1. Saving Private Ryan
2. Armageddon
3. There's Something About Mary
4. A Bug's Life
5. The Waterboy

Extreme Machines

My new *Extreme Machines* series begins its six-week run on BBC2 about now, and although there's an accompanying magazine, video and musical bog-roll holder, I thought I'd use this page to make some important pronouncements.

The Ferrari F50 is dull. The Dodge Viper is a Thomas Hardy novel on wheels. And, as far as I'm concerned, even the McLaren F1 is nothing more than a gateway to the Land of Nod, because for the past year I've been exposed to a range of machinery that is untinged with the mundane.

When Gordon Murray designed the F1, he was forced by law to fit headlamps and a horn. He needed to ensure that it met various environmental regulations and that it would last for twenty years. You see, the F1 is only a car, a device to convey some people and their luggage from A to B. And I know of a farmer in Yorkshire who uses his McLaren for daily trips, down his rutted drive, to the pub.

Now take the racing snowmobile. It is unburdened with a need to be reliable or safe. It needs no seat belts and no one will care very much if it runs on nitric acid. Its purpose is as pure as the driven snow on which it runs. It has just one job – to entertain.

And it's the same story with a one-man hovercraft. You can buy a new one for £10,000 and, I swear to God, no car on earth can provide so much fun, because in a car you know where you're going, but in a hovercraft you don't. You can turn the handlebars and lean till your face peels off, but it will just head for whatever it was that scared you in the first place.

It's much the same with an airboat. The V8 engine powers an aeroplane propeller with such enormous force that you can actually drive one down the road. But I don't recommend it because you have no say in your direction of travel. And no brakes.

People talk about it being hard to stop a supertanker but, having driven the biggest example of the breed, let me tell you this is nonsense. The Jahre Viking is 50 feet longer than the Empire State Building but can get from its 14-knot cruising speed to a dead halt in just five miles.

No way could you do that with an airboat. But which of the thirty or so machines that I tried was best? Well with 37 million horsepower on tap, the space shuttle was the fastest, but for some reason NASA wouldn't let me have a go. The USAF, on the other hand, was a lot more co-operative and handed me the controls of a Mach 2.2 F15E. Which was nice.

And I shall forever be in Steve Curtis' debt for letting me take the wheel on the maiden voyage of his new Class One offshore powerboat. We did 150mph in a 5mph speed limit, which must be a record.

Oh, sorry, Steve Curtis is Britain's leading Class One throttleman and has won the World Championship twice. But you won't have heard of him because you were too busy watching Glamorgan play Lancashire.

Strangely though, 150mph in the Solent was beaten for thrills by 70mph in a quarry in New Zealand. The people who gave us bungee jumping have now invented jet sprinting, where you race a V8-powered soap dish.

I have to say though that, all things considered, second slot goes to the Apache helicopter gunship – simply because

I want to fly one down Oxford Street on Christmas Eve. No reason; I just do.

But my favourite big boys' toy of all is the Riva Aquarama speedboat. It's made of wood, it can barely crack 50mph and it was designed thirty-two years ago – but it is the most beautiful piece of sculpture in man's entire history.

It is also made with the sort of care I shall demand from the eye surgeon who operates on my daughter next week. And it is powered by two V8s, which sound like God farting. Sure, an Aquarama costs £250,000 – twenty times more than any other speedboat – but when you see it, you'll know why. And you'll know why the list of people who had one for those wild nights in the South of France reads like the guest list at a Monegasque royal wedding: Peter Sellers, Roger Vadim, Brigitte Bardot, Sophia Loren, King Hussein, Ferruccio Lamborghini, Richard Burton.

Give me the choice between a Riva Aquarama and a Ferrari 355 and I'd take the boat. This might have something to do with the fact I already have a 355. Or it might not.

February 1998

The Jag XJR V8

When my last Jaguar arrived, it was blue. When it went away again two years later, it was a sort of bluey-brown colour.

The problem here is simple. Time. When the low fuel warning light comes on, it means I can relax. That reassuring little glow means the bulb is still working and that I've a gallon – maybe two – before I need to refill.

When I pass a sign on the motorway saying 'services 1m and 27m', I'll carry on and, 27 miles later, I'll still carry on. I will never, ever stop before the computer says I have 0 miles left to go. Even then I'll keep going. Tiff is with me on this. We've just worked out that in a lifetime we spend days hunched over nozzles filling up with fuel. And I don't have the time.

So, if I'm not going to feed the car, I'm certainly not going to waste time washing the damn thing. I was once allergy-tested and it came up with house dust, pollen and washing cars. I only need to see a bottle of Turtlewax and my eyes start to stream. Show me a chamois and I'll sneeze until my spleen explodes.

My Ferrari is still coated in a thin sheen of last November's muck and I reckon it looks pretty cool. Mika Salo is obviously a man after my own heart because his 355 could, if you squint a bit, be mistaken for a large woodlouse. It's absolutely filthy.

However, I have something of a problem with my new

Jaguar. You see, it is black by name and black by nature. It is a nightmare.

Black cars cannot achieve that all-over scum effect so, when it's dirty, it just looks awful. I have to clean it, and in a morning when the dew has evaporated, it's coated once more in dust. So I have to clean it again.

In a month, I've spent forty-two hours driving it and 420 hours washing it and I cannot even begin to tell you what a chore this is.

First of all, there's a man who comes round in the night to tie knots in the hosepipe that I neatly looped round its peg the day before. So in the morning I turn on the tap and – bang! – the build-up of pressure causes the pipe to part company with the tap.

And here's a small tip. It is impossible – not hard; impossible – to refit a hose pipe onto a tap unless you have an honours degree in astrophysics and engineering.

So I end up lugging buckets of water from the kitchen, hurling them over the roof and watching the whole bloody lot evaporate before I've had a chance to refill the bucket.

Then it's time to look under the sink, where I discover the car shampoo I bought only the week before has evaporated. I bellow at the kids, who deny all knowledge of this. I glower at my wife, who cries and I threaten to strangle the dog until she owns up to having eaten it. She never does though, leading me to the inevitable conclusion: it has disappeared into the ether. Either that or the man who ties my hose pipe in knots breaks into the house and nicks it.

I'm reduced to using Fairy Liquid, which I now discover contains salt and will, after prolonged use, turn the car into a DeLorean. Still, I apply it liberally and then hurl more buckets of clean water over the washed car to discover that huge chunks of it have not been washed at all.

How can this be? I've washed it scientifically, panel by panel and yet half the roof, three quarters of the offside rear door and a square foot of bonnet are still as dirty as they were in the first place.

So I wash it all over again, and turn to the chamois, which was sold to me in a garage yesterday and has the same ability to absorb water as tin foil. Feverishly, I attack the car with it until I'm bathed in sweat and heaving for breath. Since that car arrived I've lost very nearly two stone.

However, I always stand back after two hours to admire my handiwork . . . which turns out to be crap. The not-leather has left so many streaks that the paintwork looks like it's been stone washed. And there's only one solution. It involves a duster, more manual labour and some Turtlewax.

And for sure, the car is then clean . . . until the mist comes down in the night. I am now so fed up that we are building a garage which, it turns out, will cost about twice as much as a space shuttle.

So here's my tip. Jag XJR V8. Brilliant. Needs to be blue.

July 1998

Driving tests

Before Quentin became an estate agent and drove around talking about people's fireplaces, he lent those dulcet tones to a programme called *Driving School*. You may remember it. It focused on people learning to drive and it made a star of Maureen, whose mouth was on upside down. Sadly, she never did get the hang of driving, but that didn't matter; some civil servant in beige trousers handed over a document saying that she was legally able to drive a Ferrari F40 on the Snake Pass in winter.

Well that's just brilliant. And Maureen isn't alone. There was another woman on the programme who, having passed her test, had another lesson because she wasn't confident enough. She wouldn't be, driving around with a dog the size of a wildebeest in the passenger seat.

Oh, how we laugh . . . right up to the moment when someone just like dog-woman ploughs into a primary school playground, killing thirty under-fives.

I'm sorry, but every day I see people in cars who were born to be on the bus. Hunched over the steering wheel, airbag an inch from those half-filled hot water bottles they used to call breasts, they peer into the gloom, looking neither left nor right.

Tom Cruise could be in the car alongside, waving his meat out of the window, but these people wouldn't dare sneak a peek. They're driving along, petrified. And petrified means 'turned into stone', by the way.

They can't look in a mirror to see what's behind, they can't glance out of the side window to see what's alongside, they just plough on, oblivious to the mayhem in their wake.

I found one of them yesterday doing 30 on an open, sweeping A road. The sun visor was pulled down behind her head which meant, of course, she had no idea I was overtaking when she began – with no warning whatsoever – to turn right.

We've all seen this and we all assume the police should be more vigilant and aggressive, but be realistic. Even if they do pull someone over they'll find it impossible to charge them with 'sitting too far forward' or 'doing 30'.

No. To attack this we have to get to the root of the problem – the driving examiner. I have some sympathy with these poor souls. Think about it. If you are scared half to death while someone is taking their test, you'll pass them. That way, there's only a very small chance you'll meet them coming the other way on a dark night.

If you fail them, there's a very large chance that, in six months' time, they'll be back, ready to scare you to death all over again.

Here's the solution. First, anyone who fails their test three times is simply told that they may not apply again. They must accept that they can't drive, in the same way that I have now accepted that I'll never be an astronaut or a lesbian.

Second: anyone who has not passed their test by the age of twenty-five shall not be allowed to do so. Let's face facts here. If you're so disinterested in driving and cars that you allow eight years to slip by without trying to get a licence, then you are never going to make a good enough driver.

Fact: if you are not interested in something, you will be no good at it. Proof: I am no good at cricket.

Basically, the driving licence will become a privilege and not a right, and in order to get one, I'm afraid that the test will need to be modified. You'll still be expected to brake sharply and reverse round a corner; town driving will remain to ensure you have good spatial awareness.

The written test will survive too, and don't worry if you live in Norfolk or Cornwall. I have no proposals for motorways to be on the curriculum, so you won't have to come to England.

However, you will be taken to a circuit which you will be expected to negotiate in a certain time – nothing mad; just fast enough to make the tyres squeal on the corners. We need to see that the car doesn't scare you and that you're able to take it to the red line once in a while.

We don't want you to break speed limits – they're there for a good reason – but, on the A44, we want to ensure you'll go at more than 30. And if you don't, you blind, deaf, old bat, we'll come round one night and fit a turbo to your Rover 400. A turbo with the wastegate jammed shut.

December 1998

CAR OF THE YEAR: FORD FOCUS

1999

TOP 5 BESTSELLING SINGLES
SONG TITLE – ARTIST

1. Baby One More Time – Britney Spears
2. Blue (Da Ba Dee) – Eiffel 65
3. The Millennium Prayer – Cliff Richard
4. Mambo no. 5 (A Little Bit Of . . .) – Lou Bega
5. 9PM (Till I Come) ATB

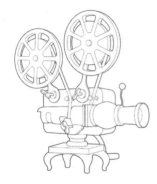

TOP 5 BOX OFFICE MOVIES

1. Star Wars: Episode 1 – The Phantom Menace
2. The Sixth Sense
3. Toy Story 2
4. Austin Powers: The Spy Who Shagged Me
5. The Matrix

Leaving *Top Gear* TV

To a great many people, *Top Gear* presenters have very possibly the best job in the world. Free cars, club class travel, no repurcussions when you crash and large dollops of fame, fortune and *foie gras*. So I'm sure a few readers may be a little perplexed to hear that I have resigned. Here's why.

Now that I've gone, I don't need to drive a razor around my face every single morning. I don't need to buy new shoes every time the old pair start to look scruffy and, best of all, I have no need, ever, to set foot again in the armpit that masquerades as Britain's second city.

Much as I liked Pebble Mill, I really did grow to hate, with unbridled passion, the city that surrounds it. Until you've driven through King's Heath on a wet Wednesday in February, you have not experienced true horror.

You may have seen footage of the Columbian towns devastated by the recent earthquake. Well, King's Heath is like that, only worse. In seven days, God created heaven and earth and then, just to keep his oppo amused, he let Beelzebub do Birmingham.

I pity James May, the man being touted as my replacement. He has been lured by the promise of untold riches, of motor industry obsequeousness on a biblical scale and of bathing in an intoxicating mix of public adulation and Dom Perignon. But he has not considered that his drive from England to Pebble Mill will mean getting through King's Heath.

There are, of course, other reasons why I needed to go.

There was, for instance, surprise when I described the Corolla as dull and, yes, even shock when I was seen to fall asleep while driving it. And then, there was surprise again when I savaged the Vectra, refusing for seven minutes of televisual time to say anything about it.

By the time I got round to the Cadillac Seville STS, the Clarkson attacks were only mildly noteworthy. You had grown to expect them. The shock tactics had become predictable and so weren't shocking any more.

And it was the same with the metaphors. The first time you heard me liken some car to the best bits of Cameron Diaz, you probably sniggered about it at school all the next day. But now, it's tedious.

I never tired of trying to think up new ways to describe a car, and could regularly be found at four in the morning scribbling new lines on a piece of paper by the side of the bed.

I thought of one only last night. 'It's like being left outside the pub as a child with a crisp drink and a bag of coke.' Great, but now I've nowhere to put it.

I will of course carry on writing for this magazine, and there's always Mr Murdoch to stand bravely between my front door and the wolf, but already I'm starting to miss *Top Gear*.

I miss the banter with Quentin and Tiff, as we sniggered about Steve Berry and what he'd crashed that week. I miss Vicky's eyes and her ability to bring sex into absolutely everything. I miss climbing into a new car and thinking, Right. What have we got here then.

You may think that the best bit was the endless succession of new cars. But it wasn't. The best bit was sitting down at the computer with an expectant, winking cursor and then, four days later, handing over seven minutes of video tape to the producer.

The actual driving was always a drag. You sat in some godforsaken hedge on a blind bend, waiting for the walkie-talkie to say the road was clear. And then you set off to find it wasn't or that the cameraman had lost focus and that you'd have to do it all over again, and again and again.

I promise you this. It really isn't much fun driving a Ferrari when you're accompanied by a cameraman, a ton of equipment and a bloody great blinding light on the bonnet.

I'm often asked what qualifications you need to work on *Top Gear* and I've always given the same advice. Like cars by all means, but love writing. Love it so much that you do it to relax. See the new Alfa or whatever as nothing more than a tool on which your prose can be based.

Don't worry about how fast it gets from 0–60. Worry only about how you will explain this meaningless figure to your viewers or readers.

So what am I going to do to fill the void left by *Top Gear*? Simple. I'm going to write and write and write until the smiles come back.

March 1999

The Mercedes S-Class

Last weekend, Andy Wilman, that human carpet you sometimes see on *Top Gear*, asked if he could borrow the keys to a Mercedes S-Class I had on loan.

No surprises there. People who come to stay are always asking if they can try out whatever cars are parked in the drive. And the S-Class is big news. Some say it's the best car in the world. Some say it's even better than that, so Andy wanted to get out there to see if the reality lived up to the legend.

Strange, then, that after just a few minutes, he was back inside the house having not driven the car at all.

'Why?' I asked him.

'Because there's no need,' he said.

And he might be right. When you're presented with a new Mercedes S-Class, you sort of know it's going to be utterly silent and effortlessly fast. You can be assured there will be no twist in the tale or, thanks to the traction control, the tail. So really, what's the point of actually driving the damn thing?

What you want, frankly, is to be amazed by the toys – and believe me, the S-Class amazes, and then some. I mean, the seats come with a grand total of forty motors apiece and small fans which cool or heat your buttocks as you move along.

And it gets better, because as you adjust the temperature a small bank of blue and red lights illuminate. That's great. You don't have to sit there thinking, Is my arse hot or is it cold? A simple glance will tell you.

And then your attention is drawn to the television, telephone, stereo and satellite navigation system, all of which are fitted into a 6x6 box that lives on the centre console.

Now, to those of us who are over thirty years old, this is deeply impressive – when we were growing up, your amp was the size of a washing machine, your TV was black and white, there were no satellites and your phone number was Darrowby 35.

Obviously, having been brought up in a pre-calculator age, I am completely baffled by computers. But that didn't stop me stabbing away at the various buttons, responding with an excitable shriek when the readout on the TV screen changed. Simply getting the radio to come on, and play music, gives hope to the world's old people that maybe one day they could buy an Internet and make it mow the lawn.

For all I know, the air-conditioning system in an S-Class could mow the lawn and a whole lot more besides: bikini-wax your wife? Make a pizza? Who knows? I certainly don't, because the controls made no sense to me at all.

In American cars, the function performed by a knob is written in English on the knob itself. The button to open the sunroof actually says 'sunroof'. Now in the rest of the world, people recognize that there's such a thing as a language barrier, and as a result, they use symbols instead.

Again, this worked fine. Find a button with a drawing of a sunroof on it and, unless you're in an Alfa, it'll open the roof when pressed. But what happens when a car offers a new function you've never heard of before? The symbol on the switch will be meaningless.

There's one button on the S-Class dashboard that appears to have a corn circle drawn on it. So you press it and guess what? A small red light comes on. There's no whirring noise, no soft whoosh such as you'd get when the doors open on the *USS Enterprise*, just that little red light.

And next to it is another button with what looks like a Breville snack and sandwich toaster stencilled on it. Again, when you press this, absolutely nothing happens. I would say that, of all the buttons in the S-Class, and there are hundreds, 80 per cent appear to have no function whatsoever.

Obviously the solution can be found in the handbook, but look, it's the size of the Bible and makes even less sense. By the time you'd got to the chapter marked 'How to Walk on Water', your car would have rusted away.

And anyway, I sort of know what all those buttons do. They change the driving characteristics slightly, making the car perhaps a little more lively in the bends or a little more prone to rear-end breakaway. And honestly, this is silly because you can't induce power oversteer when you're still at home, with all your friends in the back saying, 'Hey, what does that one do?'

Certainly, you should attempt to drive an S-Class by yourself. What with Maureen lunging at you from every side road, and school children surfing on your back bumper, you have enough to worry about without having to translate ancient Egyptian hieroglyphics every time you want to turn the radio up a bit.

Of course, no one who buys an S-Class ever actually does the driving – you have a driver. But from now on you're going to need two: one to drive the car and beat up pedestrians who want your autograph and another who must be computer-literate, skilled in satellite guidance and fully conversant with road-going avionics. So, that's Andy Wilman and me out then.

May 1999

CAR OF THE YEAR: TOYOTA YARIS

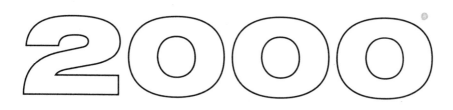

TOP 5 BESTSELLING SINGLES
SONG TITLE – ARTIST

1 Can We Fix It – Bob The Builder
2 Pure Shores – All Saints
3 It Feels So Good – Sonique
4 Who Let The Dogs Out – Baha Men
5 Rock DJ – Robbie Williams

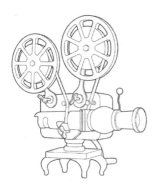

TOP 5 BOX OFFICE MOVIES

1 How the Grinch Stole Christmas
2 Cast Away
3 Mission: Impossible II
4 Gladiator
5 What Women Want

England

More news from Rover on the 75 front. With 8,000 sold, it's outperforming the Alfa 156 here in the UK while, over in Italy, it's been voted the 'most beautiful car in the world'.

Furthermore, a bunch of Middle Eastern motoring observers have voted it their car of the year. So, there we are then. It's brilliant.

Well, sorry to be the one who relieves himself all over the bonfire, but I'm not convinced. I don't care how many LCD read-outs they put on the dashboard, or whether the K-series power plant is an engineering masterpiece, the Rover name still smacks of post-war austerity; as a result, the 75 is a sort of wheeled Werther's Original.

And then there's that advertisement where the new 25 is seen driving round a roulette wheel. What's that all about? It should have Dr Finlay behind the wheel, not some bird in a silk nightie.

And I don't see how the situation will ever get better, not so long as BMW remains at the helm. It's a bit like Manchester United buying Liverpool FC and telling them: 'Be good . . . but not as good as us.' The best Rover can hope to achieve is second place and that's why they are about to post losses of around £600 million. A sum described in City circles as 'a lot'.

Then there's Marks & Spencer who, like Rover, have a middle-aged, middle-England appeal and who are also about to announce some catastrophic results. Meanwhile, we have a £758 million dome that no one wants to visit, a river of fire that didn't happen, a big wheel that broke and a flame of hope, which was designed to burn all year in Birmingham, but fizzled out after five days.

In Brazil, some of our football players lost an important game of football and I understand that our cricketers, too, failed to do well in South Africa. So, all in all, it's not been a good start to the third millennium for the Mr Smiths and Mr Robinsons of the world.

Some, of course, would say that this is predictable, that we should accept the fact that these days England is just a 44 dial code, .uk on the Web, the fifty-first state of America and the thirteenth member of the EU. They would argue that the empire is gone, along with Scotland, Wales and Northern Ireland and that we are nothing more than a two-bit island race in a global village.

I, however, am proud of being English, in a passive, now-that-you-mention-it sort of way. I like the fact that it's always 57 degrees and drizzling because this means we spend more time at work and less on the beach. And this, in turn, makes us richer.

I mean, look at France. Yes, they won the World Cup and yes, they came damn close to taking the ultimate rugby crown, too, but so what? Their idea of a luxury car is a Peugeot 406 and their students have to get jobs in London since there are none in Paris.

And Germany? Think how delighted they must have been when they bought Rover, how they'd put one over on Tommy. But now it turns out their longest-serving Chancellor was corrupt and their little acquisition is costing them £600 million a year.

Sure, I'm no great fan of phoney Tony, but then he's Scottish. As is his Chancellor, his Lord Chancellor, the Chief Secretary of the Treasury, his Foreign Secretary and the new bloke at Transport. Then there's Prescott, who's Welsh, and most of the rest are homosexual. England's contribution to the cabinet is Mo Mowlam, and she's the best of the lot, by far.

And then there's Richard Curtis, Marco Pierre White and Tara Palmer-Tomkinson. There's *Notting Hill* and *The Full Monty*. I even had some British wine the other night and it was bloody good.

But best of all, there's Jaguar. My old XJR has just gone back after two years and 20,000 totally trouble-free miles. No, really, in all that time not a single thing went wrong, whereas life with my Toyota Land Cruiser is a non-stop return trip to the dealers.

I've looked at all the alternatives. There's a Jeep Grand Cherokee outside my house right now but it's too jiggly. The Mitsubishi Shogun is too brash and the Merc M-Class is just too Guildford. Which means that, some time this year, we shall get either a Discovery or a Range Rover, because they're still the best 4x4s by far.

And what about sports cars? I know the new Boxster is a fine-handling machine that now goes as quickly as its badge would suggest, and I'm aware that six-cylinder SLKs are about to burst out of the pipeline. But, come on, neither of these is a match for the sheer brutality you get from a TVR. These things are so aggressive they could almost be Scottish.

But if they're out of your price range, then it's off to Mazda for an MX-5, a car that wouldn't be half as good if it weren't for the Lotus Elan.

And anyway, we do still have an empire. It's a small island in the Pacific Ocean and last time I looked the population was 8,000. And all of them, curiously, have Rover 75s.

March 2000

Publishing

Last year, an old school friend stopped by to relive old times, drink some whisky and ask if I'd write a book about Ferrari for his new publishing company. 'It'll be great,' he said.

It isn't. I saw a copy last week and would have to say that it's a complete rip-off and that anyone thinking about buying it should flush the money down the loo instead. It'd be more rewarding.

The reviews have been bad but they don't go far enough. With the possible exception of *Captain Corelli's Mandolin* and A.A. Gill's *Sap Rising*, it is the worst book in the whole world.

Last week, I flew in a jet that went out of control at 42,000 feet, spiralling like a sycamore leaf to a height of 20,000 feet before the pilot regained control. I emerged to say that this was the worst thing I'd ever done, only to be told by a photographer, 'No, your chat show is the worst thing you've ever done.'

But in fact, we were both wrong. The worst thing I've ever done is that bloody Ferrari book. All I can say in my defence is that I've received no cash for this ridiculous tome and that if, by some miracle, any should be forthcoming at some point in the future, I shall give it away to the poor and needy.

But I am at least heartened by the latest crop of all-road, off-road, on-roaders from Audi, Volvo and BMW. It goes to show, I guess, that we all make mistakes.

I should make it plain at this point that I have driven none of these cars, but I do know why they've burst on to the scene, offering what appears to be the protection of chocolate from the searing heat of the fireplace. Johnny Motor-Mogul obviously got it into his head that if a normal estate car could be infused with a bit of off-road cred, it would become a resounding success throughout school-run Britain. Good idea. But flawed – people don't buy off-road cars to go off-road. They are not impressed by big ground clearance or knobbly tyres. No, they think, with some justification, that if a car is built to handle the vast heat that is Africa, it will offer more protection than a normal car should it be involved in a prang at the end of Laburnum Drive.

They also like the big, rumbustious interior, screwed together with sheep in mind and using plastics that are therefore better able to deal with the scuff marks from a million Clarks Trackers.

And they will not be fooled by a BMW X5. This, they will quickly determine, is a normal 5-Series that is now being asked to wobble around town on stilts. Road testers have commented, 'It's remarkably car-like to drive.' To which I say, 'Not half as car-like as it would be if it weren't so high off the ground.'

Let's stop at this point, however, and consider the advantages that an all/off/on-road car has over its normal brethren: 1) er. 2) um. 3) I suppose it's better able to go down cart tracks.

Now, stop again and think when you last needed to go down a cart track.

Even if you do sometimes need to see friends whose drive is unmade, when was the last time you had to park up and walk? What kind of track is too bad for a normal car but not bad enough to warrant the full Range Rover?

And even if such a road exists, would you seriously buy a raised-up car to deal with it? Really? You'd pay the excess purchase price and the extra fuel bills and put up with the choppier ride for that one day a year when you're confronted by a farm track?

I wouldn't mind, but these new cars seem to have exactly the same interiors as the executive expresses on which they're based. So each time you pop into a shop, leaving your children inside to play hide and seek, your car will be reduced to its component parts.

The simple fact of the matter is this: off-road cars and MPVs are designed with children in mind. The 5-Series BMW and others of its ilk are not.

So why then do I think these new all/off/on-road cars are so fantastic? For a time I thought it might be because I fancied that bloke in Volvo's television commercial who leaves his wife to the bears and goes for a pizza.

I mean, these are cars that like to hang around bars wearing white vests. They go to the gym and work out in front of mirrors. And all that ironmongery at the front is like a moustache. A big Freddie Mercury lower-nose bush. Give these cars their head and they won't head for the M1 or the A38. No, they'll make a beeline for the Bovril Boulevard.

But the thing is, it's only a short hop in the world of vest culture from Peter Mandelson to Bruce Willis in *Die Hard* and that's what I like to think we have with the Audi all-road in particular. A normal city car that finds itself stuck in the countryside and must fight its way back to civilization.

Unlike a normal off-road car, which doesn't work in town, or a normal A6, which doesn't work on the school run, the beefed-up Audi does, strangely, manage to work in both environments. On paper, it's the worst of both worlds, but in practice, I bet it's the best.

Buy one. It's probably cheaper than my Ferrari book and, even if it comes without wheels, a lot more enjoyable.

September 2000

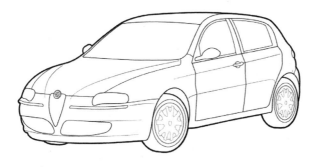

CAR OF THE YEAR: ALFA ROMEO 147

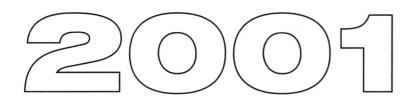

2001

TOP 5 BESTSELLING SINGLES
SONG TITLE – ARTIST

1. It Wasn't Me – Shaggy
2. Pure and Simple – Hear'Say
3. Can't Get You Out Of My Head – Kylie Minogue
4. Whole Again – Atomic Kitten
5. Hey Baby – DJ Otzi

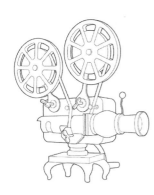

TOP 5 BOX OFFICE MOVIES

1. Harry Potter and the Philosopher's Stone
2. The Lord of the Rings: The Fellowship of the Ring
3. Shrek
4. Monsters Inc.
5. Rush Hour 2

Off-roaders

Imagine how you'd feel if you'd bought a tin of custard powder, added it to water and found the resultant explosion put the entire gable end of your house in Humberside. You'd be cross if it said custard powder on what was actually a tin of fertilizer, sodium and ammonia.

And I'm sure I'd be cross if I bought a BMW X5. It looks like a big off-road car. It feels like a big off-road car. And at £45,000, it's sure as hell priced like a big off-road car. But if you go off-road in it, you'd better hope there's a stout pair of shoes in the boot for the walk home.

What normally happens when you go off-road in a big four-wheel-drive car is that when it gets stuck, you stab away at the various levers and push whatever buttons you can find on the dash until eventually it starts to move again. But in the X5, apart from a hill descent speed control, which they nicked from Land Rover, there is nothing. You may as well poke away at the heater vents. Or pick your nose.

And it's the same with Toyota's entry-level RAV4. It looks good and, with a price tag of £18,000, seems like good value. But it only has two-wheel drive.

When I asked Toyota if I could have one for a test drive, someone rang back to say, 'Er . . . we'd love to help but we only have one on the press fleet and it's been marooned by the floods in York.'

Great, so you buy an off-road car, you put up with its

performance and handling shortfalls and then, when the flood of the century arrives, it gets stuck.

And Honda can stop laughing too. As you may have spotted, I've had one of these on test recently, and while I can report there's plenty of space in the front, there is almost none at all underneath. The exhaust is perilously close to the road and would, for sure, be torn asunder should it ever be dragged over a sweet wrapper of some kind. The problem here is simple. Car makers have noticed that most people with four-wheel-drive cars don't ever drive off-road. So why bother equipping them to do such a thing?

On the face of it, this seems like a sensible question, but really it's up there with 'Why is the Moon made of cheese?'

It's like asking why anyone wants to go out to a restaurant for dinner. It's much cheaper to stay at home and suck dust mites out of the carpet. And why do vicars need churches? Surely, it would be easier to hold their religious knees-ups in a scout hut somewhere. Or the way congregations are going these days, in the vicarage cloakroom.

The computer I'm using to write this is also capable of putting me through to a Thai ladyboy in Saigon. But even though I never wish to use this facility, it's nice to know I could.

Worse. Buying an X5 or a RAV4 or an HR-V with their big, rambunctious, macho handles is like buying a computer that promises to deliver hot sex directly into your office, and then getting home to find that the best it can manage is a mocked-up Britney nipple slip.

And it isn't just off-roaders that are failing to deliver what it says on the tin. Look at these silly mid-range people carriers that are starting to burst forth. 'I see, so with a body shape like that, it's obvious I get a great many seats in there.' 'Er, no, sir, just the five.'

They point out that these cars are tall, but what precisely is the advantage of that? How many people do you know who drive while standing up?

It's like those targa-topped cars that were all the rage as punk gave way to the new romantics. They were sold as convertibles, so you went through six fingernails and fourteen Band-Aids, and after eleven hours you finally removed the roof to leave a hole the size of two bats.

They called this wind-in-the-hair motoring. They were right. There was one hair that'd get some breeze, so you'd arrive everywhere with what looked like a twig sticking out of your head.

Other offenders? Well there's Vauxhall and Ford, who hide behind the Union Jack while making most of their cars in Germany. And then there's Nissan, who said the Micra was as English as meat pie, even though the engine, gearboxes and body shells were shipped in from under the rising sun.

So far as I can tell, the only British stuff on those early cars was the bog roll that the men who made them used to wipe their bottoms.

Even Ferrari has been a culprit. Back in the early Eighties, it laboured under the misapprehension that the name was good enough and that the cars could handle and go like seasoned oak. Happily, it didn't take them long to figure out that this simply isn't the case.

Let me put it this way: you take a girl out and all night long you get the come-on. But when push comes to shove, she shoves off. How many times do you think she can do that before the whole town starts to steer clear?

BMW says that its X5 is a sports activity vehicle. And they're right. It is far more sporty than any other car of this type, but then if they'd bothered to fit it with all the stuff you need for green laning, it wouldn't be.

So I guess it does do what it says on the tin. But if you read the ingredients carefully, you'll find it doesn't have any.

January 2001

Car manufacturing

When BMW reversed out of Rover, everyone ran around the countryside waving their arms in the air and wondering what on earth happened to the British Motor Industry. Indeed, I'm ashamed to say, I may have been party to some of that running and waving.

But then older, cleverer people rose to their gouty feet and, with measured tones, pointed out that, actually, more cars were being made in Britain at the time than at any point in history.

Not any more. Honda has said that it will not be making something or other in Swindon, Nissan is about to cease production of Micras in the North and Vauxhall has said that no more cars will be made at Luton. This came as a surprise to me since I thought they'd stopped making cars there years ago. And started making the Vectra.

There is, however, some good news in all of this. If foreign firms stop coming over here and building factories on flood plains, our traditional autumn rains will have somewhere to go other than the vault in York Minster or Mrs Miggins' tea shop in Telford.

Plus, remember that we have been telling the auto makers for some time that we'd like lower prices, so if the opportunity arises for General Motors to save a few quid by making its cars in Bongo Bongo land, then they'll take it.

These people are US businessmen and see the world not as a planet but as dots and dashes on a balance sheet. It costs

£5,000 to make a car in Luton, wherever the hell that is. And £3,000 to make it in Lahore, wherever the hell that is. So they will make it in Lahore.

Yes, a few thousand car workers in Bedfordshire get thrown out of work. But who cares, apart from the man in the local toy shop who sold rather fewer *Thunderbird* dolls this Christmas than he had been expecting? It's a global village, remember, and a job lost in Luton is a job gained somewhere else.

In the past, GM paid its workers in England and the workers put some of that money in charity boxes. Well now they've cut out the middle man. They have put the whole job in the charity box, and very nice too. You and I get cheaper cars and Mrs Miggins doesn't get raw sewage in her tea bags.

Except, of course, Luton's decimated.

'Yes, I want a cheaper car, but could I, in all conscience, buy such a thing if I knew it had brought misery to someone?'

Now, generally speaking, I have little truck with those who throw furniture through the windows at McDonald's, and plant herbs in Parliament Square. I was not in Nice recently sporting dreadlocks and a bandanna. And it was not I who led the charge in Seattle. I've never been able to understand the protesters' grievance. If I'm going to get hit in the face with a policeman's truncheon, I'd like it to be for something more worthwhile than the commonality of hamburgers throughout the world.

When I wake up in the morning, this comes way, way down on my list of things I must address in the day. It's below fox hunting. It's below the sodomy of sixteen-year-old boys. It's below everything. I just don't care. In fact, sometimes, when I'm hungry and in a country where the ice cubes can kill, it's good to stroll under that big yellow M and get a tasty Big Mac with fries.

And it's the same with banks. Men in suits lend men with bones through their noses some money and then want it back with some interest. This, it seems to me, is good business practice.

But banks, we are told by those of an anti-global-capitalism nature, have a great deal of money while there are countries in the world that do not. This is unfair, they say. Yes, but Barclays, so far as I can tell, does not run an army and does not spend 90 per cent of its income on shiny new AK47s.

However, I've been forced to question these tweedy, middle-England views this month by the news from Detroit.

Yes, I want a cheaper car but could I, in all conscience, buy such a thing if I knew it had brought misery to someone?

Would you, for instance, buy a jumper if you knew that it had been knitted by a five-year-old girl in leg irons, who got paid in Rohypnol?

No. So why should you rush out to buy the next generation of Vectra when you know its low price is a direct result of GM shutting down car production in Luton and putting thousands on the dole. You save £100 and to hell with the poor bastards who are having to feed their children on soil. Or each other.

So I find myself siding with these people who worry about the globalization of everything. Sure, some kid in Guatemala may benefit from Luton's loss, but do you know what? I don't care about some kid in Guatemala. The world is not a village, as anyone who's flown to New Zealand will testify. It's enormous and Guatemala is miles away. In the same way that Luton is bloody miles away from Detroit.

I believe that there must be some reminder for the world's car makers that the blips on their computer screens are lives and children's Christmas presents.

Maybe they should only be allowed to close a factory if the chairman himself walks onto the shop floor, butt naked save for a pair of fluffy slippers, and delivers the news himself.

February 2001

Used Rollers

Several years ago, someone called Quentin Willson went on television and explained that it was possible to buy a serviceable Rolls-Royce for as little as £6,000. I remember it well. I remember it so well in fact that I recall thinking for a femtosecond that we must have one.

Think. If nothing else, the Rolls-Royce is a tough and imperious old bird that would demolish anything that dared to get in its way. So that would make it a safe place to put our children on the school run.

But since the children in question are not called Ahmed, this was a ridiculous idea. So as this mysterious figure, with hair that seemed to be receding one moment and growing back again the next, rabbited on about how to buy Rolls-Royce gearboxes for 28p, I started to throw things at the screen.

Shut up, I wailed. I have no interest in what you're saying. For six grand I'd rather have a frontal lobotomy, which is actually what you'd need to even think about putting a Rolls-Royce on the drive. These cars are button-backed sofas for the sort of irretrievably vulgar people who see uPVC as a worthwhile and sensible addition to a period house.

There's more too. The Roller he was waffling on about – the Shadow – has exactly the same styling as a Lada. It does! Straight bonnet, straight windows, straight roof, straight boot. The only waviness you find in a car of this type is on the over-carpets that its previous owner had put in the footwell.

And then there's the engine, that 6.7-litre V8 which, according to the people who made it, provides 'adequate' levels of power. Adequate for what, though? Put your foot down to exploit a gap in the traffic and the last thought on your mind was, Oh, that's adequate. Quite the reverse, in fact. You tended to think, Oh s**t. It's broken. And don't for one minute believe that these cars are even remotely quiet. Oh, they're quiet compared with the noise molten lava makes when it's just landed after a thousand-foot fall on a sea of Icelandic ice. They're quiet compared with the sound you'd get from Brian Blessed if he were being gang-raped by forty-two Tunisian market traders. But don't fall for that guff about only being able to hear the clock ticking at 100mph. The car wouldn't do 100 anyway, and even if it could, the only clock you'd be able to hear was Big Ben.

However, the other day, that idiot A.A. Gill, who does restaurant reviews and O-level essays about starvation in Africa for *The Sunday Times,* called me and said he wanted to buy a brown Roller. Now this is the bloke who bought a TVR despite having no clue what it was. It could have been an egg whisk, or a wood-burning stove for all he knew. And when it did turn up, and turned out to be a car, he asked the salesman why it had two speedometers. 'It's a rev counter, you buffoon.'

Still, since he gets me into good restaurants, it was the least I could do to help him with a car. I therefore called Damon Hill, who's got mates in the trade, put the two in touch and now A.A. has his brown, 1978 Shadow II.

It cost £10,000, and for that he's got gold badging and a gold spirit of ecstasy. Every single thing works, even the little lights that illuminate the vanity mirrors in the back, and it's only done 68,000 miles. Well, I'm sure it hasn't really. I'm sure it's been clocked, but the V5 doesn't lie and it's only had one owner.

Yes, it's still noisy, slow and stupidly cramped in the back, but you have to admit that, for this kind of money, it is a lot of car . . . except for one thing. This business about style and taste.

Well, it turns out that, once again, the start of a fashion has passed me by. It seems that John Diamond, the journalist who recently died of cancer, had bought a Roller as a sort of 'what the hell' final gesture and that this one thing had made the old dowager cool.

And it's true. I've noticed that every Roller in town is now being driven by Nick Hornby/Guy Ritchie types – shaved heads, forty-odd, all in black and with a pair of Bono glasses to get them past security at the Met bar.

The old Roller has become the car of choice for the sort of people we saw in *Lock, Stock and Two Smoking Barrels*. Youngish, bright, on-the-edge urbanites. Check out the area around Charlotte Street where all the ad men hang and it's choc full of choc-brown Rollers.

Amazing, isn't it? VW brought out the Beetle, and Chrysler the PT Cruiser, to try and win the hearts of precisely this sort of person and both have failed spectacularly. Jim Davidson, for instance, has a PT, and the only people I ever see in Beetles are school teachers.

Whoever would have guessed it? Quentin Willson was not only ahead of his hair, but ahead of the times too. I should have bought that Roller when he told me too, because prices will soon be shooting through the roof.

It's no good thinking that any similar car from this period

will do, because it won't. Forget Stag, Aston or old Rover because the Seventies roller is perfect for the dawn of Mr Blair's bright new century.

All the animals are equal. But some are more equal than others.

May 2001

Ageing

I feel nineteen. I think I have the body of someone who's nineteen. I think I look nineteen. In fact, I only know I'm not nineteen when I try to act like I'm nineteen.

The trouble is that the deterioration of my lungs has been gradual. When I was nineteen I could have run to Las Vegas and arrived with perhaps a bead of perspiration on my brow, and only because of the heat. Now, I don't do the stairs two at a time but in two stages. With a cigarette break on the first landing.

It's the same story with my stamina. When I was nineteen I could go to parties that went on for a week, whereas now I get sleepy by eleven. And hangovers? Jesus. I'm only just over Boxing Day.

But it wasn't like I suddenly woke up one morning and found that one glass of dry white was enough. It happened s l o w l y. One day it was fourteen pints, then it was thirteen and a half and then it was twelve, until now, after twenty years, I'm cross-eyed after a sniff of Ribena.

I bring all this up – and believe me I do that too if I have more than a pint – because I've just spent the last week driving a 1990 Audi Quattro. And I'm sorry, but it was like bumping into an old girlfriend who's had three kids since you last saw her, and got a job in a chocolate factory. For crying out loud, how on earth did I ever fancy this?

Really. When I wrote for *Performance Car* magazine in the late Eighties, the 20-valve Audi Quattro was the equivalent of an M5, a Ferrari, a Subaru Impreza and the Lloyd's Building, all rolled into one. I made it my car of the year every year because there was nothing – and I mean nothing – that even got close to it.

Well, it may only have been eleven years ago but, heaven's above, things have changed. Driving it nowadays is like listening to *Tubular Bells*.

I mean, where are the wheels? How did I not notice that the old thing was connected to the road by four Smarties. Honestly, they're only 14 inches in diameter – four less than on an RS4.

And then you have the wipers, which aren't hidden under the leading edge of the bonnet. They stand proud, in the air flow where they can increase drag, not work at speed and, as a bonus, fracture the skull of anyone you run down.

Moving inside, there's the digital dash, which Honda has unwisely brought back on the S2000 and er . . . that's about it. Answer me this. How in God's name did we ever manage without air-conditioning? In that mid-May heatwave I had to drive along with the bloody window down and I still got home every night in need of a bath.

Then there's the stereo. A Blaupunkt Melbourne with buttons that you have to press. And when you press them, a red line moves mechanically up the dial. That's the stuff of Brunel.

But worst of all were the door panels. Today, even the cheapest and most horrible Hyundai has sculptured lining, whereas the Quattro simply has material to stop you seeing the metal – metal which clangs when the door is closed. Honestly, I've seen cow sheds which can be sealed with more aplomb.

I was amazed. I would never have believed that car design had come on so fast in the last ten years that things we take for granted now weren't even available as an extra on an all-singing all-dancing supercar from just eleven years ago.

However, in one important respect, modern cars still cannot hold a candle to the old bruiser. And that is the way the damn thing moves.

At this point, I know, the editor of *Top Gear* magazine will be finding something important to do, which involves being in Chile for a month, but he once moved a 20-valve Quattro into a cornfield. Backwards at about 85. And I still don't know how.

Yes, there is a touch of understeer to start with, but if you lift off or brake or even die, the tail starts to come round so gradually that even a man with no arms could get it back again.

Needless to say, the 2.2-litre turbo five is down on power compared with the RS4, but in a drag race – and I know this because I did it – you simply wouldn't believe how close the older, lighter car gets. At the half-mile marker, there was just a car's length in it.

More than this, the Quattro is a car that begs to be driven hard. The RS4 is stupendous – one of the world's great ground coverers – but when you're just driving along, it turns into a pussy cat. The Quattro, however, doesn't know the meaning of 'just driving along'.

My wife said after a drive from Chipping Norton to Wiltshire that she'd averaged XXX miles per hour (censored because I need someone to drive me home from parties) and, frankly, I didn't believe her. But the following day, without really trying, I managed the same thing. Even though I had to have the damn window down.

It made me wonder about the direction modern cars are taking. Obviously, they are more comfortable, kinder to the environment and equipped with far more in the way of toys. But when it comes to excitement, the old Quattro is an easy match for even a Subaru P1.

Imperceptibly, I've got older and slower, but the Quattro is still nineteen. Moby may be all the rage but Mike Oldfield did it first. And better.

July 2001

The Trabant

As Europeans everywhere blanch at the notion of a single currency, fearing that such a thing will turn us into one giant amorphous blob, I have at last found one thing that does unite the entire continent. We may speak different languages, eat different food, practice different nocturnal perversions and keep different dogs, but believe me, a local car show in Zwickau is the same as every local car show you've ever been to anywhere.

You get the same blokes in stone-washed denim mooching about buying things that their wives would rather they didn't: bits of steering wheel, rear light assemblies, CJD burgers. You get the same unintelligible public address systems and the same line-up of bored girlfriends in inappropriate outfits.

Zwickau is in the former East German Democratic Republic, so named, of course, because there was no democracy. What there was, just outside the pretty old town, was a huge and useless car factory where they made Trabants.

When the wall came down, there was a drive to rid the roads of these hopeless little cars with their 26bhp two-stroke engines and their woeful safety record.

It wasn't so bad when everyone had a Trabant, but in a unified Germany they were sharing the roads with Audis, and it was a mix as devastating as Baileys and lime juice. You may remember that in 1995 an entire East German family in their Trabant was killed when it hit an A8. And the Audi driver? He went home with a broken radiator grille.

Trabants did not sit well with Germany's philosophy of environmental protection either. I have done some mental arithmetic here: an S-Class Mercedes produces the same amount of toxic waste over 30 miles that a Trabant chucks out in three seconds.

The only good thing about this Commie oxbow lake in the river of capitalism was watching the Green party agonize. The Trabby had to go, but this would be seen as Western arrogance. They couldn't deny the poor Easterners their wheels, planet killers though they may have been.

Wait, there was another good thing about it. It spawned the first German joke that didn't involve poo. A cartoon appeared in a newspaper showing a Trabant salesman knocking on someone's door, saying, 'Your car is here!'

Don't get it? Well, there was a twenty-year waiting list for Trabants when the wall was up, and here was a car being delivered long after it came down.

Anyway, twelve years after Checkpoint Charlie was abandoned, most of the Trabants have gone but there is now a movement afoot to preserve a few for posterity. Hence the car show.

Not being the slightest bit bothered about Western arrogance, I rocked up in a Mark 1 E-Type Jag. Roof down. Dido on the CD player. And they didn't pay me any attention.

This is because I'd parked next to the longest car I'd ever seen. I think the owner said it was 15 metres long. Though he might have been giving me his mother's recipe for baked Alaska.

I was much more concerned about the fact that I had started to sink. It is a well-known fact that the weather at any car show can do what it pleases, but the ground will always be like a quagmire. Zwickau was no different. Then there's the onion problem. There were stall holders selling pizzas, beer, hot dogs, more beer and beer. But still, there was the same all-pervading aroma that blankets every car show from Portugal to the Baltic. Fried onions.

There was confusion with the music too. Trabants can be bought in working order for just £30, which makes them very popular with young men who then spend £30,000 equipping them with stereos that can blow the doors off a police van at 400 paces.

Thus, the sound at the car show is a pulsating cacophony of bass. The organizers know this will happen, so why do they provide music for the tannoy?

It was the usual fayre. We started with the Scorpions and then Brian Adams, Toto, Europe and whatever else made the DJ feel like he was working for some God-awful soft rock KZFM west coast radio station.

We can't hear any of it, moron. Your puny loud hailers are no match for a Trabant pickup that's been turned from a dog into a giant woofer.

It's amazing what you can do to a Trabant. I found one with a VW 16v engine, and another with the two-stroke tweaked to deliver 68bhp. Then there was Michael Schumacher's idiot cousin who'd tried to make his Trabant look like a F1 car. It hadn't worked.

But that didn't stop every person stopping to take a photograph of it.

Everywhere I went, macheteing my way through the bass 'n' onions, the story was the same. I was told that none of the best cars had made it. Which put me in mind of those crabs on Christmas Island. Millions set out for the mating grounds, but only the fittest survive.

A bit like society really. They tried communism but it didn't live long. And neither should the cars it spawned. The solution's simple. Put one Trabant in a museum and shoot the rest.

August 2001

Murder

Given the choice, most of us would like to die peacefully in our sleep or heroically at the helm of a doomed airliner. But unfortunately, for every 100,000 people reading this, 1.4 are going to be sorely disappointed. Because you're going to be murdered.

If that doesn't appeal to you, move to Argentina, where the rate is just 0.1 for every 100,000. Niger looks good too, at 0.2, but that's mainly because murderers, like everyone else, have such bad diarrhoea, they're never off the lavatory long enough to do the deed.

At the other end of the scale we have Swaziland where, for every 100,000 people, 88 arrive at the Pearly Gates sporting a smouldering Dunlop necklace. Murdering is now so popular in Africa that America isn't even in the premier league any more. Despite a big push from drug dealers in Detroit and Chicago, the former champions came away with just 14,000 hits last year, thanks mainly to a pathetic showing from New Hampshire, where murderers only scored four times.

However, if you're going to be murdered, America is still best. Nearly half the killings last year involved speedy and fairly painless handguns. Even speedier rifles, shotguns and automatic machine pistols took out another 2,000. Axes and chainsaws saw to the rest.

Being murdered in Britain is much more grisly. Here, one of the most popular methods is 'hitting and kicking'. Oh dear. I think I'd rather be eaten than hit and kicked to death.

But more worrying still is that the eighth most common murder weapon in the UK is the motor vehicle.

Now I know we're famed throughout the world for our sense of fair play: we don't shoot pheasants on the ground and we prefer to chase foxes on horses rather than in Range Rovers, but really, if you want to hit and run, the car is awfully hit and miss. If you decide that you really do have to kill the man at the newsagents, why not simply set fire to him? Or use a Flymo?

Let's face it, there are innumerable problems with making your getaway in the murder weapon. To have killed the man, you must have been doing at least 40mph. At that speed, your car will have sustained serious damage. And it's not so much the complication and expense of getting this repaired as the fact that while Plod might not have noticed you driving down the pavement, he sure as hell will spot a broken indicator lens and pull you over.

The other problem is that cars are now being designed with pedestrian safety in mind so that even if you do get him right between the headlights, he will almost certainly walk away with nothing more than light bruising. Look at the figures: of the 43,000 people knocked down last year, fewer than 900 actually died from their injuries.

Modern wipers are tucked away under the leading edge of the bonnet so that a flailing head is unlikely to connect with the bone-shattering nut that holds them in place. Modern bonnets are designed to be flexible and soft in the middle but hard where they cover the unyielding suspension mounts. Bumpers are shaped to ensure a body is thrown up and over, rather than down and into the path of the wheels.

So if you must use a car as a murder weapon, choose the model carefully. Certainly, you should avoid the Daihatsu Sirion which, in a recent Euro NCAP test, achieved a three-star rating for both pedestrian safety and occupant protection – in other words, you're going to end up in the same shape as the man you hit.

But the absolute worst choice you can make is the Honda Civic, which was found to offer nearly twice the pedestrian protection of any other car.

So what's good then? Well, you may be tempted by something with a pointy bonnet ornament, like a Rolls-Royce. You may also be interested to know that in Switzerland, the Spirit of Ecstasy is banned; Rollers are sold with smooth-topped radiator grilles.

But don't get your hopes up because in the free world, where there is no Nazi gold, it's designed to retract in the event of an impact. And you thought this was to stop people nicking it.

It turns out that what you really need for killing newsagents is a short bonnet so that his head hits the windscreen. Good cars singled out in crash tests are the Ford Fiesta, Renault Clio and Volkswagen Polo. The Audi A4 does well too – at last, a reason for buying one – as does the 5-Series BMW. Top of the tree, though, seem to be people carriers. The Peugeot 806, Chrysler Voyager and Vauxhall Sintra are killing machines to rival the Uzi 9mm.

I'm sorry if you've found this month's column distasteful, but let's be honest: if I'd written it the other way round, lavishing praise on safe cars, you'd have switched off in the second paragraph.

And rightly so. While it's hugely laudable for the RAC and others to push for bonnets like duvets and inflatable headlamps, in Britain today you stand a roughly equal chance of being knocked down and killed by a car as you do of being murdered.

September 2001

The Dutch

You join me this month in Holland, where the people are high, the country is low, the men are gay, the women are naked and you're exhorted, as you walk down the streets of Amsterdam, to step inside every building for some sleaze and filth.

I'm making a TV series about the major European countries and the people who live in them. And to be honest, it's a piece of cake.

There's a good reason to dislike or distrust every single one of the tribes on this side of the water. The Spanish nick our fish but have no clue how to cook it. The French know how to cook it but can't be arsed to serve us. Then you have the Italians who have no sense of humour, the Germans who can't play football and the Belgians who can't play football either, mainly because they think they're fish.

It's easy to be smug too because there is almost no country in Europe that we haven't creamed at some point. Except Belgium, of course, which was invented by the British as somewhere to play our military away fixtures.

This argument, however, doesn't hold water with the Dutch. They once had the barefaced cheek to sail right up the Thames and sink our entire fleet. They even killed Lord Sandwich. However, in the ensuing peace treaty they made the mistake of swapping Suriname – a two-bit hell-hole in South America – for a place called New Amsterdam. We then changed its name to New York.

The thing is, though, that rather than fret about it, Johnny Dutch simply points out that Britain got no footballers at all from America whereas their entire national team is Surinamese, or whatever it is you are when you're from there. So, in their eyes, they kind of won both the war and the peace as well.

I like the Dutch. I like their tolerance. I like their relaxed attitude to sex and drugs. Only last night, a chap I met told me he was a little late because he'd been downloading some porno movies from the Internet. He said it like he'd been shopping.

And then there was a girl in a bar. An aid worker. Respectable. Late thirties. A bit plain. And within five minutes she was extolling the virtues of the cock ring. I was flabbergasted.

Obviously, I want to dislike them and have cast about frantically for a reason. They are a little tight perhaps, and will wreck a perfectly good car by adding a raised roof to make it, technically, a van. This cuts the tax bill in half.

They also have quite an absurd penchant for caravanning. Think about it. Think of all the amazing places you've been to. The remote craggy outpost of Western Spain. The high Alpine passes or Switzerland. The very top of Scotland. What's always there to spoil the view? Yes! A Dutch family in chunky jumpers and a camper van.

Then you have Dutch traffic lights, which are green for half a second, orange for half a second and red for three weeks. And there's an absolutely idiotic law here which says you must always give way to people on bicycles.

But I can forgive them this. I can forgive them anything for what they are doing about the only thing they have ever given to the world. The Gatso speed camera.

Holland is infested with the damn things. On the motorway

from Amsterdam to Eindhoven yesterday, I counted eight in the space of one mile. Eight! And they're painted an even more invisible shade of grey than ours.

However, even though the Dutch don't get penalty points for speeding, and the fine is usually £20, they have reacted to this explosion of Nanny Statism with a fury that has left the whole country gasping.

Basically, someone is going around at night, blowing them up. He gives the police fair warning, painting the camera pink. And then, a few nights later, using heavy fireworks imported from Belgium – BANG! – the whole £25,000 shooting match is blown sky high.

As you cruise around, you will see evidence of his handiwork everywhere. Grey stumps with frazzled wires poking out of the top. Shattered radar equipment in the tree tops.

And now there are copycat crimes. Tyres full of petrol are slung around the box on top. Four-wheel drives are bending the mounting poles so they only photograph passing ospreys. No, really. If you don't believe me, there are photographs for your viewing pleasure at www.tuftufclub.com.

I don't doubt that many of you will check out this site, and you will maybe e-mail the pictures to your friends who, just like you, will laugh and say, 'Hey, wouldn't it be great if someone else did that here in Britain'.

I'm not suggesting anyone should, of course. I mean, it would be wholly irresponsible to attack a speed camera. Or relocate those which are positioned behind bushes on open stretches of road to somewhere more appropriate, like outside a children's play area or a school, for example.

Were you to do any of this you would be interfering with the chief constable's business and you may well end up in court. Unless of course you did it at night, dressed in combat fatigues with lookouts posted.

So, sadly, it seems like the speed camera is here to stay in Britain, whereas in Holland, it really does look like the war on fast driving may well be lost.

That's the best thing about the Dutch. They do not elect people to govern them. They elect a leader who does as he's told. And what they're telling him over here at the moment is simple: 'Get off our backs.'

November 2001

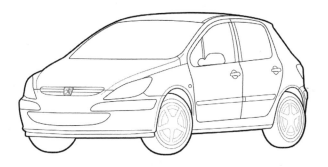

CAR OF THE YEAR: PEUGEOT 307

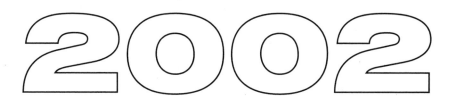

2002

TOP 5 BESTSELLING SINGLES
SONG TITLE – ARTIST

1 Evergreen – Will Young
2 Unchained Melody – Gareth Gates
3 Hero – Enrique Iglesias
4 Dilemma – Nelly featuring
Kelly Rowland
5 A Little Less Conversation –
Elvis Presley vs JXL

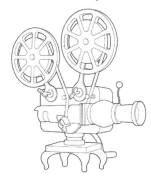

TOP 5 BOX OFFICE MOVIES

1 Spider-Man
2 The Lord of the Rings: The Two Towers
3 Star Wars: Episode II – Attack of the
Clones
4 Harry Potter and the Chamber of Secrets
5 My Big Fat Greek Wedding

The Euro

Since the whole of Europe has now become one, I thought we'd talk about the Euro. Sorry.

Thozzzzze in favour say that it will make price discrepancies more obvious, that we'll be able to see how much cheaper a Ford Focus is in France if they're using the same money. But this is rubbish. Even I, with the mental agility of a horse, can convert pounds into Francs without moving my lips.

They also say it will increase trade. No it won't. If we all have the same currency, the playing field is level and companies will simply buy whichever product is best. That means German, usually.

Sure, British companies are being hurt now because the pound is strong, but it can't be long before His Tonyness does something silly and it comes over all weak again.

Then they say that if we join the Euro, business transactions will be simpler. This is undoubtedly true, but do you really want to put the Queen's head in the dustbin, along with your blue passport, just to make life a little bit simpler for some spotty bank clerk?

I do. I think the Euro is a fabulous idea. It puts power firmly in the hands of the Europeans and that means less control for the idiot Blair – the only man ever to have lived who believes you can have a 'caring' war.

Give me Berlusconi any day. When the skyscrapers came down, the Italian said it was a struggle between a people who live in tents and a people who gave the world the high renaissance. Then he went for lunch. What a guy.

Three days after the plane crashes – I refuse to say 'the events of September 11' – one newspaper in Italy carried a report of anti-terrorism developments at the bottom of page one. The rest of the page was given over to a new Piaggio scooter launch. Marvellous.

I really do believe the civilized world is at a crossroads right now. We can either go down the American route: busy, busy, busy, no time for lunch, eat on the move, cupholders in the car, golf, working breakfast, working supper, work out and styrofoam food. Or we can go down the European route: style, pasta, more style, some red wine, smoke, laugh, style, friends, drive fast, see more, do more, eat more and take longer over doing everything.

There are those, I know, who say that if Britain must become part of something bigger, we should apply to be the fifty-first state of the USA, but I cannot think of anything worse. There are millions of reasons, but there's only space here to deal with one – their cars.

Think about it. The only people in the entire world who buy American cars live in caravans and have one functioning eye. We never see what sort of wheels have been chosen by the *Deliverance* 'squeal like a piggy' chap, but we just know that it's an IROC-Z.

Then you have America's only sports car – the Corvette. Oh please. A Corvette is a ship.

Anyone in America who earns over three dollars a year buys European. There are ritzy clubs on both coasts where you simply won't get past the meat machine at the gate if you turn up in a Chevy or a Dodge. It must be a Benz or a Bimmer or, best of all, a Range Rover.

There is, of course, a jolly good reason for this. American cars are, by and large, absolute rubbish. When you're behind the wheel of a Lexus, you sense that its engineering tolerances are measured in nanomicrons. Whereas when you're in an American car, you get the impression it was built to the nearest foot.

There's some evidence for this too. Look at the Euro NCAP safety test results. Even a humble Euro car like the Renault Laguna gets five stars, whereas the old Chrysler Voyager was the worst car they'd ever tested. And other Yank tanks don't do much better.

We must also consider America's automotive breakthroughs over the years. Cadillac developed the electric starter – presumably because its customers were too fat to get out of the car and do it themselves – and Ford came up with the production line. So that its workforce could build cars without moving.

Great, but we Europeans came up with the wheel and haven't stopped innovating since.

Part of the problem, of course, is that the American motorist doesn't really demand more from his car than four wheels and a seat. We in Europe want to feel we're the organic part of the machine, but over there, he is so disinterested in the driving experience that the car has to chime and bong all the time to tell him to do things.

This is why he's happy to have a truck. Never mind that it has medieval cart springs and an engine that develops 4bhp despite being the size of France. To Hank, it's just an auxiliary transport module; a device that will get him from A to B until someone invents a *Star Trek* beaming machine. He views driving with the same disdain that he views root-canal work.

Do you want to be a part of that? Or do you want a Noble M12 GTO? Well, good. When we finally get round to the referendum on the Euro, vote yes.

February 2002

The E-Type

I'm intrigued by the notion of that Ford GT40 that was shown at the recent Detroit Motor Show. It's new in every way and so meets all the most lunatic safety and emission requirements. It's modern-day fast too, and yet it looks exactly like the old GT40.

What a fantastic idea; to combine the style of the Sixties with the ease and convenience, and power, of life in the twenty-first century.

Jaguar's stylists will, I'm sure, be dispirited to hear this as they slave away over the new F-Type. It'll probably be a lovely car, but imagine how good it would be if it had a super-charged V8 engine, anti-lock brakes and styling that wasn't simply reminiscent of, but identical to, the old E-Type.

I know what a head-turner the E-Type is because last summer I did 20,000 miles round Europe in a Series 1 4.2 Roadster.

I went so far across Germany that I bumped into Poland and then all the way back to Brittany. I went to the south east corner of Spain and then right across the middle to the north western tip. I did Amsterdam to the heel of Italy in a day. So, believe me, I know that car inside out.

Of course, you're now picturing it, aren't you? You are visualizing the lustrous navy paintwork and the brilliant chrome. You can see it glinting on the sea front in St Tropez and blasting past the spaghetti western backdrop of central Spain. Might I dare to suggest you're a little bit envious?

Rightly so, but realistically, behind the tip-top aesthetics, an old car like this is going to be a let-down if you're used to something modern like a Daewoo Leganza. Or a Ford Sierra.

Mine had been mildly tweaked by Eagle E Types of Sussex, so that it had a better cooling system, better brakes and modern tyres, but that didn't stop everything heading off to hell one fine evening on the German autobahn.

People started honking their horns as they blasted past, but this, I figured, was just an acknowledgment that my car was better than their slate-grey Teutonic missiles. So I waved cheerily to them, and I was still waving when the Jag's rear tyre exploded.

It turned out that it was a tubeless Pirelli, which had been fitted with an inner tube because the wire wheels leak. That's fine if you coat the tube with talcum powder but I'm a child of the modern age. If I'm going to break out the lubricant, I can think of better things to smear it on than my wheels. Same goes for the white powder.

As luck would have it, however, I was just outside Koblenz, which is where Pirelli have a factory. So an hour later I was on my way. Rather more slowly than before. Even though I was fully dusted down, I never really trusted the tyres again and kept my speed down to . . . well, I don't know actually because the speedo was broken.

And so it was that on one fine day, just outside Biarritz, I was cruising along at 60 or 80, or maybe it was 40, when I became aware of a strange noise. Obviously, being used to modern cars, I did nothing, and I continued to do nothing up to the moment when I noted the temperature needle was bent like an arthritic finger round the top of the dial. Shit. And just to make matters worse, the oil pressure gauge was reading the sort of score that former presenters of *Top Gear* get on *The Weakest Link*. One.

Even I, with the mechanical sympathy and understanding of a Visigoth, knew this meant something was up, so I coasted into one of those rural Renault garages off the autoroute and went in search of 'A Man'.

He didn't actually have a beret and Gitanes, but he should have done. He had that demeanour as he sauntered over to see the Rosbif's broken car. But when he saw what it was, the top of his head came off in delight. Certainly, he developed a hitherto unseen ability to speak perfect English.

I was taken to his workshop to see his own cars: a Mark 2, a Mark 10 and an XK120. And by the time we went outside again his mate, who happened to be passing and who also happened to be chairman of the French Historic Jaguar Drivers' Club, had stopped by in his XK150.

Did I feel lucky? Yes. Did I understand what was wrong with my car? Nope. But they fixed it and charged me nought for the privilege.

To be honest, this was the extent of my breakdowns. And that's not so bad in 20,000 miles.

What is bad are the things that used to be considered normal; the refusal for the front end to go where you'd like it to go. The steering, which seemed to be set in concrete. The hood, which chopped off your fingers or ripped the seats. Or both, but never neither.

Then there was the stereo system. I'd installed a CD player without realizing the old slot was right next to the heater, which was permanently on – handy when you're stuck in a Madrid traffic jam in August – but the savage heat hammering away at my bald patch was nothing compared with the searing agony of touching a CD fresh from the slot. It would have caused grave injury to my fingertips had they not been severed by the roof.

Think though. These are simple problems which would be easy to address if they started again with the E-Type. Or the Mustang. Or the Ferrari Daytona. Keep the style the same, but replace everything else. It'd be like buying *Sgt Pepper* on mini disc. It'd be great.

If you want to see the programme that features the Jaguar, it's called *Meet the Neighbours* and it will be on the television.

March 2002

The Impreza Turbo

Strange but true. More people watch *Top Gear* in India than there are people in Britain. Yup, every week, the world's premiere motoring television show attracts an audience on the sub continent in excess of 60 million.

It's much the same story in the Middle East too. So when I went to Dubai the other day, I was prepared for the onslaught of autograph hunters at the airport.

There weren't any. But no matter. At the hotel it would be a different story. There'd be hundreds and hundreds of salivating fans queuing up to meet the motoring guru from the centre of the Empire.

I was shown to my room by a butler who explained how the Internet worked, how to draw the curtains without getting out of bed and how the jacuzzi would relax me after my long flight. Then, rather nervously, he asked if, perhaps, I might give him my signature.

'Of course,' I said, reaching for my pen and a scrap of paper on the desk. Taking his name from his lapel badge, I wrote 'To Ahmed, with very best wishes, from Jeremy Clarkson.'

He looked a bit bewildered and after a discreet cough said, 'Er, no, I meant, could you put your signature on the registration form.'

Well I was devastated. I realized that I'm living in a world far removed from reality and that I must catch the bus and the underground train back to 'real world central'.

And so, while driving down Regent Street in London yesterday, I didn't even look up, let alone grin inanely into the lens, when a Japanese person on the pavement started to film me on one of those high-tech Oriental cameras that's also a phone, and a computer, and an Internet, and a house.

But hang on. Why is he filming me? *Top Gear* was never very big in Japan. He doesn't know who I am. So, if he's not interested in me, he must be interested in . . . the car.

My suspicions were confirmed 200 yards later when another Japanese person, in another Burberry mac with another phone, Internet, WAP, house, garage, computer camera started to film my progress. Well, I couldn't believe it. These people were within a stone's throw of Piccadilly Circus, one of the most recognizable landmarks on the planet, but they were ignoring the Coca Cola signs and Eros and choosing to film a Subaru WRX STI GTi IT Nutter Bastard Xi RS Turbo AWD Impreza instead.

Let's not beat about the bush here. On the absolute raggedy edge of adhesion, on a track, when someone else is paying for the tyres and Tiff is at the helm, then yes, a Mitsubishi Evo MMCVII is better, but for everyday use, be in no doubt that the Subaru is completely and totally stunning. I f***ing loved it.

But it's no oil painting, is it? If you were a Japanese person on holiday in England and you only had so much tape to record your visit, you'd be better off pointing your WAP camera house at Blenheim Palace or Big Ben than you would at a WRX STI IT Nutter Bastard Xi RS Turbo AWD Impreza.

I mean, that spoiler on the back, and those decals, in pink if you please, and that colour scheme. It's not exactly the vision the folks back home have of little olde England, is it?

But there's something about the techno wizardry of the Scooby Doo that seems to make a Japanese person priapic with excitement. And this is interesting, because just five days earlier I'd driven across London in a new BMW 7 Series. Yes iDrive blah blah, 700 functions blah blah Chris Bangle blah V8 power blah. But could Tojo give a damn? Could he hell as like. I may as well have been driving the invisible car so far as his Cinemascope view on life was concerned.

The brothers, on the other hand, went berserk. Every black guy from the Elephant and Castle to deepest Balham acted like I was cruising past in Bob Marley himself.

The driver of one bus left his seat, opened the doors and beamed the beam of a tropical crescent moon. Man. He loved that car.

I know that since some American rap artist whose name I can't remember bought a Lexus, the LS430 is supposed be the car of choice in South London. But believe me, nothing, not even a joint the shape and size of Ali G, could whip up as much enthusiasm as a 7 Series. It is the king of kings. Second in command to Haile Selassie. Rasta Pasta for the soul. It is, to the brothers, what a Volvo is to the ringlet and trilby boys of Stoke Newington.

Whereas in Southhall, centre of the Indian community in London, I may as well have been driving a dog turd.

Here, there's only one car and it's the Nissan Bluebird. But when things pick up, the driver will go for anything, so long as it has a three-pointed star on the bonnet. It doesn't matter if it's a one cc, diesel C-Class coupé, with vinyl seats and rubber carpetry, all Benzes, to Johnny Indian, are better than any other cars. Full stop. A 600CL is not a car. It's a deity.

So where, in this potpourri of skin tones and churches, is whitey? Well, on a bicycle, to be honest, pedalling to his civic office block, where he spends the day dreaming up new traffic management schemes and congestion charges and bus lanes and speed cameras and tow-away trucks and drink-driving rules that cause your licence to be taken away if you've inadvertently driven past a newsagents that sells wine gums.

Multicultural Britain? I'm in.

May 2002

Denmark

Automotively speaking, I think it's fair to say that Denmark has not exactly been a major player. In fact, come to think of it, I can't think that Denmark has made much of a contribution in any field. I think I went there once, and I seem to recall there were many cows. Maybe Hans Christian Andersen was a Friesian.

In fact, on really, really quiet days I have found myself wondering, what exactly is the point of Denmark? But now I have the answer. It's called the BoCart.

Made in a town that appears to have been named by someone who simply ran amok with a typewriter keyboard, it's a sort of off-road go-kart. A modern-day Honda Pilot, if you will.

Except that the Pilot was made largely for an American audience and, as a result, you couldn't see where you were going for all the warning notices. Every square inch of the chassis was smothered with labels warning drivers that if they drove fast they would be killed, that if more than one person was on board at a time everyone would die of plague and that if you tried to drive across a steep bank, you might trip the missile silos in Kentucky and instigate a nuclear winter that would last a thousand years.

The BoCart is mercifully free from such prophecies of doom, though the handbook – well, hand-pamphlet to be precise – does make a few veiled threats. It says, for instance, that you shouldn't try to clean the vehicle while it's in motion, but it doesn't say what would happen if you did.

I like that sort of attitude to safety, though it might explain why we hear so little from Denmark. Perhaps they're all dead. And anyway, if I wanted to be nice and safe, I wouldn't be interested in a BoCart. But I am, and you should be too.

Some figures: the Panther Extreme, the biggest, fastest, most expensive model – and let's be honest, that's the one to go for here – is £2,999. Plus the cost of an acre or so of paddock. At today's prices, reckon on about another two grand.

For your money, you get a 13 horsepower Honda engine... Yes, I thought that too. I went round the field a couple of times and I thought it was fine – a sort of grown-up kids' toy, but not really capable of arousing the adrenalin gland in a man who's been to the sound barrier in an F-15.

However, I then invited some mates round for a go, and instilled with an it's-not-mine-so-I-don't-care-if-I-break-it bravery, they went berserk. Pretty soon it was three feet in the air. And then – shortly after one of them discovered that if you braked hard while going fast round a corner, it would spin – it was upside down.

This is the key. Once I'd been shown that I could hurt myself, I started to love it a whole lot more. And now, obviously, I've got to buy another. Owning one BoCart is like owning one Japanese fighting fish. Fine, up to a point. But having a pair to race would lift the excitement to a whole new level.

Now this is interesting, isn't it? Without wishing to sound completely spoiled, I've got a Ferrari in the garage and yet, give me the choice this afternoon of going for a blast in that, or going for a spin on the Hoover-powered bedspring and there's no contest. The BoCart wins every time.

Why? Well, part of it has to do with the utter simplicity of the thing. You can see the springs working and there's no heavyweight bodywork to dilute the fun. It's just you, a roll cage and a four-point seatbelt. That's it.

But I think the main reason has to do with the freedom you get in a field. You can ride it drunk – I have – and it's up to you, not Stephen Byers, how fast you can tackle the jumps and dips. Driving on the road these days is slavery. Driving off it is freedom.

Of course, it never takes very long for a crowd of ramblers to arrive and stand with their hands on their hips, looking displeased, but this just makes the whole experience even better. Because there's absolutely nothing they can do about it, and anyway, devising new ways to annoy people in cagoules should be on the school curriculum.

Actually, did you know that the Ramblers' Association began life as an offshoot of the Communist Party. That's true, that is.

Anyway, my point is that with all the speed cameras, and sleeping policemen, and wide-awake policemen, a normal road car, even a very good one like a 355, has limits. That's why track days are becoming so popular these days. But even on track days, there's always someone in a tabard telling you what you can and can't do.

And that's not quite good enough.

As humans, we are born to take risks. Put a toddler on a swing and watch their faces; they love the sensation of having the wind in their hair. I recently took my six-year-old waterskiing and he was priapic with excitement about the whole thing.

So to be told that you can't do this and you can't do that, doesn't really sit well with what makes us tick. The safer they make our lives, the more we will have to find escape routes to let off steam.

And now, if you'll forgive me, I'm off into the countryside on my BoCart to chase a fox. I understand that you aren't allowed to chase them with dogs any more, so . . .

June 2002

Domestic bliss

Hundreds and hundreds of years ago, *Top Gear* used to employ a man called Tiffany Dell. Tiffany used to drive very fast, especially when he came to a corner, and judged cars solely on their ability to slide whenever they went past a camera.

Then one day Tiffany needed to buy a car with his own money. Naturally, he was drawn to machines like the Porsche 911, but Mrs Dell said no. Mrs Dell explained that they had many children and would need something large and high.

And so it was that Tiffany found himself in the real world, worrying about baby seats, how easy it is to operate a door handle when you have a screaming child in the other arm, and whether the boot was big enough for all three push-chairs. Good handling, he found, simply made Jack's juice beaker fall over.

Oh how I laughed. I laughed and laughed for years. I kept on laughing even after Tiffany had been transported to a motoring programme that he can't watch at home, and to a magazine that likes the Vectra. In fact, I laughed until last weekend, when suddenly the same thing happened to me. Mrs Clarkson slammed my fingers in the fridge door of life and showed me that pretty well everything I'd ever said about cars was rubbish.

She needed a new car to replace her BMW Z1. It's starting to feel its age and she wants something a bit friskier, a bit more like the Caterham I made her sell last year.

Obviously, you can forget the SLK and the MR2 and the

MX-5, because they're built as only cars. They're built to be fun . . . up to a point. They're kind of like the headmaster at a progressive secondary school, or a community police constable. I like a laugh as much as the next man, but occasionally the laughing has to stop.

Well Mrs Clarkson doesn't want the laughing to stop. This is a mother of three, remember, who took her Caterham to Morocco one year and Sicily the next. Sleet? Pah. The hood's for homosexuals. She wanted, as she put it, a toy car, a car that hasn't grown up. She wanted another Caterham.

So last weekend the choice came down to a TVR Tamora or a Lotus Elise.

'Simple,' I said. 'It has to be the Lotus.'

'Why?' she asked.

'Well,' I spluttered, 'the Lotus is sushi and the TVR is a meat pie. The Elise is a better engineered car, which thanks to its extruded aluminium construction, is better able to switch between power oversteer and neutrality. The TVR, on the other hand, is brute force and ignorance. A sort of box girder bridge, if you will, with windscreen wipers.'

'She wanted,' as she put it, 'a toy car, a car that hasn't grown up. She wanted another Caterham.

'Furthermore,' I said, 'you can't reach the pedals in a TVR and you're not strong enough to fasten the roof struts. Plus, you're a girl.'

This, when translated, means the TVR is £36,000 and the Lotus is £26,000.

She wasn't convinced and spent the entire weekend pretending to make her mind up, but knowing full well from the moment they arrived which was going to win.

Except, of course, this was not a normal twin test. She is not a motoring journalist, making a decision then going home in next week's hatchback. There was no winner or loser. This was for real. And these are her conclusions . . . She liked the fact that neither came with a driver aid or an air bag, which implies that they trust the driver. And she liked the fact that both are about as British as it's possible to be without being Elton John.

To help her along, I came home from a drive in the Lotus and declared it to be perfect. This is definitely the one to go for, I told her. And every single motoring journalist would agree. Tiffany certainly does.

But it seems we're wrong. After the Caterham, she says, the Elise is just too civilized, too slow, too heavy, too tardy in its responses. For an everyday car it would be fine, she says, but for taking out because the sun's shining and you fancy a trip to the shops, or the Sudan, it's too boring.

The TVR is similarly civilized, she says, and when was the last time you heard a motoring journalist call either of these cars 'too civilized'?

However, apparently the TVR makes up for the carpets and the stereo by being really, properly loud and really, properly fast. On a track the Lotus might be the more balanced, but she doesn't go to track days so she doesn't care. She just wants something that turns a trip to the gym into an event.

Certainly, the Tamora obliged yesterday by coming out of one roundabout between here and Oxford completely sideways. 'I loved it,' declared Mrs C, which is amazing really, when I remind you that she can't reach the pedals properly.

I tried to explain that in identical circumstances, the Elise would've remained planted to the road, but it was no good. Being planted to the road, contrary to what I may have told you over the years, is a bad thing. It's dull.

So, it looks like we're going to buy a Tamora. I've tried to extol the virtues of a Chimaera, which is a bit cheaper, but this, it seems, is not pretty enough. And frankly, I'm better off admitting defeat now before she gets designs on a £50,000 Tuscan.

And anyway, it's not so bad. I end up at *Top Gear* with a TVR. Tiffany ends up at *Autocar* with an M-Class Mercedes.

STOP PRESS: I was forgetting, my wife is a woman. She has changed her mind. For reasons I don't understand, she is getting the Lotus.

July 2002

Classic cars

It was a great start to the British summer. Huge lows barrelled in from the Atlantic, bringing showers, drizzle and longer periods of rain. It was cold too, and windy. Marvellous.

But then, disaster. In the middle of July, the Azores High moved into Britain and this cued everyone with a floral dress to spark up some kind of village show.

Being a strict libertarian, I have nothing against these ancient, traditional gatherings, so long as they stick to murdering goats and don't start building wicker men in which to burn the local bobby. No really, if someone wishes to dress up as a Morris Man and dance around a pagan penis, that's fine by me. Same goes with the cake stall, the traction engine display, and the village band . . . so long as they don't attempt the 1812.

However, the trouble with shows of this kind is that it encourages people with vintage cars to take 'the old girl' out for a spin.

Why? No one looks forward to a really wet, rainy night in November so they can huddle round the fire and watch an episode of *Z Cars* on a 1950s television. 'Ooh look, Doris. Isn't it great how the picture's all fuzzy and we can't hear a word that Bert Lynch says. And isn't it fun, doing away with that horrid, modern remote control.'

NASA doesn't ever say, 'Look, guys. Let's not use the shuttle this time. Let's have a bit of nostalgia and go up there in an old Apollo.' And nor have I decided to eschew my laptop and write this column with a quill. So what's this thing people have for old cars?

I should perhaps explain at this point that I'm not talking about cars that were made since, say, the Mustang. I'm talking about cars that have running boards. Cars where you have to go outside to change gear.

You see them, whenever the sun comes out, cruising around the Cotswolds on their way to some kind of Fred Dibnah village show. Except, of course, 'cruising' is entirely the wrong word. They're 'spluttering'.

And what on earth does the *de rigueur* woman in the back look like? Honestly, you could wrap her in tin foil and stick her on the bonnet. She'd look a lot less daft.

For God's sake, woman. When you're invited out for a spin in 'the old girl', just say no. Tell your husband you have a heavy period. Tell him you're eloping with Robbie Williams. Tell him any damn thing but do not get in the back of his car. As I've said before, the only person who ever looked good in the back of a convertible was Hitler.

And when your idiotic husband makes yet another wrong turning and tries to turn round, do not wave cheerily at the people who are being held up, or they may get out of their cars and stab you in the heart with a tyre iron. The back of a convertible can be a very dangerous place. Ask Mrs Kennedy.

Have you ever seen a vintage car trying to do a three-point turn? You sit and watch the driver wrestling with the wheel, spinning it round endlessly, and you want to scream from the air-conditioned, power-assisted luxury of your own car, 'Hey, Fool. That wheel. It's not connected to anything, so stop pretending otherwise.'

Then there's the bothersome business of changing gear. Would someone please write in and explain exactly why it's fun to have a crash box, with a clutch pedal in the boot and a brake near the radiator. All the driver gets, every time he moves the lever, is the noise of sixteen cogs eating them-selves for breakfast. And once again, you have to lean out of your car and shout, 'That's not connected to anything either.'

Only the other day, I was taken for a spin in a Blower Bentley, which is valuable for all sorts of reasons I will never be able to fathom. It was hell, but then it would be, since it had medieval springs, pre-Byzantine gears, the engine out of a Spitfire Mark 9 and tyres from a Raleigh Chopper. If you want to offer people a lift home from the pub in 'the Blower', buy a bloody XJR. At least a Jaguar can pull up in a few yards, rather than in a few counties.

Of course, fans of the old car will explain at this point that 'the old girl' is so much more stylish than anything made today, as though everything old simply must be better than anything new. Right. Well, why don't you go to work tomorrow in some doublet and hose? And when your boss says you're expected to have a video conference with the New York Office at one, explain that you'd prefer to write it all down in a letter.

Actually, my biggest problem with old cars is that they don't really mix on modern roads. Fans of motors with external radiator caps may think, as they splutter about the Cotswolds, that up here, with the lovely old stone barns and peaceful sheep, all is tranquil and folksy. Well it isn't. Some of us have to live and work here, and we can't if you're on your way to buy some jam in a 1932 Potterton.

Let me put it this way. How would you like it if, when you were trying to get some old-fashioned peace and quiet in your garden on a Sunday afternoon, I came along in a Max Powered Renault Turbo and imposed some gangsta rap on you?

You'd hate it, wouldn't you? You'd say I was being selfish. Well quite.

Old cars, I'm afraid, belong in museums. Or the Saturday supplement of the *Daily Telegraph*. Which is the same thing.

September 2002

The DB7

Imagine, just for a moment, that no car firm had a history. Imagine there'd never been any racing at Spa or Le Mans. Imagine there'd never been a film called *The Italian Job* and that *Bullitt* was a spelling mistake.

Suddenly, every car would have to be judged, not on pre-conceived ideas or expectations, but on what it's like in the here and now. Where would that leave the Aston Martin DB7 Vantage?

You'd look hard at that £94,000 price tag and think, Hang on a minute, what exactly am I paying for here? Not space, that's for sure. Because the engine's whopping great computer is located under the driver's seat, the only person who could get genuinely comfortable behind the wheel is Anne Boleyn.

Performance? Hardly. It may have a six-litre V12 engine under the bonnet and it may make the noise of every thunderstorm there's ever been, but the speedo doesn't exactly move round the dial like lightning.

So what about the driving; the sheer string-backed, tweedy thrill of hurling this 420bhp British GT car up some mountain pass? Well the car I drove this month was by far the best I've ever tried. It had a nimbleness I've never encountered in a DB7 before. It braked straight and true. It was nice.

But it still wasn't as nice as the competition.

So perhaps it's loaded up to the gunwales with expensive electronic trickery? Nope. You get air-conditioning and a woman in the radio who tells you where to go, but that's it. Can I even set a temperature and expect the cabin to remain just so? No, I can't. No matter what you do with the knobs, which come from a 1940s gramophone via the XJS, all you're offered is either an icicle in the eye or a jet of invisible flame.

Have you ever tried moving the seat in a Vantage? The only people who might be capable of doing such a thing are those surgeons who can remotely operate delicate equipment while watching a television screen. The switches, you see, are in a quarter-inch gap between the handbrake and the seat.

I could go on. So I will. You can't open the boot unless the ignition is on. The satnav woman is only interested in taking me to Letchworth. And oh no, I just banged my head again, getting out.

Then there's the gearbox. While it's nice to have a six-speed manual bolted to that wonderful engine – I wish they'd do it on the Vanquish – I wonder why they've chosen to fit something that was plainly designed for a combine harvester.

We can't forget either that, before the V12 came along, DB7s were exactly the same, only badly made and much slower.

Which brings me back to where we started. Why is this the most successful Aston Martin of all time? Why does anyone buy it at all when it's so comprehensively thrashed by the Mercedes SL, the Porsche 911 and even that big Fiat called the Ferrari 360?

And why is it just about impossible to find any DB7, even an early one, for less than £50,000 in the second-hand sections. They just seem to get to this point and stick, no matter what you do with them. 'For Sale. DB7. Five years old. Regularly raced and rallied. Two million miles. Used as a hen house for past two years. £50,000. No offers.'

Why? Well let's re-introduce the name at this point and see what happens.

For sure, as you leave the house of an evening it sounds good to say, in a Leslie Philips voice, 'Shall we take the Aston?' But what does that mean exactly?

None of us is old enough to remember Aston Martin's heroic but usually doomed attempts to win Le Mans in the Fifties. And if we are old enough, we should be in bed by now, with some Ovaltine.

James Bond leaps into the frame, of course, but let's be honest, he hasn't used an Aston since he stopped being Scottish and became Australian. All through his English, Welsh and Irish years, he's been in something else.

Whatever, I don't think the name is it. It'd be easy and comfortable to think people buy the DB7 because of some past glory on the race track or some heroic moment in the cinema, but that's only a small part of it.

I think a big part of it is that styling. This is one of those cars that you simply cannot walk away from without turning for one last look. It's like sitting opposite a stunning girl in a restaurant; you can't concentrate on your food, and you don't even notice that your wife has got up in a temper and left.

Some say that the new Giugiaro concept car – the Alfa Romeo Brera – has stolen the DB7's beauty-pageant sash, but I say pah. Italian cars, and particularly Alfas, only ever look good when they are launched. They date as well as milk. The DB7, on the other hand, looks as good today as it did when it first nosed out of the factory. And it will continue to look as good forever.

It may even improve. New laws, due to be imposed in 2005, mean cars must offer the same level of protection as they do now, even if the occupants aren't wearing seat belts.

Couple that to proposed new rules about pedestrian safety and, in future, you're going to be sitting six feet from the windscreen in a car with a bonnet like the cow catcher on a trans-Nevada express train.

Never again will we see the classic long nose and short tail which have, since the Sixties, been the hallmark of truly good-looking cars. The original Mustang. The Ferrari Daytona. The E-Type. And, best of all, the DB7.

But can styling alone justify the price tag? Well it must do. There's no other reason I can see why someone would buy such a car.

And £94,000 for a piece of art is nothing. I went to that Henry Moore park up north where the fields are littered with his meaningless sculptures – one looked like a giant piece of sheep shit – and I'll bet that every single one was worth half a mill. Maybe more.

I recently bought a steel wolf, which sits in the garden frightening the children, and it was, how can I put this, expensive. Not DB7 expensive, obviously, but it's not as pretty.

Nothing is, apart perhaps from the Humber Bridge and the Blackbird SR-71 spy plane.

If I were rich enough, and contrary to what you may think, I'm not, I'd be happy to buy a DB7 and put it on a pole outside my house.

As a driving machine it's worth about £4.50. The name adds another 40p. The looks make it worth a million.

December 2002

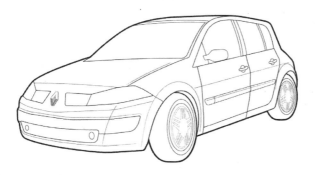

CAR OF THE YEAR: RENAULT MÉGANE

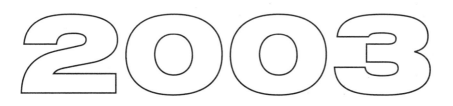

2003

TOP 5 BESTSELLING SINGLES
SONG TITLE – ARTIST

1 Where Is the Love – Black Eyed Peas
2 Spirit in the Sky – Gareth Gates Ft. The Kumars
3 Ignition Remix – R. Kelly
4 Mad World – Michael Andrews featuring Gary Jules
5 Leave Right Now – Will Young

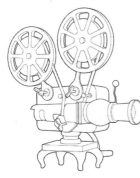

TOP 5 BOX OFFICE MOVIES

1. The Lord of the Rings: The Return of the King
2 Finding Nemo
3 Pirates of the Caribbean: The Curse of the Black Pearl
4 The Matrix Reloaded
5 Bruce Almighty

The Cool Wall

The easiest way to make a fortune is to pick a small rural market town with lots of outlying villages and start a taxi firm.

I live in the perfect place – Chipping Norton – and, let me tell you, it is nearly impossible to move around out here. Obviously, I wouldn't dream of using a bus, even if there was one, and even if it was going in my direction. But there isn't, so that's that.

Christmas has been interesting. We get invited to lots of dull parties, and the only way to get through them is to get drunk. That's fine, but how can we then get home again?

There's only one taxi and it's booked up from now until November. What's more, because he has a monopoly he can charge £100 to go five miles. What are you going to do? Pay or walk?

You would imagine that the taxi driver in question has a Maybach, with a new Rolls-Royce on order. But, no. He has a Citroën C5 and he was interested in what I thought of it. 'Well, it's rubbish,' I said.

But of course, it isn't. It's a large, five-seat diesel that does 2,000 miles to the gallon and only costs £10,000 to buy new. It may be rubbish to you and I – soulless, ugly and uninspiring to drive – but it is a good cab.

'I'm thinking of changing it for a Skoda Superb,' he added. 'What do you think?'

Well, I suppose if I were in Kingham St Michael at 3 a.m. and I was drunk, the back of a Superb would live up to its name. Certainly, there's plenty of room to be sick back there. But in the morning, I'd be sober and it would still be a Skoda.

He didn't get it. So far as he's concerned, £15,000 for an elongated VW Passat is great value. Plus you get VW build quality, VW engines and, apparently, good service from the dealer. Great, but where's the coolness, man?

This is why I came up with the Top Gear Cool Wall. It started out as a bit of fun, a device to explain why the Chrysler PT Cruiser and VW Beetle are 'so last week', but it seemed to strike a chord. Seven days after it was shown for the first time on television, we'd had 20,000 emails about it. (To put that in perspective, all the gardening programmes put together only get 800 emails a week.)

I'm sorry to say I have not had a chance to read all the messages – in the time it took to read one, forty more arrived – but one thing was clear. One man's cool car is another man's hot potato. No one agrees on anything.

So let me explain the rules. A car can be cool even if it's horrid to drive and wilfully ugly to behold. The Audi A2 is a classic case in point. This is a dreadful car in every way, but there's something about it that marks the driver out as being a little bit separate, a little bit stylish.

Similarly, a car that's wonderful to drive and built with Japanese precision can be hopelessly uncool. The Nissan Skyline GTR stands out here. Why? Well that's where my Kristin Scott Thomas litmus test comes in. She's possibly the coolest actress around. British-born, public-school educated, she lives in Paris and has a French attitude to nudity.

Now I don't know, but I'd imagine she isn't terribly interested in cars and, as a result, she'd find the Skyline daft. No, really. What would you say if she asked why it had a meter to show how much 'g' you were generating in the bends. Answer that and try to sound cool. See? It can't be done.

Which brings me on to the Ferrari 360. It's uncool. Why? Well, think about it. Have you ever seen one being driven by someone you'd have round for dinner? In London, they all look like Albanian mafia and up north they look like they own carpet shops in Dewsbury.

But at the other end of the Fiat spectrum, the Punto is super cool. Icy cool. And it's the same with all small European hatchbacks. The Peugeot 206, the Golf, the Clio, the C3 and the Ibiza; they're all freezing. And yet the Fiesta and the Corsa are not. The Europeans are like the coffee you get at Caffè Nero. The Ford and the Vauxhall are like the coffee you get at Starbucks. And there's a big, big difference. Then there's the new Nissan Micra. Oh, dear.

Moving up a notch, all mid-range four-door saloons are uncool. A Vectra or a BMW 5 Series, a Mondeo or an Audi A4, all medium-sized saloon cars, with the possible exception of the Saab 9-3, suggest you're more interested in practicality than style. End of story.

Coupés? Everyone's saying the Nissan 350Z is hot, and they're absolutely right, it is. Boiling. All Japanese coupés are uncool. In fact, there are only two cool coupés that spring to mind: the Peugeot 406 and the Alfa GTV. The TT was cool for ten minutes, but now they're far too common, and as a result, it's gone.

Other cars we need to dismiss at this point include all MPVs, all BMWs (except the new Z4), all Mercs (including the SL55), all diesels and all TVRs. Funnily enough, the Porsche 911 is cool. It wasn't in the Eighties when it was all stripy shirts and braces, but now the image is repaired and it's almost up there with the Aston Martin Vanquish, which could give a man frost bite at 400 paces.

It, along with the Land Rover Defender, the new Mini and the Renault Avantime are, in fact, the only cars that sit in my 'sub-zero' section on the Cool Wall.

There is another car that could get into this section – providing it's driven by the right sort of person. The Mitsubishi Evo VII. What do you need to make this cool? Simple. Breasts.

Sit down, Subaru Impreza fans. Sorry. You could have tits like Zeppelins and it's still not coming in. It's a great car, the Impreza, but it's not cool.

At the top of the tree, it's almost impossible to be cool. As well as all BMWs and the Ferrari 360, the Lamborghini Murciélago is also down there with the Beetle. And if you turned up at Kristin's house with a Zonda, she'd hide in the wardrobe. You're much better off using a Volvo V70 estate, mainly because that's what she actually uses herself.

Jaguars have an air of coolness about them. Not the X- or S-Types, obviously, but the XJ has a certain something and so does the XK. But for super coolness at the top of the tree, you're hard pressed to beat the Range Rover, which has performed a 911-style turnaround.

Skoda, on the other hand, has not. Those of us who read car magazines know how it's come on in leaps and bounds. But let's be honest, shall we? Those of us who read car mags are the least cool people in the world.

Perhaps the only way to be more uncool is to start up a taxi firm in a rural market town.

February 2003

Choice

Have you tried to buy a pair of training shoes recently? I have and I don't want to sound like I'm a million years old, but when I was at school, it really was terribly simple – for indoor work, you had the simple black pump and for outdoor activity, the Green Flash tennis shoe.

I'm aware, of course, that fashion has goose-stepped its way into the world of leisure footwear in recent years and that certain brands are now very uncool. This, however, was not the problem. Whether I'm identified with the bassist from Travis or one of the Sugarbabes does not interest me overmuch.

No, I had flown to New Zealand and realized that the penny loafers I had packed might be a trifle unsuitable for scrabbling up a chunk of giantized magma, so I hurried into a sports shop hoping that I might buy a pair of comfy size tens.

But it wasn't that simple. What did I want them for, asked the man in the shop. 'Well, my feet really,' I replied. No, no, no. What was I going to do in them? 'Well, sort of walk about'.

This wasn't good enough. He needed to know what sort of walking and on what sort of terrain. So I explained that I'd be starting off on a road, then I'd be walking up a well-trodden path, which would become progressively more rocky and Janet Street-Porterish.

This elicited a sucking in of air through the teeth. 'Hmm,' he said. 'Road, track and rock. Now that's a tricky combination.'

By this stage in my shopping trip, my car had a ticket and the New Zealand parliament was sitting to decide whether or not they should introduce some kind of tow-away scheme for persistent offenders.

I couldn't believe it. And I especially couldn't believe the shoes he produced. Finished in suede and leather and equipped with a price tag that appeared to have fallen off the space station, they had soles of such enormity that even a Ukrainian prostitute would have blanched.

'I can't drive in those things,' I said incredulously.

'No,' he replied, laughing. They're not for driving. You need another pair for that . . . and another for getting out of the car and another for getting to the side of the road and another for the light track and then . . . I could change into the leather and suede breeze blocks that would make me about 27 feet tall.

And what's more, none of these shoes could be used should I abandon the policy of a lifetime and do sport of some kind.

You don't just buy a shoe for running any more. You have to be specific. So you must say whether you want to do short, fast stints, or a long slow plod. Nike, for example, bills its Air Structure Triax as a shoe for the runner who needs motion control and cushioning without any sass.

What does that mean exactly?

There are now magazines devoted to the myriad of choice and in 'road tests' the 'journalists' talk about high-rebound compound, rubberized GTO cushioning pads, thermoplastic devices in the midfoot, composite wave plates and, my favourite, the DuoSole forefoot with blown rubber.

Did you know that training shoes are now so technologically advanced that there are industry recalls. I mean it. In

July 2001, Nike recalled 425,000 pairs of Jordan Trunners because a piece of metal could protrude from the heel, causing injury.

It's all jolly interesting, chiefly because it's all rubbish. You simply don't need this amount of technology, or this amount of choice, in a bloody shoe.

And I suspect it's much the same story in the world of cars. Honda develops variable valve timing – the automotive equivalent of composite wave plates probably – and the damn thing is bought by a little old lady who never exceeds six miles an hour and doesn't know what the radio is for.

Then there's the question of choice. In the beginning, you had three cars to choose from: the saloon, the estate and the off-roader for farmers. Then along came the MPV. Then the mini MPV. And then the mini MPV with four-wheel drive. And strangely, in the case of the Honda HR-V, the four-wheel drive with two-wheel drive. Whoa there, boy. This is all too complicated. And that was before we got to the Renault Avantime, which is an MPV coupé. Or, to put it another way, impossible.

It got to the point where the simple saloon was looking awfully forlorn. Small children would climb inside and enquire, 'Where are the wings, Daddy, and how do we turn it into a submarine?'

The fact is, however, that the saloon, for all its alderman Fifties austerity, is actually a pretty good compromise. You get seating for five, a boot in which things can be locked and an engine in the front. You get, as a by-product of this, refinement, because the noisy rear end is outside, and you get, if the stylist knows his onions from his swede, good looks too. I like a nice saloon car.

And that's why I was delighted to see the Ford 427 at the

recent Detroit Motorshow. Most people, of course, were drawn away by the air sole blown rubber Aston Martin V8, but I liked the simple Ford.

Finished in black to make it look sinister – 'We want people to feel like they're doing something wrong even when they're not,' say the designers – it has a 7-litre V10 engine. So actually, chances are you will be doing something wrong anyway.

The main reason why this car was there, though, was to remind people that Ford still does saloons. Because with all the sports utility vehicles and mini sports utility vehicles and sports utility vehicle multi-purpose vehicles, it's easy to over-look the *Terry and June*-mobile in the far corner. Overlook it at your peril, though, because let's not forget, shall we, that Ford's best car is the Mondeo.

Furthermore, the car everyone buys when they make it is not a Ferrari or a Lambo. It's an S-Class Mercedes-Benz saloon, and the best new car I drove last year was the Mazda6. Which is a Green Flash tennis shoe with windscreen wipers.

The saloon car is like the saloon bar. You may be drawn to the fancy new bistro with its crisp white wines and its exotic nuts. But for a pie and a pint . . .

March 2003

Luck

I want to start this month by talking about luck. On the one hand we have Ringo Starr, who wakes up every morning in a huge house on a bed made of money. And what's he done to earn this?

Someone once said to John Lennon that Ringo wasn't exactly the best drummer in the world, to which John replied, 'Not the best drummer in the world? He isn't even the best drummer in the Beatles.'

Ringo is king of the lucky club. A club that also includes his wife, Barbara Bach, former Bond girl and possibly the worst actress ever. Then there's Roger Moore, all the super-models, the Marquis of Blandford, Richard Branson and, of course, Ray Mears, who makes a fortune every year because he can cook snot on a beach. These are the people who won joint first prize in the lottery of life.

Then, at the other end of the scale, there's me. I make the orphans in the engine room of a Malaysian paddle steamer look like Flavio Briatore. The forgotten families of Brazil go to sleep every night on the rubbish tips of Sao Paulo saying, 'Well, at least we're not Jeremy Clarkson.'

In Monopoly, I go directly to jail and stay there. In bridge, I'm the three of clubs. And at the races, my horse goes home in a butcher's van. In any game of chance, I'm the paper to your scissors, the stone to your good fortune. I always, always lose.

Strange to report then that I love gambling in general and

blackjack in particular. It's the thrill. Being dealt an eight and hoping, praying, sinking to my knees and whimpering like a dog, that the next card will be a three. Then I could double my bet, get a picture, and win!

It never happens, obviously – it's always a five – but that's all right because what non-gamblers don't understand about gambling is this: winning is not important.

If all I wanted was more money, I'd plonk myself at the roulette table and play one of the systems. But what's the point? That's doing maths for a guaranteed pay back. And that's not fun. That's called accountancy.

Being there is what it's all about. The agony of choice, the *frisson* of hope, the black shroud of despair. P.J. O'Rourke once said that his idea of heaven would be watching the entire Mexican air force crash land on a petro-chemical refinery. But for me, I can think of nothing better than those days back in the Eighties, playing cards at my little underground casino on Lower Sloane Street, with its roaring fire and its fresh coffee. The joy was unparalleled.

This is why I've never enjoyed playing in Las Vegas. Oh, I'm sure it was fun in the days when Robert De Niro was in charge and Joe Pesci was in the back room, putting someone's head in a vice. But today Vegas has changed and it feels like you're playing against corporate America.

The dealers are simply a far-flung tentacle of that amorphous, unseen being known as the corporate shareholder. And their job is to get your money into the Nasdaq system as fast as possible. It's as impersonal, and as fast, as a backstreet hand job in downtown Saigon.

I was thinking all this last night as, once again, I found myself driving home with the fuel needle bent double over the bump stop of empty. Thinking about the appeal of gambling was a sort of answer to the perennial question: 'Why do I do this?'

It's not just me either. Tiff Needell, formerly of this parish, went everywhere with both the rev counter and the fuel gauge in the red zone. He never went into a filling station with the engine still running.

And why not? I genuinely worry about people who fill up whenever the needle drops below half. How empty must your life be, and how unimportant your journey, if you have time to stand and watch the pump dispense the fruits of your labours in a digital blur?

It's not the expense; oh, we may moan about the price of petrol these days, but that's not the issue here. It's the tedium. It's hard to think of anything, apart from being dissolved in a bath of acid, which is less enjoyable than standing in a filling station, pumping fuel.

It's particularly awful when you have a Jaguar, because unless you have the nozzle arranged just so, it cuts out every second and a half. Then you have the pumps, which deliver fuel at the rate of a gallon an hour, and those with stiff grips that give your hand cramp, and those that deliberately deliver exactly 1p more than you'd planned.

The whole event is an affront to the senses. The fluorescent half light, knowing that the smell is giving you cancer and that when the tank is finally full, you'll be in a shop that only sells carcinogenic pies and radioactive drink. Why do petrol stations have to be like petrol stations? Why can't they be like Victorian railway stations or cricket pavilions? Why can't they be designed by Conran with splashes of zinc here and there? Who says that I must have a Fuse bar every time I fill up? What if I want a lobster?

And as you look about, the whole place is full of people

who don't really need to be there, people who are filling up long before the engine actually coughs. I bet Norma Major keeps the diesel tank topped off. And I bet Ozzy Osbourne doesn't.

I don't either. When I'm driving up a motorway with the fuel light on and a sign says, 'Services 1m and 29m', I always, always, always go for the furthest target. And when I get there, I'll often drive past that one too.

Now you probably think this is a pointless game. You think that there's no prize if I win and a long trudge in the rain if I lose.

You will also explain that even if I do make it home, on fumes, the car will not miraculously fuel itself overnight. It will have to be filled eventually, so why not now?

True, but on a motorway with nothing but Gareth Gates for company, things can get dull. Playing fuel-light bingo brings a bit of excitement to the monotony. The will I/won't I gamble puts some fizz in my blood stream and an extra boing to my heart beat.

I am now the world expert on which cars go how far below empty on the gauge. Fords are good, but Porsches are bad. When a 928 says it has no fuel on board, it has no fuel on board and you judder to a halt.

That's not bad though. One failure in twenty-five years on the road. I'm surprised they haven't asked me to be the new voice of *Thomas the Tank Engine*.

April 2003

Marketing

When I was growing up, in the dark and dismal days before Mr Sony invented his PlayStation and comedy on television centred around Mrs Slocombe's pussy, I used to enjoy nothing more than curling up at night with one of Enid Blyton's Famous Five books. The bits where Georgina got tied up were especially exciting.

They were wonderful stories and there's no reason why they wouldn't work today. Four kids and a dog called Timmy, staying with an eccentric uncle in a land of caves, smugglers and pre-pubescent bondage is as pertinent now as it was back then.

My eight-year-old daughter, however, can't quite get it. She read a few pages with the sort of rapt attention adults reserve for spam email, decided that she didn't know what ginger beer was and went back to her stories about Bad Girls.

That's fine, of course. At least she's reading. But there's no point saving her Bad Girl books for her younger sister because, by the time she's old enough to read, there'll be something new.

This is marketing. Yes, Harry Potter is cool now, but the absolute last thing the Big They want is for parents to pass on the tapes and the books and the videos. There's no money to be made out of hand-me-downs. So Harry will be eaten and something bigger and better and more Beyblade-ish will come along.

I'd love to jump up and down about this and make a heart-felt call for a return to the old simpler days, but actually I don't care. Money is what oils the economy and if publishers want to keep the machine working by dreaming up an endless succession of stories, great. I mean, if we only had Dickens to read, no one would read at all. Bob Cratchett? What a twat. If ever a man was born to drive a Nissan Micra, he's it.

That said, I do wish Porsche would stop inventing niches and developing marketing opportunities with their infernal 911.

I should state right now that I don't like 911s in the same way that I don't like marzipan, Lisa Riley, America, traffic news on the radio, the M6, flies, people who say 'off of', Radio One, motorbikes, Ken Livingstone's adenoids, bores . . . the list is endless really. And that's fine.

These are my opinions. You may wish to try them on if you like, as you would a suit, and you may decide that you don't like them. And that's fine too. Money makes the world go round, but individualism is what makes it interesting.

So you may adore the 911 and I respect you for that. I accept your argument that it is the only supercar which you can use every day and that the enormous traction offered by putting the engine in the back easily outweighs a certain trickiness beyond the limit.

I agree with you that the 911 Turbo is an immense car and that, for the money, nothing gets anywhere close. But I simply don't like it and I'd never, ever have one, even if it were served on a bed of swans by Kristin Scott Thomas herself.

What I especially don't like about the 911, though, is not the arse-enginedness of it, or the fact that the driver seems to sit too far forwards. I prefer a long bonnet, in the same way that I would prefer to have a big penis than a big arse.

No, what I really don't like is the way that Porsche so very obviously milk one car. They're like Golden Earring endlessly touring with their one hit single. Or Jo Brand, who has made a living from describing a Tampax in 3,000 different ways.

We've got the Carrera 2 for those who want a 911, no questions asked. Then we've got the Carrera 4 for those who want a 911 but have plenty of questions about their own driving ability. Good, so that's a Carrera for everyone then.

Then there's the Turbo, which is a Carrera 4 for those who want to arrive at their destination before they set off, and the GT2 which has two turbos and is for people who want to arrive at their destination before they even thought about going there.

And we mustn't forget the new GT3 – not to be confused with the old GT3, of course – which is a lightweight, lowered, hard-riding track-day car that can be ordered with a roll cage, bucket seats and six-point seat belts.

There's plenty of choice here. If you want to go from 0–60 in five seconds, get a Carrera 2. If you want to do it in 4.9, get the Carrera 4. If you fancy the idea of doing it in 4.5, the GT3 is your answer, and if you want to take it down to 4.2, go for the turbo. If you want to do it in 4.1, however, you must have the GT2.

But what if you want to do 0–60 in 4.95 seconds? Well, don't worry. Porsche has thought of you too, and come up with the C4S which is a Carrera 4 fitted with the turbo's body and brakes, but not the spoilers.

I spent a few days with the C4S this month and must admit it made me feel a bit Cheshire. People would point and say, 'Is that a turbo?' To which I'd have to say, 'Er, no. It's just made to look like one. And would you like to see my fake Rolex while we're chatting?'

Given the choice, I'd take the Carrera 4, which is £3,000 cheaper and a tiny bit faster. Except, of course, I wouldn't. I'd have the 2 because the whole point of having a 911 is telling people what you drive. In which case, you may as well buy the cheapest.

You must remember, at this point, that I'm talking about the 996, 993, 911 or even the 964, which was both a 964 and a 911 also.

Confused? Well, that's before we get to the thorny question of whether to go for a convertible, a Targa with a glass roof or the straight coupé.

This brings me back to Harry Potter. What we have here is one bespectacled little boy who fights the forces of evil in an endless selection of different ways. Everyone knows that when JK Rowling finishes the fifth book, she'll hang up her juices and let someone else pick up the baton.

I think that's what's happening with Porsche. They've tried every conceivable trick in the rear-engined book, and now they've decided to move on to the Cayenne.

I'm very much looking forward, in forty years' time, to driving the two-wheel-drive, low-rider, desert-raid convertible version.

May 2003

Sports cars

So, does a sports car have to be fast? I only ask because parked on my drive are a Smart Roadster and a Ford StreetKa which, superficially, are two of the most confusing machines ever to see the light of day. It's not just the speed either. It's everything. These cars have forced me to ask a very big question indeed. We know what an off-road car is, and we know what a saloon car is, but what, exactly, is a sports car?

Sport implies speed and excitement, but let's not forget, shall we, that a sport is any game that requires specialist clothing. If you can do it in jeans, it's a pastime.

On that basis, this duo of steel and plastic and canvas are pastime cars. However, let's not forget, shall we, that you need specialist clothing to play that symphony of tedium and sloth called cricket. So even though it moves with the vim and vigour of a Jane Austen plot, it's a sport.

Perhaps sport, in the case of cars, derives from 'sporting'. And a sporting car is one that can be used on a track, in some kind of competition. So on that basis, yes, unless you want to be last, a sports car has to be fast.

And yet if we look back through the history of MG, which is like reading *Emma* in slow motion, we find an endless succession of cars that couldn't have pulled a greased stick out of a pig's arse. The TF, for instance, could only do 80mph, whereas its rival, the Triumph TR2, could do over a hundred.

Then we find the MG Midget, which waded into the

gunfight with a small butter knife under the bonnet. It had a top speed of 86mph and took more than twenty seconds to get from 0–60. But was it a sports car? Yes, and so is the Mazda MX-5, which isn't exactly a streak of lightning either.

Maybe looks have something to do with it. And now the Daimler Dart has just popped into my head, so maybe they don't.

Then there's the Triumph TR7. That was a fairly speedy two-seater convertible. But not a sports car. And yet the tin-top GT6 most definitely was. Curiouser and curiouser.

Strangest of all, however, is the Mercedes SL. It comes with a big engine, bundles of power, two seats, two doors and a folding roof. It's even known at women's lunch groups from Houston to Harrogate as the Mercedes Sports. But it isn't a sports car.

Indeed, if I were to make a list of the five least sporty things in the world, it would go something like this:

5. Me
4. The monkfish
3. A gate-leg table
2. The Mercedes SL
1. Terry Wogan

I think it's mostly a question of attitude. A sports car doesn't have to be fast or pretty. It need not have a folding roof and it can have seats in the back. But it does need to be uncompromising in some way, shape or form. It needs to be hard riding and noisier than necessary. It needs to remind its owner every single yard of every single journey that he or she bought the car to be exciting.

It needs, therefore, to transmit its interaction with the road with a series of semaphore signals in the driver's pants.

It needs to telegraph every burp of its engine, every squeak of its tyres. A sports car is a state of mind.

And that's why the StreetKa misses the mark. But I like it. I think it's fun to drive.

It also manages to be cheap and cheerful, which is quite a feat since the words 'cheap' and 'cheerful' go together like bacon and Sullivan. Or Gilbert and eggs. If a hotel is cheap, it's likely to be miserable. And if someone is cheerful, he's likely to be rich. And yet the StreetKa, with its unlined roof and fantastically flimsy glovebox, is both.

What's more, I think every single woman from the salons of Wilmslow to the fashion pages of *Vogue* magazine will kill to buy one. And yet, despite all this, it is not a sports car.

The engine isn't quite raspy enough. The steering's not quite precise enough. It's too comfortable. And as a result, it feels like a hatchback with the roof cut off. It's like a Marlboro Light. Either smoke properly, or don't smoke at all.

I thought, when I first clapped eyes on the Smart, that it would miss the mark by an even greater margin. Nothing, I figured, with a 600cc engine could possibly be called a sports car. Not even MG ever sunk that low.

And yet, it works. There's plenty I don't like. The steering wheel is far too large and the cockpit puts me in mind of a 1982 British kit car – a Midas Gold or a Clan Invader, perhaps. Then there's the gearbox. Holy mother of Mary, what were they thinking of?

It's a manual with a Tiptronic-style shift, which is never all right. In the Smart, however, it's truly terrible. Jerky is too small a word, and because the 600cc engine is not exactly the Flying Scotsman when it comes to torque, you have to change gear a lot. Or you can switch to auto mode.

That may seem more sensible – why buy a self-cleaning

oven and then clean it yourself – but in auto mode, you never know when the jerks are coming. You just turn round to see if . . . and whoops, your head's come off.

What else don't I like? Well, the boot's like a baking tray, the paintwork looks cheap and a price of £13,500 is expensive – mainly because the left-hand-drive models are only £9,999.

Also, it most definitely is not fast. It's not even on nodding terms with the vaguest concept of speediness. I mean, 0–60 in eleven seconds. How Jane Austen is that?

But you should hear the noise. To liken it to the Joneses, it looks like 'Snowman' Aled, but it sings like Tom – a loud, Welsh roar bouncing off the hillsides as you flash by.

Well, when I say 'flash', what I mean is tootle. But that's OK. You have plenty of time to enjoy the wind in your hair.

Well, when I say 'wind', what I mean is gentle breeze. But that's OK too. You'll arrive refreshed.

Well, when I say 'arrive', you'll be late almost to the point of rudeness, but no one will mind because you'll be up for a party.

And happy. There's a rightness, not only to the noise but to the steering and the handling too. It feels exciting, like a good pop song, and safe too. Because if anything does go wrong, you will have time to undo your seat belt, open the door and jump.

I wouldn't buy one, but I liked it. Because it's a sports car. Whatever that may be.

June 2003

Gardening

When I bought my house, seven years ago, the previous owners left behind what can only be described as a tropical rainforest in the conservatory. There were plants in there that would have left Attenborough breathless. Ray Mears could have filmed an entire series in one corner alone. It was wonderful. And I was determined to look after it, so every day my wife and I fed those plants and read them poetry. We nurtured them so much that within two years, all of them were dead.

Undaunted, we went to the garden centre and bought a whole new selection, which were planted and nourished with the sort of loving care normally only found between a parent and their child. They died too.

So we bought more, which were attacked by a beetle that made all their leaves sticky. To prevent the disease spreading, we moved them outside, where they were killed by the frost. Even the pots they were in shattered. You've heard of cot death? Well, this was the far more lethal 'pot death'.

Then we got serious. We sought expert help, bought books and had electric blinds fitted so that it was never too hot in there, or too cold. And that was just the start.

We ripped up the floor and installed hot water pipes beneath grates so that you could go in there with a hosepipe and all the spare water, when it hit the pipes, would turn to steam. It was a sauna and massage parlour. A little bit of equatorial Brazil in the middle of Chipping Norton. It was perfect, except for one small thing. Everything died.

Well, not everything. There's one forlorn thing that's clinging to life about as adroitly as it's clinging to the stone work. And I'm assured the orchid isn't technically dead yet, though you could have fooled me.

Otherwise, each pot is full of dead leaves, butt ends (from ffrench-Constant's last visit), a bit of cracked and wizened soil and a pointless twig. Our conservatory? It's the Killing Fields of the Cotswolds, a little bit of Passchendaele brought to North Oxfordshire.

Why? We know the previous owners could manage it perfectly well. We have the books, the know-how and the wherewithal. And we have the perfect south-facing spot. Everything is fine, and yet everything still goes and dies.

The board of BMW must feel the same sort of despondency when they look at their soon-to-be-axed Z8. When it was being born, they knew pretty well everything there was to know about sports car design. They had the best brains in the business and one of the best-looking shapes. They had the M5 engine and free use of the trick Z axle. Yet when all these ingredients were mixed together, they ended up with a bowl of ice cream and gravy.

The Z8 was the same as David Bailey getting his pictures back from Boots with a sticker on each of them: 'This picture is fuzzy because you had your thumb in front of the lens, or because you forgot to take the lens cap off.'

And it's not just the Z8. The Audi A2 must have seemed like a marvellous idea on paper – take the Audi badge and apply it to a super-light aluminium body which, despite its small size, is big enough for four and their luggage. Serve with tasty little diesel engine *et voilà*.

Et voilà, indeed. Somehow, the finished product was like my orchid. A lot of moss and roots with very little flower.

I'm told the new boss of Audi, Burnt Fishtrousers, is not a fan either. On his first morning at work, having come from BMW, he pointed at the smallest car in Audi's range and said, 'You can get rid of that for a start.' Or words to that effect.

Then there's the Peugeot 607. Take one piece of bread, one toaster, one knife, some butter and Gordon Ramsay's toast chef. That's what Peugeot did . . . and they ended up with some cream cheese, served on a bed of dark chocolate McVities Homewheat biscuit.

Actually, I feel sorry for Peugeot. You get the impression they didn't want to make the 607, but the French government said, 'Look, the Germans can turn up at EU meetings in a Mercedes and the British in a Range Rover. Even the Italians can go in an Alfa 166, so there is no way we're rocking up in a Clio. Build us something big.'

So, that's what they got. The best way of describing the 607 is 'something big'.

Jaguar falls into this category as well with the X-Type. They had access to Ford's lucky dip parts bin where every prize is a winner and they had Ford's cheque book too. They had a factory where the car could be made, and a workforce trained for the job. However, there's an X factor that went missing in the mix, so that whenever you're in an X-Type, you find yourself saying, 'I can't believe it's not a Jaguar.' But it isn't, somehow.

The problem is, of course, that you can have as many committees and as many computers as you can fit in the building, but cars, like everything else, are designed by people, and people make mistakes.

Every week, for instance, we put *Top Gear* together at the BBC. Half the office knows everything there is to know about cars and the other half knows everything there is to know about television. Between us, we can work out what should be on the show. And pretty well every single week, we get it wrong.

Last month we kicked off with the Rolls-Royce and moved moments later into the Rover P5B. It looked like a great idea on paper, covering the last word in luxury and then explaining how you can have the same sort of thing for £8,000. But I looked at my seven-year-old son halfway through the programme and he was fast asleep.

I therefore don't blame Lexus for the SC430. They tried and they made a pig's ear of it. I even feel sorry for them because they can't say 'whoops' and move on. They have to pretend it was what they wanted all along.

Only after a car goes out of production do you hear the manufacturers saying, 'Jesus Christ, we got that one wrong.'

Interestingly, I still haven't heard anyone from Vauxhall admit that the last Vectra was off beam. Indeed, it'd be nice if someone from the company said the entire range – Corsas, Astras, Omegas and Vectras – was like my conservatory, a room full of dead twigs.

It seems, though, they have a better idea. With the Aussie V8 Monaro coupé and the new sports car waiting in the wings, and the Signum and VX turbo here now, it seems they're forgetting what's done and showing the world what's to come. I am too. My fuschia's bright. My fuschia's orange.

July 2003

Soft tops

It's the fastest soft top in the world. So says the rather clever advertising for BMW's rather pretty new Z4.

Of course, it's not the fastest soft top in the world, a Pagani Zonda could get to Leeds much more quickly. But it does *have* the fastest soft top. You press a button and just ten seconds later the whole hood is in the boot.

This sounds wonderful. You can get the roof off while the traffic lights are on red. Actually, while Ken Livingstone's traffic lights are on red, you have time to take the roof off and rebuild the car, but that's another story.

The point is that Z4 drivers can exploit even the slightest crack in the clouds, sunning themselves when the rays break through then closing up again whenever the rain comes.

Small wonder with such cars on the market that British motorists buy six times more convertibles than people in Spain. Though this might have something to do with the fact that when you've spent your whole life on the back of a donkey, an open-air car might appear to be a bit plebeian.

Anyway, it's the same story with the new Renault Mégane convertible and the proposed open-air Peugeot 307, both of which have Mercedes-style, vandal-proof metal roofs that whirr noiselessly and speedily into the boot.

Great. Except it's not great at all. These clever hoods may look absolutely wonderful on television, or if you're eight. They may have a huge appeal in the showroom too, but think about it. If you were sitting in a BMW Z4 at the lights and you lowered that roof, what, exactly, do you think other motorists are going to think of you?

Do you really think they'll turn to the passengers and say, 'My, there's a sophisticated chap.' And what of people on buses, who will have a bird's-eye view of the action? Are they going to say, 'Hey everyone. Come and look at this new Beemer. Boy, it's got such a speedy roof action.'

Or are they going to hoik up the largest docker's oyster in the history of phlegm and gob on your newly exposed head.

It's not just the roof malarkey either. I'm starting to doubt whether men can actually drive a convertible at all, ever.

With some, the answer is easy. No man, for instance, can drive a Peugeot 206CC. It may look like a car. It may be priced like a car. It may function like a car with gears and a petrol tank and so on. But it is a skirt.

Men may not drive an MG either. Oh, it's not a bad motor, in the same way that Space NK is not a bad shop. It's just that men don't go in there any more than they'd go in the new StreetKa or the Beetle cabrio.

I saw my co-presenter, Richard Hammond in the new Citroën Pluriel this morning. Now I know he uses hair products, and I know he has a poodle. I'm aware too that he spends time motorcycling with his men friends. Strangely, he gets away with all this, but behind the wheel of the new five-ways Citroën, he looked so camp, even James May admitted to fancying him.

The Saab convertible is for girls and architects. Though if your architect does turn up in a topless Swede, sack him. If he thinks that's a good ride or good looking, the man's obviously useless at his job and you'll end up with cracks in the conservatory and a brushed aluminium spiral staircase that doesn't quite reach the first floor.

The new Audi A4 is awfully girly, though strangely the 3-Series BMW isn't. That's for berks, especially the M3 version. The Fiat Barchetta's for girls (Hammond used to own one) and so is the 911 and so is Audi's TT.

In fact, the only cabrios men can buy are the Mazda MX-5, the Toyota MR2, the Merc CLK, the Alfa Spider (just), the Lotus Elise, the Honda S2000, the Jaguar XKR, the DB7, the 360 Ferrari and, obviously, all TVRs.

However, while you can buy these cars, because they've a certain earthiness beneath the pretty-boy looks, you can't drive them around with the roof down if people are looking.

Only the other day I came out of a breakfast meeting with the German ambassador. Nice chap. No idea why I was there. Anyway, it was a lovely sunny day and I thought I would take the roof off the Merc for an alfresco drive to Notting Hill . . .

My finger hovered over the button, but my mind was adamant. 'You can't do this,' it said. 'You are a middle-aged man with a bald patch, yellow teeth and a stomach the size of Norfolk. What message do you think you are sending out by driving down Park Lane with the roof down?'

It had a point. The real reason we drive with the roof off is to be seen. But why do we want to be seen? That's the big question.

It's because we think we look good. But we don't. Which is why when you see some middle-aged bloke cruise by in his sports car, you don't think, Hmm, cool guy. You think, Look at that fat twat. Well, I do.

I now have a rule with the Mercedes. I drive it with the roof down in the countryside and on the motorway, but before I get to London I pull into a special little lane I've found and, when no one is looking, put it up again.

There's another issue to the vexed question of whether or not it's possible to go topless. Because you're English, the chances are that you have the complexion of forced rhubarb and hair like wire wool. So, when you've arrived at wherever it is you are going, your barnet will have an unusual new parting and the texture of a breeze block, and your nose will be a huge glowing tomato. Yes, your arms will be lovely and brown but you'll likely have had a shirt on, so there'll be a line above the elbow where it all goes milky white. Is that what you want? Raspberry ripple arms, bad hair, a big gut, yellow teeth, a bald patch and a nose as big and red as the starter button on God's Vanquish.

The car will have made you deeply unattractive to your wife or girlfriend, not that you'll be speaking anyway because, in my experience, women like the idea of toplessness on the road, but dislike the practice as much as they dislike some of the odd sexual practices one reads about.

If you have a soft top, a typical conversation with a girl goes like this. 'Can we take the roof off? Can we take the roof off? Can we take the roof off? Can we take the roof off?' . . . Brrrm. 'Can we put the roof up? Can we put the roof up? Can we put the roof up? Can we put the roof up? I hate you.'

Welcome, then, to convertible motoring in Britain today.

August 2003

Goodwood

God it was a good Goodwood. The sun didn't just shine, it fried my eyes. Elle Macpherson smiled at me. I went up the hill in the passenger seat of a McLaren Mercedes and someone wrote, 'Jodi was faster', in the dust on the bonnet of Jay Kay's Ferrari Enzo,

Best of all though, at the Saturday night black-tie party, with Chrissie Hynde on vocals and half a ton of fireworks on bass, a man invited me to step outside for a spot of pugilism.

He was the motoring historian from the *Daily Telegraph* who dragged *Top Gear*'s name into the tabloids, saying we'd trashed a historic C-Type Jaguar and that we were hooligans, blah blah, louts, blah blah, no place on television, blah.

Anyway, to cut a long story short, I responded by saying, in the *Sun,* that we knew where he lived, and that if he wanted to see some real hooliganism, he should try complaining again.

Boy was he cross. So cross that he waded into the Goodwood showdown sporting what I can only presume was a protest beard. Or maybe he has got it into his head that beards grown under the face are somehow cool and interesting.

Whatever, he poked me a lot in the chest, said I was fat and over the hill and that he could take me any time. I would dearly love to report that at this point I shut him up by punching him in the middle of the face, but it would have been like hitting a goblin. So I'm afraid I just laughed at him and went off to get drunk.

By eleven I was really very sozzled indeed, so very little of what happened subsequently has stuck. I remember Eddie Jordan saying he'd got a new engine, and meeting Edsel Ford, who was great. I also remember fancying the wife of the new boss of Ford in Europe, but somehow I ended up dancing with Dave Richards.

At one point, I distinctly remember discussing unnatural and illegal sexual acts with the hostess of the party, Janet March. But since Janet is one of the nicest people I know, this must be wrong. Maybe she'd got a new engine and I'd been talking bottoms with Eddie Jordan. Oh, and Jenson Button was there too, in a purple suit.

Then it was three in the morning and I was back at the hotel, clinging onto the bed for dear life because I knew it to be upside down. Why does room-spin do that? Stop spinning when you're the wrong way up.

Unfortunately, on Sunday morning I was still drunk, so when I found the SL had a puncture, I became convinced the historian had done it. 'Bastard,' I shouted, running around with a red face and sweating. It was my wife who pointed to the dust cap and said, 'If someone had let your tyre down, they wouldn't have put that back.'

Good point. Less good, however, was trying to find an SL tyre on a Sunday. Eventually, the local Merc dealer came – and then dropped the car off the jack. Happily for the man who came and told me, I'd already started rehairing the dog, so I didn't really care less.

To cushion the blow, he said I could take a passenger ride in the 612bhp McLaren Mercedes that had turned up at the event unannounced. What can I say? Unlike some motoring journalists, I'm unable to tell you what a car is like from the right-hand side of a left-hooker, except that it makes a great noise and is a laugh pissed.

I sobered up enough to help judge the Cartier concours competition, although I must say, it's jolly difficult to say which is the best Fifties stock-car racer. They all looked the same: broken.

Furthermore, one of the other judges was David Linley, who just the week before had been giving me a lift across London when I saw a Bugatti Veyron parked outside the German Embassy.

'Ooh', I said, 'that's the new Bugatti Veyron. Can you stop.' I piled out and bumped into the German ambassador with whom I'd had breakfast back in April.

Anyway, he invited me inside leaving the Queen's nephew standing on the street outside. It was all hopelessly embarrassing.

But then I'm good at that. Another judge was the DJ Johnny Walker who, when I asked how he was, said, 'Fine, apart from the cancer.' It's difficult to know where you go with that, so I asked where it had bitten him. 'In the arse-hole,' he said and that really was the end of that.

Then, more trouble. Standing between me and my place at the lunch table was David Coulthard who, I have said many times, is like one of those aliens from *Men in Black*. He looks human on the surface, but beneath those overalls I'm sure he has eight flippers and webbed legs.

If anyone has a damn good reason for punching me in the stomach, it's him. But unlike the historian, he's a gentleman, so things were cool.

Then I bumped into Jodi Kidd. Superstar, Supermodel and the fastest person ever to have gone round the *Top Gear* test track.

Unfortunately, the day afterwards, she'd been rung by someone from the *Guardian*, who'd said I was furious that a girl had beaten everyone. Absolutely not true, so we made up with a hug, which was one of those life-changing moments. I am now completely in love with that girl.

Over lunch, Sir Terence Conran told me that he has an Audi. Sorry, Tel, but this was like saying you have ears. You are one of the country's most important design masterminds, and there was no way in hell you'd drive anything else.

I never had the chance to mention this, though, because from the other side of the tent, Elle had waved at me. This was amazing. We'd once had dinner, and here was proof that she'd remembered. I mean, *crikey*. When I got back from the lavatories, lunch was over, so I sauntered over to the super-car arena, half-inched the keys to Merc's SL55 demonstrator and went home.

And that was my day and night at the Goodwood festival of speed. A fight. A drinkathon, the Pretenders, two super-models, a McLaren Mercedes and five minutes discussing some Fifties stock cars with Her Majesty's carpenter. You don't get half of this at Henley or Wimbledon or the Chelsea Flower Show.

I loved it, but it wasn't until I was halfway up the A34 that I realized I'd forgotten something. I hadn't watched a single car go up the hill in a blaze of noise and tortured rubber.

It seems, then, that the festival has come of age. The point has become a side show.

September 2003

Coupés

There is no argument more guaranteed to make my eyes swell up and my teeth move about than the one which says you pay more for a coupé and get less space.

About a hundred years ago, when I was nineteen, I bought a Scirocco GLi and spent the next two years with my hands in my pockets in a desperate bid not to punch the next person who explained, through tortured adenoids, that I'd paid a £1,000 premium for what, after all, was just a Golf GTi.

Aaaaaaargh. That's like telling someone who's just paid £22 million for a Van Gogh masterpiece that underneath all the paint, it's only canvas. And that he may as well have bought something for a pound from the church fayre.

If I were to tell you that a Bang & Olufsen home cinema system is basically Phillips kit in a sleek box, would it make you want one less?

Genetically speaking, those men who crop up on *Wife Swap* every week, with their tattoos and their penchant for lying on the sofa, are almost completely identical to Henry Kissinger. More than that. They're almost completely identical to Skippy the bush kangaroo.

But it's the little touch, the final flourish, that makes all the difference. And so it was with the VW Scirocco. Yes. I could have bought a Golf GTi and saved my £1,000 but then I would have had less sex.

Eventually, the Scirocco was replaced with a BMW 3.0 CSL, which gave way to a Honda CRX, which was kicked back on to the forecourt by an Alfa Romeo GTV6. So as you can see, I've always had a soft spot for coupés.

Why? Because the designers only had to worry about boot space or rear headroom in the same way they worried about their biro running out of ink, or Tenerife falling into the sea and creating a tidal wave. Subliminally, in other words.

What mattered most of all was design that verged on being art. With a house, the three most important features are location, location and location. With coupés, it's style, style and style.

Why do you think that the Audi TT sells in such vast numbers? For a lot less money you could have a Skoda Octavia, which is basically the same car, but it's one that you could drive without fear of being thrown backwards into the Armco every time you twitched the wheel on an autobahn. But you do like those air vents, don't you? And rightly so.

There's another reason, though, why it has been such a hit. There wasn't really any competition. Nissan abandoned the 200SX, VW dropped the Corrado, Vauxhall ditched the Calibra, Fiat tucked their coupé away as soon as the man who designed it upped sticks and left for BMW, William Hague bought a Ford Cougar and in doing so gave it the kiss of death as surely as Gareth Cheeseman had done for the Probe, and Honda gave up selling its Prelude to old ladies in Lancashire.

The disease spread far and wide. The Puma came and went. A serious pity, given that the girly Ka's still here – they're the same thing underneath, and the Puma was as hilariously entertaining on the road and easy on the pay cheque as they come. BMW dropped the 6 Series and made a 3 Series coupé, which only looked different to the saloon when viewed from a helicopter, and all the Rover 200 coupés (or Tomcats, as the boisterous Brum engineers nicknamed them) hit trees.

Now, though, the coupé is coming back with a vengeance. We've got the new BMW 6 Series waiting in the wings and I for one hope it stays there. If this were a house, it'd be that one in the middle of the M62. I've seen more style on a Surrey patio.

Then there's that Mercedes-Benz SLK in a Wilbur suit, and the Chrysler Crossfire, which looks like a dog doing a shit. You know – that arched-back thing pooches do when they're squeezing one out.

And let's not forget the Mazda RX-8. Now this is one of the best-handling cars I have ever driven and I just love telling friends of my mother that it has a Wankel rotary engine. But the styling's chintzier than a pair of council house curtains. It rather looks like they had a 'design' suggestion box at the factory and decided to adopt everyone's idea. So as a result it's a two-door four door, with the boot of a saloon, the front of a Humber, gills and some triangles. And this from the same company that brought us one of the most heavenly-looking creations of all time, the last RX-7.

Finally, there's the Nissan 350Z. Now this is more like it. In many ways, it reminds me of the old De Tomaso Mangusta – muscular, beefy, solid. Not prepared to back down from an argument. You don't want to spill its pint, that's for sure.

On looks alone, this is the easy choice, but typically, the best looking is the least desirable to own. It's one of the most tiring cars I've ever driven. If I were to pop into town in one, I'd need to check into a hotel for a lie-down. After a drive in the 350Z from Sheffield to London earlier in the year, I had such a bad headache that I considered chopping it off. In the end I ate so many paracetamol pills, I grew a second penis.

So what would I buy if I were in the market for a coupé now? Well, there's the Toyota Celica T-Sport I suppose, which is a laugh a minute with its mad-arsed million valve, rev-happy engine, but even that seems a bit girly somehow. Then there's the good old Alfa GTV, which used to be agonizingly pretty, but since its recent collagen injection now looks like Leslie Ash.

The Peugeot 406 is not to be forgotten, especially in metallic pale green. But do you know what? I think I'd go for the Hyundai Coupé.

Some criticize it for looking too like the Ferrari 456, but isn't that like being criticized for painting like Turner. Driving an £18,000 car that looks like it cost ten times as much cannot, even in the warped imagination of the most cynical observer, be anything but a good thing.

December 2003

CAR OF THE YEAR: FIAT PANDA

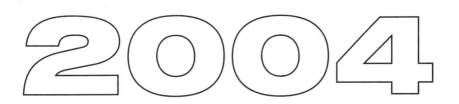

2004

TOP 5 BESTSELLING SINGLES
SONG TITLE – ARTIST

1 Do They Know It's Christmas –
  Band Aid 20
2 I Don't Want You Back – Eamon
3 Cha Cha Slide – DJ Casper
4 Call On Me – Eric Prydz
5 Yeah – Usher featuring Lil' Jon and
  Ludacris

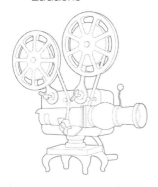

TOP 5 BOX OFFICE MOVIES

1 Shrek 2
2 Spider-Man 2
3 The Passion of the Christ
4 Meet the Fockers
5 The Incredibles

Concorde's death

At 7.51 a.m. local time, Captain Mike Bannister eased the throttles forward, ignited the burners and I became one of the last hundred people alive today to go to the far side of the sound barrier without the benefit of a parachute.

Three hours later, as we neared the coast of Wales, we dropped back down to a gentle 500mph. And that was that. Supersonic transport for the paying customer was over.

By now, you will have read much tear-stained prose in all the newspapers about the premature death of Concorde. I fear I may have written much of it myself, saying the decision to can it was one giant leap backwards for mankind.

Everyone seemed to think the same way, even the *Guardian* and the *Independent*. And it was all summed up beautifully by the ballet dancer Darcy Bussell. 'Why', she asked, 'can it not be run at a loss? The National Ballet is.'

At New York's JFK airport that morning, even the epsilons who load the bags onto Delta flights to Iowa stopped for one last gawp. All around the airfield, the emergency vehicles turned on their flashing lights. And with a crackling rumble, the last great reminder that Britain was once a force to be reckoned with was gone.

At Heathrow, they came in their thousands to see the New York flight, and two others, land in line astern. There was live coverage from all the television networks. And none of them mentioned the fact that the day before, on Concorde's last outbound flight, four of the paying passengers, who'd remortgaged their houses and sold all their furniture to be there, had forgotten their passports.

Even this heart-rending (but bloody funny) tale of people trudging back to their empty houses was overshadowed by the death of an icon.

But hang on a minute. Why exactly did we all feel so sad? I mean, I don't feel sorry for the businessmen who used it like a bus. It was their meanness in the latter years that got it killed. I don't feel sorry for the people who serviced it, or worked in the cabin. They'll get other jobs. And I don't feel sorry for British Airways, either.

No, what I feel sorry for is the machine itself. For twenty-seven years, it's flown back and forth across the Atlantic, never putting a foot wrong. And then one day, no one came to its hangar to hoover its carpets or replenish its fuel tanks. One day, for no reason that it could possibly understand, its owners decided they didn't want it any more.

I don't want to sound soft, but think how your dog would feel if you did that: tickled its tummy and filled its bowl for twenty-seven years and then one day, locked it in a kennel and never went back.

Concorde doesn't understand profit and loss. It has no concept of risk or airworthiness certificates and it sure as hell wouldn't understand Richard Branson's ludicrous claim that he could keep it going. It's a machine. It knows only how to fly very, very fast across the Atlantic.

But. Some machines become more than a collection of wires and glass and metal. They take on a personality and this is what makes their death hard to stomach.

I once visited the Davis-Monthan airbase in Arizona. We were there to film a giant guillotine cutting B52 bombers into small pieces and, I'm telling you, it hurt. Here was a machine that was built to deliver death and destruction. But it never knew that. It was created to do a job, and it did that job without complaint. So it would have to wonder, 'Why are they cutting my arms off?'

Titanic was another machine that warmed the corners of your heart, and so is my coffee machine. I'm also hugely fond of my noise-cancelling Bose headphones. But you could take a hammer to this damn computer and I'd thank you for it. Same goes for my television and my mobile phone. But not my barometer, strangely.

We see the same sort of thing in the world of cars. Why do I think the Renault Clio has a soul when I know for sure that a Toyota Corolla does not? And why would I be saddened to see a Rover SD1 crushed, but unmoved completely by the death of its successor, the 820?

Last month on *Top Gear* we bought a Toyota pickup truck that had already covered 190,000 miles. Ten of which, probably, had been done on the road. After just a few hundred yards, I knew this was a car with some soul, it was the dependable labourer who's been building dry stone walls for forty years, and I began to hate myself for the pain I was going to inflict on it.

Over the next two days, I smashed it into trees, drowned it in the sea, crashed it into Bristol, dropped a caravan on it and set fire to it. And after each torment, it would cough back into life with a diesely working-man's rumble. And sit there with half of the Bristol Channel in its eyes asking, 'Why are you doing this to me?'

Once, I fed a Volvo 340 into a crushing machine and felt nothing as the metal jaws ripped it to pieces, but each time I see our burned-out, half-dead Toyota sitting in the studio, it brings a tear to my eye. Weird.

Do not confuse this with an attachment that you might build towards your car. When you've had a few bumps, and a few bonks in the back, it's easy to form an attachment. But I'm not talking about your relationship with the machine. I'm talking about the machine's relationship with you.

When I had the Ferrari, I felt it was sad, sitting in the garage all winter, and yet I can cheerfully leave the Mercedes in the cold for weeks on end and not give its feelings a second thought. I don't think it has any.

My wife's Lotus, though, manages to look miserable and doe-eyed when it hasn't been used for a while. Sometimes, and I'm not joking, I'm tempted to go out there and give it a blanket.

No car, however, gets close to the aching sadness I feel for Concorde. Next time I'm passing Heathrow, in this season of goodwill, I may drop in and buy it some soup.

Speaking of the season, have a jolly time and thanks for being a petrosexual.

January 2004

Clothes

This month I shall be writing about clothes, so I should mention, at the outset, that I have absolutely no idea what I'm on about. I tend to wear whatever happens to be nearest to the bed and don't really care if my socks don't match. The other day, by mistake, I went to a party in odd shoes.

People write to *Top Gear* occasionally saying that my teeth appear to have got a sun tan and that my hair's a mess. Clearly, they're mistaking me for someone who gives a damn. Some bloke last week wrote to say my brogues were dirty.

How empty does your life have to be for you to care? And how doubly empty for you to be so enraged that you turn on your PC, write a letter of complaint and then go to all the bother of finding a stamp and an envelope? I have never, ever, cleaned a pair of shoes. I wear them. They disintegrate. I buy some more. The End.

If you find me offensive to behold, put something in front of the right side of the screen and look at the adorable little Hammond with his flowery shirts and his puppy-dog eyes instead.

Just the other night I was out for dinner with the Blonde (*Sunday Times* readers will know who I mean) when she leaned over, grabbed my wrist and said curtly, 'Oh. Novelty cufflinks'.

I am aware that novelty underpants and novelty socks bearing the legend 'I'm not wearing any knickers' are a bit of a no-no. But did you know that cufflinks shaped like typewriter keys are also social death? No. Neither did I.

Why, some people ask, do I wear jeans all the time? Well, let's have a look at the alternatives. Combats? I'm forty-three. Slacks? Er . . . I'm forty-three. Cords? I think not. Cords are for people who have given up on sex, parties, girls, flirting, everything. They are truly for people who are looking forward to dying. I confess I sometimes wear a suit. But it's six years old now and a bit knackered.

Yes, I could buy a new one, but this would involve going to a shop. And being heterosexual and male, that's really not the done thing, is it?

So, the upshot is, I don't care about clothes, I have no interest in clothes. I don't know what goes with what and reckon that if you can't see my genitals, I'm well dressed.

However, my wardrobe is far from a potpourri of any old rubbish. There are rules in there. Well, there's one, but that's all you need. My rule is: no car-branded stuff of any kind.

My father used to have an M Power belt, which was hideous enough. 'Dad,' I used to say, as we trundled around in his Cortina, 'it would be better if you wore your trousers round your ankles.' Even back then I knew that advertising a car you didn't actually own was poor form.

It's true that wherever you go on holiday, everyone on the beach is wearing a T-shirt saying they've been somewhere else. But 'I've been to Florida' is better than 'I don't own an M3'.

There is, however, something that's even worse. Advertising a brand of car that you do actually own.

I saw on the Web the other day, an MG tiepin and cufflink set for £30. But if you're the sort of person who wears a tiepin, we already know you have an MG, and are likely enthusiastic enough to have avoided the rubber bumper model.

But worse. Much, much worse, is the Subaru anorak. What exactly are you trying to say here? Women, even if they are Penny Mallory herself, will not be interested. This is a cast-iron guarantee. So you must be doing it to impress other men. And that leads us to some interesting speculation about those of a Subaru disposition.

Does it mean that because your power goes either way, front or back, you do too?

If this isn't it, then what's your message? Obviously, I think the anorak is a fine garment, windproof, waterproof and warm, but I am aware that it has a reputation for geekiness. One imagines people who live with their mothers and spend their spare time downloading make-believe wives from the Internet wear such things. Is that the image you want for the Subaru owner?

Maybe you're hoping men will come up to you in pubs and say, 'Hey, I've got one too.' Well, maybe in America, but here? In a country where not knowing your neighbour is the national sport? I think not.

I don't want you to think I'm singling out Subaru for particular criticism. Regularly, people come to the TG studio in their RS T-shirts, and I'm bound to ask why. I don't care that they have elasticated sleeves and that they're made from petrochemical by-products, but I know there are many millions out there who will.

And that's a massive problem. Because, you see, it's not just yourself you're letting down here. It's not just the RS Club either, or even Ford. You're letting the whole car world down.

And you're not alone. One of the chief reasons why F1 can't be as glamorous or socially acceptable as it should be is the clobber worn by the back-room boys. There they are, on our TV screens every week in their Ferrari anoraks and their Merc bomber jackets. They look like nerds.

Why in God's name are they not allowed to work in whatever takes their fancy? And why does Ron Dennis tuck his T-shirt in? It looks ridiculous. If I were a Martian, visiting Earth in search of cool sports to steal, I'd take one look at Ron and abduct some snooker players instead.

Cars are under attack from all quarters. The government is trying to force them off the roads. The environmentalists are on the news every night with their lopsided views. The car makers themselves all seem to be on the brink of going bust. And those who are sitting on the fence, undecided, are not going to side with a bunch of people in branded anoraks and tiepins, with their T-shirts tucked into their trousers.

They're going to side with Swampy. Is that what you want? Because unless you have a huge clear-out of your branded clothing, that's what you're going to get. I know I started by saying I didn't know what I was talking about, but, really, it won't be the lack of oil that kills the car. It'll be Michael Schumacher's trousers.

February 2004

Parking

It is a fact that 80 per cent of all aeroplane crashes are attributed to pilot error. So the safest thing we could possibly do is get rid of the humans in the cockpit. The only trouble is that if we did this, we'd also get rid of all the humans in the passenger compartment as well. No really. Would you get on a plane that was being flown entirely by computer?

Weird, isn't it, that we take comfort from being in the hands of fallible beings who may be drunk, or menstruating, or tired, or bored out of their wits.

And the thing is that fully automated planes are science fact. I've actually filmed on board an Airbus that was told, by Chicago airport, which runway to land on at Gatwick, 4,000 miles away. It cruised right across the Atlantic on its own and landed not just on the runway, but so perfectly dead centre I could feel the catseyes bumping against the nose wheel. All the pilot did on the entire journey was throttle back after we'd touched down.

And don't think this was some stunt. Because sitting behind me were 300 or so passengers. It was a normal, everyday trans-atlantic flight. This is remarkable technology, up there with the 2580 phone service that can identify any record ever made, just by listening to it as a series of ones and noughts. Or the phone network that now routinely turns your words into a series of tiny packages. Some are then sent through cables, others go up into space, but whatever the route, they're all reassembled perfectly at the other end, even if it's in Wichita.

So, if it's now possible to do all this and make a satnav system steer, in perfect safety, the entire population of a small village halfway round the world and drop them off precisely where required, how come we have not yet made a car that can go from the middle of the road into a parking space two yards away?

I'm talking about parking this month for two very good reasons. First, because I'm about to get a Ford GT and, second, because I'm forty-three.

Because I'm forty-three, bits of my body that worked perfectly well yesterday do not work so well today. Things just break in the night. And the latest component to come over all hopeless is my left buttock, which suddenly has the give of elm.

Getting into an armchair hurts like billy-o. Getting out again is pretty much impossible. And I do wish friends would stop recommending chiropractors and osteopaths because (a) I don't want to pay a man to rub my bottom and (b) how the hell am I supposed to get there? Unless someone can invent a pair of hover-shoes, I'm marooned on my own little island of pain.

Which brings me on to the Ford GT. Yes, passers-by will nod appreciatively as I burble by, but, boy, will their nodding turn to open laughter when they see me trying to get out.

Exiting any supercar is an undignified process, no matter how old and fit you may be. If I ever parked the old Ferrari 355 against a high kerb, I found the easiest way out was to crawl onto the pavement on my hands and knees. I'm aware, of course, that this looked a bit poor.

But the GT adds to the problem because, when you open the door, half the roof comes with it. So even when it's open, it's not, if you see what I mean. In a tight parking space (and the one at my flat in London is barely wide enough to accommodate Kate Moss on a Microscooter), I'll have to turn round and slide sideways, head first out of what may as well be a letterbox.

This would be difficult at the best of times, but when your torso is joined to your leg by a buttock made of solid wood, I fear it may be impossible.

There are some solutions. I could grit my teeth and see the bum-bandit osteo-wotsit. Or I could move house. Or, I suppose, I could cancel my order for the Ford and buy a Kia Rio instead.

But would this help? In the olden days, when my bones weren't brittle and my muscles rippled like pythons in a sack, I could rotate my head almost as well as Linda Blair in *The Exorcist*. I'd pull up in front of a space, swivel in my seat and, whoosh, I'd have the car alongside the kerb. After eighteen years in London, people would come from all over the world to watch me do it.

Not any more. Now, no matter how small the car, or how light its steering, or how good its visibility, I just don't have the physical dexterity to turn round any more. And if I attempt to compensate for this by swivelling my eyes, I end up looking backwards at my own brain.

I therefore have to use The Force. And weirdly, this doesn't work very well. I don't understand why, because on the last census, I put my religion down as Jedi Knight and yet, I can never 'feel' the car behind until I really do feel it. Parking sensors are not the answer. For some strange reason they start beeping when you are half a mile from the obstacle and then become a solid wall of sound when you're two feet away. That's no good. In a crowded city like London, parking is measured to the nearest 2mm.

Very quickly, you learn to ignore the warnings in the same way as you ignore an empty fuel tank: 'Oh, it doesn't mean I have to stop now. I can just keep going another . . . crunch!' If you look at my Volvo, there's a crack in the bumper and a smashed light right above one of the sensors.

There's another problem too, which is that they cry wolf. Driving slowly, they scream away at every pedestrian or every gust of wind, so you'll be guaranteed to tune them out on the very day you really are reversing over a pram.

No. What we need is fully automated parking. We need to pull up, push a button and then read a book until we're stopped. How hard can it be? Radar could measure the space and feed the data to a computer, which simply calculates how much lock is required at any given moment. It's not like there are any variables; a 14-foot space will always require the same set of actions, whether it's in Barnsley or Barnes.

Much is being done to make cars easier to drive fast. But as middle age sets in, I need an equal amount being done to make them easier to stop.

April 2004

Beautiful cars

I see Charles Saatchi, who has a London art gallery full of dead cows and pickled sharks, has recently bought a painting of Princess Diana, by a former stripper, for £600.

Now, everyone with Harry Hill collars and a subscription to the *Guardian* is running around saying she's the new Constable Turner, the greatest find since Tracey Emin refused to get out of bed for less than £10,000.

Of course, I had a long hard look at this new painting and nodded sagely. Yes, I thought, it's an exquisite something or other and I love the way the artist has discombobulated the notion of Princess Diana as a mother, while punking up her owl as a lover and national icon. It's important, I find, when discussing art to talk absolute crap.

The only trouble is that we sometimes sink to similar depths in the world of cars. Go back through old motoring magazines and you'll find that in almost every road test of an Italian car, the writer will kick off with some nonsense about the Renaissance.

Why? Yes, there are some pretty buildings in Italy – some of them are nearly as pretty, in fact, as some of the buildings in France. And yes, there have been some great artists. But what about Rembrandt and Van Gogh, both of whom were Dutch? Does that mean cars from Holland today must be exquisite to behold? Really? So could someone explain the Mitsubishi Carisma?

And anyway, just because Italy used to be good at knocking

up a building doesn't necessarily mean the genes have been passed on. We used to be good at building bridges and tunnels and trains. Now, you can't even get from London to Manchester without being bankrupted and killed.

Sadly, I'm as guilty as the next man at perpetuating this Italian myth. I've argued many times that they can't help but design beautiful cars because they are surrounded by beauty. This is rubbish. Ferrari is based in Maranello, which is one of the ugliest towns in the world.

We need to forget this notion that Italian cars are designed by handsome Italian men whose offices overlook the twelfth-century piazza and whose secretary's legs go on for 2,500 miles.

Giugiaro is a good-looking man with some lovely jackets, but what of the man who did the Fiat Multipla? Perhaps he worked in an office that overlooked a bus station and was brought coffee in the morning by a woman who was part human, part Scammell truck. For all its cleverness, it really was an ugly son of a bitch.

And it's not alone. The original Fiat 500 was more like a mollusc than a thoroughbred, And let's not forget that the Morris Marina was converted into the hideous Ital in Italy, or the 1970 Alfa 1750, which looked like a Triumph 2000 that had been at the pies.

Yes, the Fiat Strada Abarth was a sensational road rocket, but was it beautiful? Even if it were the last girl in the nightclub and you'd washed down a handful of Viagra with sixty-four vodka-Red Bulls, you'd still want to go home on your own.

Even when the Italians get it right, they still get it wrong. Take the Alfa 164 as a prime example. When it came along, everyone thought it was just the most stupendous-looking saloon the world had ever seen. But long before the first one had turned a wheel in Britain, it was already out of date.

It's a common problem with the Italian design houses – they're good at coming up with solutions in the here and now, but their ideas, like Jason King sunglasses, never last.

Think. What are the best-looking cars ever made? Well there's the Aston Martin DB7 for sure, and that's about as Italian as a Barnsley chop. Then you have the original Ford GT40, and the E-type Jag – notice a trend yet?

Yes. They are all British, but I have never heard anyone say, 'Ah well, you know the reason the British can't help designing such good cars is because of the Shambles in York and the High Street in West Wycombe.'

It's nonsense, this notion that the surroundings have a bearing on the shape of anyone's next car. The fact is that the Jag came out of Birmingham, which is even more hideous than Maranello, and the GT40 came out of Slough. God knows where the DB7 was penned. In one of God's wet dreams probably.

Even America, a country with the aesthetic appeal and the artistic ability of a wood louse, occasionally gets it right. I was thumbing through an old motoring annual from 1969 the other day, laughing at the silly cornering angles cars used to adopt when pushed in those days, and generally marvelling at the black and whiteness of it all when I happened upon a photo of the Corvette Stingray. Jesus, in the context of the time, that thing was astonishing.

I used to think the Countach was the greatest shock to the system the car world had ever seen. Having one of those outside your house in 1971 must have been like having an F22 Raptor on your drive today. But the Stingray predated the Lambo. In 1969, it must have seemed about as far-fetched as the *USS Enterprise*.

I look at the cars made in Italy today and I see nothing that sends a shiver down my spine. The Ferrari 360 looks like a surprised frog. That 612 looks like a Bristol and the Gallardo appears to have been drawn using nothing but a ruler.

Further down the scale we find the Fiat Panda, which is just fabulous, but it fails to delight the eye like its predecessor, and the Stilo five door, which can make small children sick. I actually think the current Lancia Thema is the ugliest car made today.

This doesn't mean the Italians have lost their touch, partly because they never had a 'touch' in the first place and partly because the modern design department of a car firm is as international as Visa's mailing list. Put simply, the Panda is no more Italian than a McDonald's is Scottish.

The fact is that Italian cars do have a soul. But beauty? That can come from anywhere.

May 2004

Fuel light bingo

I guess we all hate filling up with petrol. Yes, the sheer cost is bad enough, but much, much worse is the notion that you're standing there, in the freezing cold, catching cancer and watching your life ebb away in a digital blur.

This is why I'm so partial to playing fuel light bingo. The needle is already in the red zone as you pass a sign on the motorway saying 'Services 1m'. But you don't stop. You go to the next one, and when you get there, you go past that one too.

Besides, there's always the hope, the slimmest chance that somehow, the car will run on fresh air until you get home. And then next morning your wife will fill it up.

Much to Mrs C's annoyance, I play fuel-light bingo all the time and I'm very good at it, but this month, even I thought I'd overdone it. The yellow warning light had leapt into action as I passed Nottingham on the M1. And I had no intention of stopping until I got to London – which was 130 miles away. One hundred and thirty miles of unpredictable traffic on reserve. Not possible, surely?

This, in fact, was a test of the Audi A8 diesel, which will be shown on the first episode of the new series. We all marvelled at the sheer performance of its four-litre twin turbo V8; I mean, 0–60mph in 6.6 seconds – that's good for any big car. But for a big diesel car, it's truly astonishing. Surely, though, all those force-fed cubic inches will erase the point of having a diesel in the first place – fuel consumption, and therefore the distance you can go between visits to the pumps.

There was only one way to find out. And so, early one Tuesday morning back in the depths of winter, I rocked up at the Tower filling station on the Hendon Way in north London, a mile or so from the bottom of the M1. There, I brimmed the tank with 19.7 gallons and set off on what became the most extraordinary journey I've ever done in Britain.

I planned to drive to Edinburgh and back again without filling up. Which is 800 miles and that meant doing 40.4mpg. To begin with, things looked bleak. I'd driven pretty carefully out of London and once on the M1, had settled to a nice 60mph cruise. But even so, the Audi's onboard computer said that in the first 10 miles I'd only managed 35mpg.

At Milton Keynes, it had only risen to 37 and I really felt there was no point going on. I mean, television viewers are used to *Changing Rooms* and *Ground Force* where, in the nick of time, Titchmarsh and Smillie always just get the water feature working before Maureen gets back from the shops. I wasn't even going to get close.

Still, I eased it down to 55mph and turned off the climate control, which seemed to increase the average. And by the time I turned off on the M18 – about sixteen days after I'd left London – I was on target. By the time I was at Newcastle, I'd done 42mpg – five more than Audi said was possible. Things were looking great.

But then, disaster. In Northumberland, the A1 turned into a farm track, there were more roundabouts than sheep and my average, as I endlessly slowed down and sped up again, was plummeting. Nevertheless, as I arrived in Edinburgh at dusk, the fuel gauge told a happy story. It was slap bang on the half mark.

The only thing that worried me was that I'd used half a tank plus whatever was in the pipe. I wouldn't have that luxury on the way home. On the way back the following morning, the traffic was a nightmare and the single-lane road down to Newcastle meant I arrived in Geordieland with just a quarter of a tank left. Newcastle to London on a quarter of a tank; the computer said I was going to miss by a whopping 80 miles.

What started out as a test of an engine had, at this stage, turned into a test of my driving ability. Despite the cold, I still hadn't turned on the heater, and I'd even shut down the radio and the satnav. Everything that used power was a no-no.

On the hills, I was easing off a tad, and then accelerating when gravity was on my side. But never harshly. Never, not once, did I let the revs creep above 1,200rpm. I'm telling you, if people concentrated as hard as I was concentrating that day, no one would ever crash. Be assured, driving slowly is much, much harder than driving fast.

You have to read the road, not only spotting inclines, but also trying to anticipate who was going to do what next. Braking would mean washing off preciously earned mph, so I could never touch the left pedal. But I admit, I was ready to throw in the towel when that fuel warning light came on at Nottingham. It all just seemed to be so hopeless.

I kept trying and was amazed when I was still going at Milton Keynes. It seems I've been a wimp with this fuel-light bingo in the past. But then the thing I'd dreaded most of all loomed out of nowhere. A big fat, three-lane lump of stationary metal. Bugger. I cruised to a halt on the inside lane as the range reading on the trip computer dropped from five to zero.

For fifteen minutes I inched forward in that jam, waiting

for the tell-tale cough. It never came. This was bad news, because past Luton the hard shoulder was coned off. The only thing that could be worse than this was a contraflow.

Then the contraflow started. If I broke down in this at rush hour, on a cold March evening, I'd be lynched. Especially if I told everyone in the queue that I knew it was going to happen.

By this stage, I was properly, properly cold but I couldn't feel it. I was leaning forward in my seat, begging for just another drop, treating that throttle like it was a Fabergé egg. And then, suddenly, there it was: the end of the M1. Hendon Way and yes, yes, yes, just one set of lights and the garage where I'd started. I made it. With an average speed of 47mph, I'd averaged 40.4mpg. I know this because we plugged the car into an Audi service laptop, which said the tank was bone dry. All that was left was maybe half a litre in the pump.

So there you are. The awesome Audi V8 diesel. Thrilling when driven hard. But nowhere near as thrilling as when you drive it carefully.

June 2004

His greatest ever drive

I think there's a consensus that driving is only good fun when the sun's out, the roads are empty and there are no cameras. In other words, driving is only ever really good fun when you're in France.

It's true. The recent race from our *Top Gear* studio to Monte Carlo in an Aston Martin DB9 was epic. Satisfying too because, contrary to what you saw on television, I arrived in Monaco ninety-five minutes before James and Richard wheezed into town on the train.

Other good drives? I shall never forget taking a Jeep Wrangler over the Sierra Nevada mountains in California, or an E-type from one side of Spain to the other. And to prove my theory about the importance of blue skies and empty roads, one of the best times I ever had was blasting through a deserted Portuguese forest in a Toyota Starlet.

This month, I disproved the theory with one of the greatest drives ever. None of the ingredients were clichés. The sun wasn't shining. I wasn't driving the latest whizz-bang white-line snorter. There were loads of cameras. The traffic was awful. It was a Tuesday evening. And all I could find on the radio was some harridan, droning on about not eating lettuce in Mexico.

She was so dull that I turned her off, and turned up the wick just a little bit on my Jag.

It was an XKR with the full drug-dealer kit: big wheels, a

crap ride and a colour that could be described as British racing green, but was more a sort of Cheshire bling.

Still, no one could see me in it. Partly because I was at the
far end of Wales where there are no people, and partly
because it was dark. And throwing it down, cold, windy and
utterly, utterly miserable. To make matters worse, I'd been up
since dawn, filming in the pissing rain, and home was at least
four hours away.

As a little garnish, I'd misread the map leaving Saunders-
foot, or wherever the hell I was, and wound up on a sea wall
in some godforsaken hellhole, where all the signposts were
in Welsh. By the time I eventually found the right road, I felt
like those inmates at Camp X-Ray. Dejected. Lonely. Miserable. And too far from my bed.

So to blow away the blues, I turned up the wick even more.
And with the supercharger whistling like a demented milk-
man, went berserk. On the M4, sheets of water cascaded
across the carriageway, so every now and again the rear end
would kick sideways with a sickening lurch.

And to compound the problem, every time I emerged
from the lea of an escarpment, the wind would thud into the
side like a depth charge.

I needed to be wide awake. Also, it would have been good
if I'd had a rudimentary knowledge of Welsh. When one of
those digital motorway warning boards is showing a collection of consonants, it's downright dangerous. Surely, if the
message is important enough to be flashed up there, it's
important that everyone should be able to read it. 'DFRGH-
LLYLLYH', it said, as I belted down to the Severn Bridge,
feeling like the commander of a U-boat.

Back in England, the traffic jammed up like week-old

cereal on the bottom of an unwashed bowl. The guy in front braked every fifteen seconds like clockwork and then, just when I'd become used to the metronomic pulse, he'd switch and brake randomly, just when I expected it least. Had the Jag been equipped with guns, I'd have sawn him in half.

Soon though, it was time to turn off the M5 and head for home. To celebrate the moment, the rain stopped falling in drops or stair rods and started coming down in sheets. Even with the wipers going at full tilt, I could barely see where I was going.

And now with a camber to worry about, the Jag's rear end became livelier than a terrier's tail at feeding time. Time and time again, the nearside back wheel would drop into one of the potholes at the side of the road, sending a massive shudder through my spine. Had there been rivets, they all would have flown out. It was so like a submarine in there, I was surprised the glass on the instruments didn't shatter.

A Jag is supposed to cushion you from the road and provide a safe haven for the weary motorist. But that R on a sports suspension and Humbrol-thin tyres was a bastard. It wanted to let me know just how much effort it was making to stay straight. Sometimes, I got the distinct impression that it wanted me dead.

A sane man would have checked into the nearest pub until the storm passed, but I kept my foot down because, strangely, I was enjoying myself. This was not me and the machine working together to create all those physical sensations we enjoy from a good drive. This was me, on my own, fighting a bolshy car, biblical weather and about 400 years of underinvestment in the roads.

I was also fighting other road users. Sensibly, everyone

going my way had slowed to a crawl, so I figured it was always safe to overtake, on the basis that everyone going the other way would have slowed to a crawl as well.

It seemed to work. Occasionally, I would see a starburst of halogen light smearing across the windscreen, but it was impossible to tell how fast the car was going, or whether it was a car at all. It could have been a spaceship. All I know is that I pulled out to overtake the car in front many times and there was no sickening thud.

When I finally crunched onto my drive, I felt absolutely drained, mentally knackered. The next day, I was stiff. I suppose I'd been tensed up like a piano wire for the whole journey, waiting for the impact that never came. And that's what made this drive so special. They say you never feel more alive than when you're staring death in the face. I believe it. And if you had been out that night, in a hurry and in that Jag, you'd believe it too.

You can keep your sunny days and your perfectly tuned Ferraris. Real drivers do it in the rain.

July 2004

Teaching kids to drive

Ooh, I'm feeling pleased this morning. Pleased and a bit smug. So smug, in fact, that I'm going to begin this column with the traditional snort of a victor: a simple 'ha'.

You see, when I went to junior school, I learned all about rivers and how to spell 'paraphernalia'. It seems things have changed. In her first six years of schooling, my daughter has learned that trees are a girl's best friend and that the Brazilian rain forest is being murdered by McDonald's. At one stage, a year ago, it would have been easier to get her to eat a dog turd than a Big Mac.

She also knows that baby seals are slaughtered for fun and, while she doesn't know her six times table or the capital of France, she can give you chapter and verse on every single ingredient in a packet of cigarettes and exactly how each one will rip the very fabric from her tender nine-year-old lungs.

At this age, a child has a quest for knowledge that will never be matched in adult life. They will absorb information like a sponge, but so far as I can see, these days, the only information they're actually given is eco claptrap.

And it's not just school, either. When I turned on the television thirty-five years ago, I had the national anthem or Valerie Singleton showing me how to make a robot from cereal packets. Today, children have subliminal environmental cries for help in every single pop video and cartoon.

As a result, my daughter knows for a fact that global warming is caused by man. Which, when you think about it, is pretty clever, since some of the best brains in the scientific world aren't so sure. She also knows that there are no fish in the sea, that all coral reefs have been killed by jet skis and that if she eats food made from GM crops, she'll grow another eye.

Then there's Africa. Oh, my God. Given half a chance, she would have the entire population from western Sudan in her bedroom, and her views on the evil Swiss drug companies that won't give away medicine to the needy of Zimbabwe are astonishingly uncompromising. In essence, she wants heads, on spikes, in the garden.

Needless to say, it's been thoroughly drummed into her tiny head that the car is a particular menace. The class all sits around making up songs about their awfulness, and there are plays at the end of every term in which motorists are pilloried for killing not just thousands of children, but the whole planet too.

So you'd imagine that when I suggested we cycle into town yesterday, she'd have jumped at the chance. 'Oh yes, Daddy, and we can go to the organic farm shop while we're there and buy some fair-trade parsnip crisps.'

Not a bit of it. 'You must be joking,' was what she actually said. 'I hate bicycles. I want to go in the car because cars are, like, so cool.'

So 'ha' to the environmentalists. You can drip feed our young until you are blue in the face, but all of your work can be undone in one afternoon. How? Well, all I did with my daughter was take her to the local airfield in the family Focus and toss her the keys. Ten minutes later, she was in third gear, and ten minutes after that, she really couldn't give a toss about what was coming out of the exhaust pipe. She was hooked.

Her face, the first time she timed the clutch pedal and throttle just right and the car began to move was an absolute picture. It's a power trip, to be in control of a car – especially when you're nine. But, unfortunately, it's the exact opposite when you're a parent in the passenger seat. It is sheer hell.

The first time I ever drove a car on the public road, my mother was alongside and I distinctly remember the high-pitched, keening sound she made when I emerged for the first time onto a roundabout. The problem being that I didn't pull out when there was a gap in the traffic. Being seventeen, I pulled out when I figured I had been waiting long enough.

Quite how the lorry missed us, I have no idea. Maybe it was deflected from its previous course by the ultrasonic noise waves being made by my mother.

I made a similar sound shortly after my daughter had snatched fourth. We were doing probably about 40. This doesn't sound all that fast, but trust me, it is when you suddenly remember that you haven't explained how the brakes work and therefore how we might miss the enormous mound of earth that's bearing down on us at, well, it felt like Mach 4.

Quietly, so as not to cause alarm, I told her to take her foot off the accelerator and gently move it to the pedal in the middle. 'Why?' she said in that inquisitive, annoying way kids have when there's a solid wall of soil heading towards the windscreen.

Eventually, the row ended and she looked down between her legs to see if this previously undiscovered middle pedal was for real. To celebrate its location, she slammed her left foot onto it, as though it was the clutch and, as she pointed out afterwards, 'The car stopped, didn't it.'

Later, after I'd had a little walk, and a small cigarette, we turned round and thought we'd have a go at cornering, which turned out to be even scarier than braking. At least in the emergency stop, we didn't end up – and I swear this is true – on two wheels.

The problem is that I learned to drive by watching my dad. My daughter, on the other hand, learned to drive by racing her brother on the PlayStation. And out there in the silicon jungle, there's no need to slow down for bends, or bumps, or bumps in the middle of bends.

What's more, she knew that if she were to brake, I'd wail like a banshee again, so she figured it was best to keep clear of the middle pedal altogether. It was, quite simply, the most nerve-wracking hour of my life. At one point, I even considered using the eco tool to get her out of the driving seat again.

I still think children should learn about the rudiments of driving as early as possible, but I now think that their parents should be banned from teaching them.

I also have a message for the makers of Gran Turismo. Replicating the exact handling characteristics of a particular car is very clever, but I'd also like to see some realism when those handling characteristics are exceeded. In other words, every crash should be followed by a time-consuming insurance wrangle and the loss of all the player's pocket money.

August 2004

Bumpy rides

I was wrong. Back in the last series of *Top Gear*, I mocked the new Jaguar S-Type turbodiesel, saying that its power, economy and comfort were all irrelevant because it's such a monstrosity. I suggested it was the ugliest car on sale and that if you parked one outside a cathedral, the gargoyles would faint. I still think it's a lousy looker, with its dumpling backside and its Daniella Westbrook nose, and I still think its extraordinarily good new engine is not enough to turn it into a worthwhile choice. But if it's a comfortable car you want, you'll have to put up with the styling because nothing else in the class gets close.

I drove one the other day and thought the back road that connects my house with civilization had been resurfaced because the S-Type didn't transmit any of the bumps into the cabin. It was like driving a hovercraft. There's a sense of gliding around on a cushion of air. 'Why', I wondered, as I floated past another slow-moving Rover with the speedo on 90, 'do more cars not feel like this?'

For some time now, James May has been banging on about the obsession car firms have with making their cars sporty – and I've long harboured the suspicion that he was, by any rational definition, mad. He has tried on many occasions to explain that sports cars are allowed to be sporty but that saloons are not. I've listened in the same way that a psychiatric nurse will listen to the rantings of a lunatic. But only for so long. Eventually, I had to give him his crayons back and slip away.

Now, though, I'm beginning to think he has a point. Being a keen driver, I like to feel connected to the road. I like to be able to tell, when I run over a white line, whether the paint came from Crown or Dulux. I like to feel the ugly and unwelcome intrusion of understeer the instant it walks through the door, not when I'm five millimetres from the tree. But – and maybe this comes down to an age thing – if there's any shock absorbing to be done, I'd rather it wasn't undertaken by my buttocks.

And here's the problem. Gradually, over the last decade or so, cars have been getting firmer and firmer and firmer. It's got to the point now where the harsh ride of an Audi A6 is considered normal rather than unacceptable, and the bone-shaking rigidity of an Evo VIII a small price to pay for the panache and poise.

Rubbish. I drove a BMW X3 this week and, put simply, it would be impossible to live with that ride for more than three or four minutes. Yes, the handling is startling for such a tall and ungainly looking brute, but the downside is such a massive chasm, the whole car is ruined.

Think of it as a man who stands at his garden gate giving passers-by five pound notes. And then stabbing them in the heart. The goodness in the package is completely overwhelmed by the utter awfulness.

Another recent test car to arrive at Telly Towers was the long-wheelbase £115,000 Audi W12 A8. Now this, to all intents and purposes, is a limousine. It has enough space in the back for an orgy and lots of toys too, so plainly it's aimed at the businessman who has a driver.

Such an owner is unlikely to be fourteen years old, so I'm assuming he'll want to glide from place to place in as much comfort as is technically possible. He doesn't slump down in front of the television at night in a Bentwood kitchen chair.

He flops onto the sofa. So why, you have to wonder, has Audi tuned the suspension as though it were fitted to a rallying Quattro?

I could go on. The Jaguar XKR you saw being hurtled round a beach in Wales was fitted with sports suspension that made the ride impossibly hard. The Mitsubishi Warrior pickup truck is so unforgiving it's undriveable. Even the new Golf has a firmness I don't want.

There are many reasons for this, chief among which is the Americans. For them, suspension has always been a black and white art. Comfortable cars have always wobbled like a slapped fat woman, and sports cars have always gone about their business with the rigidity of pig iron.

So, if you want to sell a 'sporty' car in what is the world's biggest marketplace, it must ride like a sports car. Which means it must ride like a Corvette. Which rides like it's going down the Spanish Steps on ice skates.

The next problem is the computer geeks. If a car is sold with shock absorbers and springs, it can't be fiddled with by those of a BIOS persuasion. They need air, and then they can set to work with their laptops and electronic nonsense. 'Look,' they will wail, 'we have made a car which maintains a constant ride height.' Well done. Very impressive. But as is the way with science, being able to do something does not necessarily mean it's a good idea.

I mean, if it were technically possible to genetically fuse a piranha fish and Hitler, would you let the boffins go ahead?

I'm told by Jaguar's engineers that it is possible to make air suspension absorb the impact of pot holes and ridges, but I'm not so sure. Because if this were so, why does no air-sprung car ride properly? The S-Class Merc. The new long-wheelbase XJ. They are as gritty as sandpaper.

The final, and biggest problem, are run-flat tyres. We're told by car makers that they're being fitted for our own good. Why, they ask, waste money on fuel simply to lug around a spare part that you'll hardly ever need?

This argument would hold water if we were being offered a few quid off when we bought a car with bugger all in the spare-wheel well, but I haven't noticed any reductions of late.

What I have noticed is that my vision goes all blurred when I'm in a car on run-flat tyres. Of course, they have to have stiffer sidewalls but this, combined with the need for 'sportiness' means an intolerable piledriver ride. The BMW Z4 is a notable example of the problem. The Lexus SC430 is even worse.

One day, someone will fit run-flat tyres on an air-sprung American sports car and then we'll be in real trouble. Because it'll take off every time it runs over a catseye.

Jaguar has proved with the S-Type that it is possible to lock away the computer geeks, and sell a car that glides but still manages to handle properly. You'd never call it sporty, but you can call it brilliant because it suits both the James Mays of the world and those, like me, who like to drive everywhere as though we have eight seconds to save the world.

What would be nice now is a car that goes as well as this but doesn't frighten the horses.

September 2004

Speeding

Of course, we all know in our heart of hearts that the vast majority of radar detectors don't work. Some will beep when you are approaching a speed camera, but they'll also beep when they hear civilian air traffic, remote central-locking plippers and gamma-radiation signals from the outer moons of Jupiter. Others remain resolutely silent when you are near a speed trap, but are very good at opening supermarket doors and changing the channel on your neighbour's television.

In an attempt to demonstrate that its detector is a cut above the rest, Snooper is currently using a quote in its commercials from British Touring Car Champion, Jason Plato. He says he drives on the very limit, but only on the track. 'Good driving on public roads isn't about getting there fast,' he argues, 'it's about getting there safely.' Which is why, apparently, he uses Snooper on every journey.

This brings me to the thrust of this month's column. You see, the real reason we are attracted to radar detectors has absolutely nothing to do with safety. It's because, theoretically, they allow us to drive at a million mph through a village, safe in the knowledge that Plod isn't hiding round the next corner in his Fiat van.

The trouble is that Plato couldn't actually say this in a commercial. He couldn't say that he likes to use Snooper on every journey because he likes to hang the tail of his 911 out as he drives through the countryside.

Go on. Try to imagine how much shit would hit the fan if

Plato popped up in an ad, saying he likes blowing Beemers into the weeds when he's out and about, and that's why I need Snooper. 'To make sure I don't get caught.'

He'd wake up to find a SWAT team in his bedroom. Prosecutions would come from the ASA, the UN, the EU, the RSPCA, the WHO and, providing they weren't all cooped up in the back of their Fiat vans at the time, maybe even the police themselves.

The trouble is that the glamorization of speed is exactly what you can read every week and every month in every single road test report in every single car magazine. We motoring journalists are regularly photographed doing power slides on mountain roads, and we wax lyrical in our prose about how the TVR will just edge away from the Ferrari and Lambo in third. It's all very exciting. It's what the readers of car magazines expect and demand, for us to live your dreams. But never does a week go by when someone doesn't write to me saying their toddler was mown down by a maniac in a Subaru – I got one such missive only yesterday from some poor chap whose teenage, petrolhead son had 'taken' the family Mercedes for a spin and killed himself in it. He enclosed a photograph of the wreckage, to hammer the point home. I'd love at this point to say that I simply toss these letters in the bin and scoff. I'd love, even more, to say I write back saying that in a society where ordinary members of the public are allowed to drive around at 70mph in two-ton chunks of metal, a little light death and bruising is inevitable. And I'd like to sign off by saying that actually, Britain has the lowest death rate on the roads in Europe, so it's hardly my fault that little Johnnie got wasted.

But in fact, whenever I get one of these letters my shoulders sag. Only the other day, on the television, I joked that I'd never buy a car because it protected pedestrians well in an accident. There are, I explained, more important things to worry about, like how fast it goes and what it looks like. And, of course, the next week I had a barrage of mail from people whose children had been run over and killed. Each one made me feel absolutely fucking dreadful.

What if one of my children were to be killed and then I had to watch some fat, balding oaf making jokes about it on television? I'd want to rip his throat out.

So, what's to be done? You can't review a car designed to do 215mph by sticking to 70. One solution, according to one of the letter writers, is to finish each story by saying, in a William Woollardish way, 'Don't try this at home.' But that's silly.

You couldn't drive a Porsche Carrera GT at 200mph 'at home' because you'd be forever crashing into the coffee table. What's more, I made a vow when I started out in TV that I'd never, ever say such a thing. Standing there with a serious face saying, 'Don't try this at home', implies that I am clever and talented and that you're a hopeless, mouth-breathing, knuckle-dragging oik.

And anyway, let's just assume you've come over the crest of a hill on a sunny morning and there, stretching out in front of your 360CS, is a wide, deserted stretch of A-road.

Are you a) going to drop a few cogs on the sequential paddle shift and floor it; or are you b) going to think Ooh, wait a minute, Jeremy Clarkson said I mustn't do this, and slow right down?

My case rests.

Except it doesn't, because the fact is that every year, several hundred people are killed in or by cars that are being driven too quickly. So what's to be done?

Well, I'm afraid we have to start by looking at the bigger

picture. And it's this. Speed is useful. Speed means we can get where we're going quicker, which means we can see more, do more and learn more. Speed makes us cleverer.

Speed also means we can leave work later and get home sooner, so it makes us richer, and our families more stable.

Speed means we can have a more varied diet because we can have fresher produce from further afield every day in our local shop. Speed therefore makes us healthier.

Speed means we can expand our horizons. It means we can explore strange new worlds and new civilizations, like Cheshire and Norfolk. And Wales. This gives us a better understanding of the world and its peoples, and that makes us more tolerant. Speed brings peace.

Most of all, though, speed is fun. Watch the face of a toddler on a garden swing as you push them higher and faster. It's a face that screams, I am enjoying myself. And you'll see the same face on a man who's pushing his 360 to the limit on his favourite piece of blacktop.

Speed, then, is both the face of civilization and the core of our inner primeval being. Speed is everything. So, you go and get yourself a Snooper radar detector and, in the meantime, I'll deal with the the angst of bereaved parents on your behalf.

October 2004

Car stereos

'Isn't It Time' is a song you don't know, by a band you've never heard of called The Babys. I like it very much, so the other day I was delighted when some wise and resourceful DJ played it on the radio.

My delight soon turned to rage, however, because, all of a sudden, and without so much as a by your leave, a woman with the sort of voice you hear in daytime advertisements for patio doors interrupted to say the pelican crossing on Latimer Street was out of order.

How dare she? What gives her the right to barge in on one of my favourite songs, a song that's played on the radio only once every 2,500 years, to tell me about a broken light bulb on a street I didn't know, in a town I wasn't planning on visiting anyway.

To make matters worse, she then handed the microphone back to the station's afternoon DJ, who was so alarmingly *Daily Maily* that, after just a few moments, I wanted to peel his face off with a linoleum knife.

Local radio stations all do this. They have the power to interrupt your listening pleasure with their irrelevant traffic reports, and none of them bothers to turn off the 'interrupt' button when the announcement is over. They hope, of course, that you'll be so impressed with their regular programming that you'll continue to listen for the rest of your life. What you actually want to do is drive over and ram your car into their reception desk.

At this point, those under the age of seven will be jumping up and down, explaining to anyone who'll listen that all car stereos have a button that can shut out the Pinocchiochial-nosed local radio traffic announcements.

True, but the button in question never comes with a symbol on it, showing a thirty-something woman with a burning rag in her mouth. Nor does it ever say, 'Press, to silence the bitch'.

In my Mercedes, for instance, you have to press the mute button for two seconds. Press it for less than this and the whole radio goes quiet. Press it for any longer and the instruction is cancelled. It's also worth noting that if you press it for two seconds while the satellite navigation woman is talking, you'll shut her up, and the local radio woman will soldier on regardless.

However, if you press it for two seconds when the satellite navigation is engaged but no instruction is actually being delivered, you turn the local radio cow back on again. And to turn her off, you have to pull over and rent a forklift truck to remove the 980-page instruction booklet from what used to be called a glovebox.

This month, then, the column is all about the bane of my life, the single biggest bugbear of twenty-first-century living: the car stereo.

Only the other day, I was in a Mitsubishi Evo VIII MR FQ-340. Trying to understand the name was bad enough but, my God, you should see the radio that slides out of the dashboard and then rattles incessantly. Obviously, I wanted to turn it off and allow myself to be serenaded by the music of that growly engine, but I couldn't. I pressed each button, for varying periods of time, but I couldn't make the system shut down. All that happened is that the screen displayed a series of hieroglyphics that were completely and absolutely meaningless.

I'll tell you how bad this stereo is. When the car was parked at Birmingham Airport for a weekend, some youths broke a rear light, but didn't even bother to nick it. I wished they had. At least it would have silenced the rattling.

Then you have the Nissan 350Z, which comes with a huge sub-woofer in the rear bulkhead. Why? This is a £26,000 car and, as such, is out of reach of those who think their music should be played through a large dog. It's bad enough being pounded by the suspension without having the booming bass line of every song being directed into your spine. I've been told that it can be turned off, but again, how? There was no button saying, 'Press, to silence the St Bernard'.

We're told, naturally, that over time we become familiar with the controls in a car, but this is just not the case. When you have a mobile phone, a BlackBerry, a computer, a DVD player, a self-tuning plasma TV, an iPod, a microwave and a CD burner, it's inevitable that sometimes you forget which button does what.

If you get the new Land Rover Discovery, you're in real trouble because it doesn't have a remote CD autochanger. In many ways this is a good thing. Certainly, if you do have one of these machines hidden away in the boot, I'd like to bet it still contains the six CDs you inserted when you first bought the car. My life is way, way too short to bugger about changing CDs, but I must admit I am becoming heartily sick of the Stones and their *Forty Licks*.

The Disco's autochanger is located in the dash itself. Brilliant! Except all the CDs are loaded through the same slot, which won't open unless you press the right sequence of buttons in the right order. Who thought that was a good idea?

In the old days, of course, you could replace a crummy standard-fit system with something from a discount store, but now hi-fis are integrated into the dash, this is no longer an option.

This therefore is a plea from the heart to the designers of in-car entertainment. Please stop it. Step away from the microprocessor and find out what real people in the real world really want.

I'm not a Luddite. My pepper grinder is motorized, and I know how to download porn from the Web, but on the average car stereo today, there are probably thirty or forty functions that I just don't need. My Merc, for instance, allows me to type in the name of the CD I'm listening to. This is madness. I know what I'm listening to because (unless the local radio woman has interrupted) I can hear it, and it's *Forty Licks*. Same as it was last week, last month and last year.

So look. By all means offer these enormously complicated modular music centres, but why not, as an option perhaps, allow customers to have a stereo that sticks closely to my needs?

I do not want to be able to scan radio stations; I only ever listen to four of them. So four pre-programmed buttons, labelled 1, 2, 3 and 4 will suffice. I do not want traffic updates. I do not want a cassette player. I do not want voice activation. In fact, I only need two other buttons: one to turn the unit off and on – this should be at least one inch in diameter – and one to adjust the volume. That's six buttons in total, and under no circumstances should any of them be capable of two things. I'll leave bass and treble up to you and your anechoic chamber.

If you find all this a bit bizarre and complicated, have a look inside a 1969 Austin 1100. The system in there worked very well indeed.

November 2004

Competitiveness

By nature, I'm a competitive man. But nurture has taught me that trying to win is a complete and utter waste of time.

I learned, at the age of thirteen, that I was no good at any ball games. My limbs were already so long that by the time the neural signals arrived at my hands and feet, the other team was already in the shower. Often I'd find myself on the football pitch, lashing out at a ball that had been bowled in a game of cricket four months earlier.

I'm not much cop at cerebral games either. The other day, I was beaten at chess by an opponent who kept asking which way the bishops go. It was humiliating frankly.

Of course, the upside of losing is that it's so much easier to get your face right. Win, and you've got to look magnanimous and proud without being smug. That's hard, even for a classically trained actor such as Alec Guinness. Actually, it's especially hard for him because he's dead, but you know what I mean.

Losing, though, is a piece of cake. You can shrug and play the fool, which comes easily. Especially if you've had as much practice as me.

I had my losing face prepared as I flew to Germany the other day to conduct a frankly preposterous experiment for the TV show. I was to try and get Jaguar's new diesel S-Type round the Nürburgring in under ten minutes. This would mean averaging 78mph, and I can't even do that on the M40 where there are no corners.

A really fast car, a Ferrari Enzo, for instance, driven by someone with the cojones of a bull elephant and an intimate knowledge of this 13-mile track, can get round in about eight minutes.

I didn't have a fast car, but I did think I knew the track. You see, twenty years ago I spent a week there as the BMW car club's guest. We were taught the correct line through each of the 147 corners and then, on the final day, we were invited to do a flying lap on which we would be judged for speed and style. One hundred and ninety-nine took part, I came 198th, and that's only because the bloke who came last crashed. My losing face got a workout that day.

However, on my first exploratory lap, I couldn't remember any of it. My instructor, Sabine Schmitz, was distinctly underwhelmed. Sabine was born in Nürburg, holds several lap records and reckons to have been round 15,000 times. She knows the place better than anyone.

'You are not 100 per cent talent free,' she said. 'but you are the laziest driver I've ever seen. I'd say you are 80 per cent talent free.' When asked if I could get the Jaguar round in under ten minutes, there wasn't even a moment's hesitation. 'No,' she laughed.

And then a strange thing happened. Instead of gurning at the camera and maybe doing some kind of Eric Morecambe deliberate trip as I walked to the car, I felt a hot prickly surge of adrenal soup course down the back of my neck. I felt, for the first time since I was eleven, competitive.

My first solo lap showed, however, that determination is no match for an absence of talent, a lack of track intimacy and a car with a turbocharged paraffin stove under the bonnet. I went round in ten minutes and twenty-six seconds.

My next lap was perfect. I kissed apexes softly, applied the power smoothly, braked to the onset of anti-lockery and, as a result, powered across the line in ten minutes, twenty seconds. I couldn't believe it. Perfection had resulted in a saving of only six seconds; where was I to find another twenty?

As it turns out, I wasn't. Because 'the Ring' is technically a public toll road, and because it was a weekend, the place was packed with speed tourists who'd paid their twelve Euros and were either in my way or up my chuff, trying to get past.

Then there were the bloody bikers who swarm past on the straights, and despite a lot of leaning, and sparks, go through the corners at a speed that can only be called glacial. What's more, they crash all the time, which means the track has to be closed while the emergency services hose their remains into a drainage ditch or culvert.

When it reopened, so many cars were out there it felt like I was doing the M25 on acid. My lap time fell to eleven minutes, then another biker fell off and, by the time they'd hosed his body – yes, he was killed; the eighth this year – into the woods, time was up and the barriers were locked down for the night.

I spent the evening poring over maps, so that the next morning, I bounded out of bed, full of confidence. Only it had rained. And on the fourth corner, my confidence, along with the rest of me, and the car, spun off onto the grass.

I wasn't alone. There was some poor disabled bloke in one of those BMW MZ3 bread van things who buried the nose in the Armco and moments later, a Ferrari 355 I was following went off hard too. It's not a good idea because your executors are made to pay for repairs to the crash barrier – at £400 a yard.

Annoyingly, I still couldn't get the track hooked up in my head. Much to the consternation of those behind, I was still braking and changing down into third on some crests, only to find the track was straight for another three miles. And conversely, I was barrelling over others, only to find myself at a hairpin bend that I could have sworn wasn't there last time around.

Then the bloody car broke down. I slammed it into second at, ooh about 100, and a warning message came up on the dash saying, 'I don't think so, matey'. The rest of the lap was done in emergency, limp-home mode.

With no real damage, and the computer reset, I went out again, trying to remember the track, trying to stay out of everyone's way and trying to remember that, because I had a diesel, corners, even tight ones, had to be done in third or even fourth. I had to use torque, not power. I had to use my brain too and I was getting very tired. But still my lap times refused to drop below 10:10.

And then, with half an hour to go before I had to fly home, I decided dying was better than failure. So I went out there and started headbutting the kerbs rather than kissing them. I was so fired up that, after overtaking a Finnish Porsche 968, I went off the track completely and never even lifted. The result, verified by time-coded onboard cameras, was a 9:59.

I'd love to say I was calm and dignified. I'd love to say there was much grace and decorum when I told the instructor. But I'm afraid I went to pieces. I beamed. I screamed. In a haze of ecstasy, I completely lost the plot.

For the first time in my life, I'd achieved a goal. I was a somebody, a driving god and, boy, it felt good. But it didn't last. Sabine then climbed into the car and, on her very first go, went round in nine minutes and twelve seconds. Situation normal then. I lost.

December 2004

CAR OF THE YEAR: TOYOTA PRIUS

2005

TOP 5 BESTSELLING SINGLES
SONG TITLE – ARTIST

1 (Is This The Way To) Amarillo – Tony Christie
2 That's My Goal – Shayne Ward
3 Axel F – Crazy Frog
4 You're Beautiful – James Blunt
5 All About You/You've Got a Friend – McFly

TOP 5 BOX OFFICE MOVIES

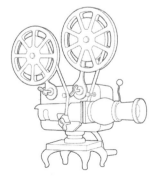

1 Star Wars Episode III – Revenge of the Sith
2 The Chronicles of Narnia: The Lion, the Witch and the Wardrobe
3 Harry Potter and The Goblet of Fire
4 War of the Worlds
5 King Kong

Women

There was a strange letter in last month's magazine. It was from a twenty-one-year-old girl who couldn't understand why her love affair with cars was such a turn-off for men.

Well, trust me on this, love, it's not a turn-off for me. There is nothing to warm the cockles of my tumescence more than the sight of a girl in a serious car. Emma Parker-Bowles, for instance, has a Mitsubishi Evo VIII, and the thought of that, honestly, keeps me awake at night.

Just yesterday I saw a middle-aged housewife in rural clothes screaming down the M40 in a Lotus Elise. I nearly grew a third leg. And when I heard that Kate Moss had bought an old pagoda roof Mercedes SL, I had to go for a lie down.

We men have learned over the last few years that it's a good idea to be in touch with our feminine side. If we cry in films, eat lots of salad and read Victorian poetry, it makes us more attractive. But there's a flip side to that argument. Women can boost the magnetism of their pheromones by getting in touch with their male side. This would mean not changing gear until they hit the red line and fancying lap dancers.

My wife is so completely in touch with her male side, I'm surprised she hasn't actually grown a scrotum. This is a woman who uses the C-word as early as possible at dinner parties to save time. Guests that shudder aren't worth talking to, and those that don't are worthy of further bottom-sniffing.

This is a woman who's just spent three weeks rallying her

Elise around the Atlas mountains in Morocco with a girl-friend. Although that said, they missed out on the ultimate prize because one night, instead of handing in their time card, they went for a swim.

This is a woman who once said she couldn't see the point of cars with less than 200bhp, who won't drive my Mercedes because it's an automatic and who loathes any car that has even a hint of pliability in the suspension. She thinks an Arial Atom is too soft and an Evo FQ-340 too slow.

When our third child was born, I suggested that her BMW Z1 might not be the most practical car and that she might require more seats. So she went out and bought a Caterham Seven as well. It wasn't quite what I had in mind.

Then came the Elise, which arrived and, after a short test drive, was sent straight back to Lotus to have a louder exhaust fitted.

And now she's bought a Land Rover.

Being mean, I tried first of all to veto the idea on the basis that she already owns two off-road go-karts, the Lotus, a Focus, a Volvo XC90 and a motorbike. When this didn't work, I tried to convince her that Land Rovers are ugly and crude and that it would just be an expensive eyesore sitting in the yard.

I had in my mind's eye a long-wheelbase, skinny-tyred pickup truck with a corrugated-iron cover and the engine from a nineteenth-century water pump. And in a list of things I wanted to buy, this would come in at about 9,450. I'd rather have gone on *Strictly Come Dancing*.

She smiled the smile of a woman who wasn't listening and two days later came home with quite the most remarkable vehicle I've ever seen.

It's an F-registered, left-hand-drive Land Rover 90 diesel,

which means it's old, and so slow it can't climb any sort of hill. That's bad, but according to the vendor it has seen service with the Swiss Army, which is good. It means it won't have seen any action at all and the engine will have been turned off at all the red traffic lights.

What's better is that all the military paraphernalia is still in place. That means camouflage paintwork, downward pointing lights that can't be seen by aircraft, four 20ft aerials, a mine prodder, an engine air-intake above the windscreen and best of all . . . a gun. Yes. My wife is now so in tune with her masculinity, she's bought a sodding tank.

To give it even more playground cred, its metal roof can be unbolted and removed completely, it has super-dark tinted windows and it sits on the widest, chunkiest off-road tyres BF Goodrich have ever produced. This thing, I kid you not, makes Lara Croft's Land Rover look like a Suzuki Vitara. It makes Norman Schwarzkopf's Hummer look like a Nissan Micra. It is butch, and then some.

Unfortunately, there are some drawbacks, chief among which is that, despite the seven seats, it cannot be used for transporting children because there are no seat belts and the interior is stuffed to overflowing with razor-sharp military protuberances that would sever a seven-year-old's head in even the gentlest of accidents.

Nor will it be much cop at transporting fence posts and Christmas trees, partly because it's a short-wheelbase 90 and partly because the back's already full of camo nets, ammo boxes and chemical-warfare suits.

Then there's the driving experience. I'd love to tell you all about this, but I made such a fuss about not getting the damn thing in the first place, my wife hasn't bothered putting me on the insurance. Still, I was taken out in it the other night and simply couldn't believe how loud and crude it was. Nor could I believe how long it took us to do three miles.

That old diesel engine really did manage to make mountains out of molehills, turning even the most Dutch piece of level ground into a sheer rock face that required another gear change to keep moving. I think we hit 40 once. I know we arrived at the party an hour late, feeling like we'd just done an SAS assault course.

'Great, isn't it?' said my wife.

'No'.

I suppose I quite like the radio which, with those enormous aerials, could almost certainly be used to eavesdrop on operations in the Gulf. Actually, you could probably use it to monitor the progress of the Voyager space probe, which left our solar system last month.

And I am interested in the piece, which is an SA-80 that's been converted to fire . . . actually, I don't what know it's been converted to fire. But I do suspect traffic wardens would think twice about ticketing a car that has a machine gun clipped to the dashboard.

What I love most of all, though, is that I don't have to drive it. If I did, people would see me coming and think, What kind of saddo would ever choose to tool around in a quasi-military Land Rover? A man in a car like this looks, at best, preposterous, and at worst like a murderer.

But a girl in a car like this looks like she's descended from the gods. A girl in a road-going tank is even more sexy than one in nothing at all.

January 2005

Car colours

Now that I've been officially recognized by *GQ* magazine as the second-worst-dressed man in Britain, I feel uniquely qualified to comment on matters of style.

You see, Jonathan Ross spends hours and thousands of pounds looking as bad as he does, and it's the same story with Graham Norton. He has to agonize for days over how much tinsel should be attached to those suits and where it should go, whereas I can achieve the same effect with absolutely no effort whatsoever.

I go into a clothes shop once every three years and buy a lot of whatever happens to be nearest to the door. I then wear it until it falls to pieces and I carry on wearing it, barging through the vicissitudes of fashion and the vagaries of climate change, until it's time to go shopping again.

Today, for instance, I'm wearing a pair of jeans that are ripped at the knee. Some would say I'm trying to emulate the Eighties boy band Bros, and that this is ridiculous for someone of my age. But I'm not. There is a hole at the knee because the denim has worn out and I'm not scheduled to buy a new pair until May.

There are other jeans in my wardrobe that do not have holes in them, but by the time I discovered this pair does, it was too late. I'd have had to take them off again and, frankly, life's too short for that. If the hole was where my penis lives, maybe. But the knee, to be honest, is something I don't mind flashing in public.

People talk about 'street' fashion and show us lots of people wearing stuff no one wears in any street I've ever been down. Whereas I blend. I look like you do. I wear the clothes you do. I hate shopping as much as you do. And that's why you can listen to me, with confidence, when I explain what colour your next car should be.

For the last few years, we've been plumping for silver or gunmetal grey. This, according to people who don't have proper jobs, is because in times of financial stability, we go for unassuming tones. Only when house prices are set to fall, and unemployment is on the rise, do we think about putting some colour and pizzazz into our wheels.

There may be some truth in this. I mean, if you cast your mind back to the late Seventies, when people were eating rats and wearing shoes made from onion peelings, orange was the colour of choice for those buying a Morris Ital. And mustard was in on the Allegro.

Today, the BMW 6 Series is available in grey, off-grey, grey with a hint of grey and dark grey, whereas its forerunner from the Seventies, the old CSL, was available in red, white, lime green or orange. And the 1970 Ford Cortina 1600E came at you in gold or aubergine.

So, what do we think is going to be the 'next big thing'. Well, we won't be wanting grey or silvery grey because we've done that, and I can't see mustard coming back in a big way either, mainly because I can't see the economy going down the tubes any time soon.

Smart has been trying to funk things up with a selection of spots and stripes, but this looks wilfully colourful, like a German game-show host's jacket. You know that underneath, all is dreary.

Then we have Honda and its pink Jazz. My mother bought

one and then added a Barbie-pink fur steering-wheel cover. It's a look that won't catch on, I fear.

This is because the colour she should have gone for is, surprisingly, white. White is coming back, just you mark my words.

Let's examine the evidence. Duran Duran recently showed the world what rock 'n' roll really means by failing to turn up for Children in Need. Girls all over the BBC are flouncing around in ra-ra skirts and leg warmers. Tony Blair has gone mad. This means we're moving back to the Eighties, and the car I had in 1982 was a white VW Scirocco.

Back then, we were coming out of the gloomy Seventies, and white, especially that pearlescent finish Audi used on the Quattro, demonstrated that we were rich and prosperous. It's why the Arabs went bonkers for white shortly after they realized they had the West by its short penis hairs. Strangely, though, the reason why 78 per cent of all cars sold in Japan are white has nothing to do with prosperity and everything to do with a lack of imagination.

Here's the deal, then. We've been buying grey and silver while we waited for Gordon Brown to make a Horlicks of the economy, but he hasn't. We're just getting richer and richer, so now we can afford to show off a bit.

The car firms are on to this sea change. I recently test drove our Car of the Year, the Golf GTi, and in red I thought it looked OK. But in white it looks sensational, especially as it has lots of black air intakes to provide some relief.

It was the same story with the old Porsche 911 Turbo. That looked good in white because it had black rear wheel-arch protectors and a big black-edged spoiler. And the XR3 pulled off the same trick using the same accessories.

Take a look at the new Land Rover Discovery. In green or

blue it looks like it's trying to be a Range Rover, and missing the mark. But in white, with all that tinted glass on the roof, it resembles an auxiliary transport module from Lunar Base X1. It looks great.

I have to say at this point that white doesn't suit all cars. Buy a white Rolls-Royce Phantom, for instance, and people will assume you are Jennifer Lopez. And then there's the Ford GT I've ordered. As is the way with these things, you give a car firm £130,000 and they spend the next nine months telling you what you can't have. Pale blue with the orange Gulf stripe? No. Black with two yellow stripes? No.

There are six colours on offer and no, we can't show you what they're like. You'll have to look on the Net. And they're not really like that either.

White seemed like a safe bet, but I decided against it, partly because it will no longer be in vogue by the time the Americans have bought an atlas, found out where Britain is and sent the car. And partly because white on a car with wide shut lines gives passers-by the impression it's been made from Lego. All you see are the joins.

Red was too Ferrari. Yellow was too silly. Black was too boring. Silver was too bland, and that left me with blue. What sort of blue is it? I have no idea, because in the pictures on the website, the photographer's used a yellow filter.

It may well turn out to be as hideous as a Linda Barker sofa, and people will laugh as I pull up. But they'll stop laughing when I step out in my white pixie boots and my ice-white skiing jacket, because they'll recognize someone who was clever enough to keep these things from when they were in fashion the first time around.

February 2005

Luck (part 2)

Without any question or shadow of doubt, I am the luckiest man alive today. With nothing but half a qualification in journalism and the engineering ability of a sparrow, I have become a motoring journalist. Which, along with being a meteorological officer in the Sahara Desert, is possibly one of the easiest jobs in the world.

What's more, I don't know what people mean when they say they can't find a free parking space, because there's always an empty meter right outside where I want to be, and it's always jammed on thirty-eight minutes. Then there's my driving licence, which has been totally clean since 1989.

This doesn't mean I drive around at 23mph with a fish on the back of the car. What it means is that I only encounter those mobile speed-detector vans just after I've dropped something on the floor and slowed down so it can be retrieved safely.

Traffic reports are meant for you. Not me. That bird on Radio Two will say that the M40 has been eaten by a dinosaur, but when I get there, he's just put it back. And it never rains on my holidays.

There is, however, a downside to this good fortune. You may remember, for instance, that I recently drove a Ferrari 612 from the Top Gear studio to a ski resort called Verbier in Switzerland.

It was all part of a big televized race against James and Hamster, who would be making exactly the same journey using trains to Heathrow, a plane to Geneva, and then the fearsomely reliable Swiss public transport to the heart of the Alps.

The figures suggested the boys would win by about half an hour. But I actually overtook them, after eleven hours on the go, literally just a few hundred meters from the finishing post.

This looked silly, like the whole thing had been rigged. And it was the same story when I tried to drive an Audi A8 all the way from London to Edinburgh and back again, on one tankful of diesel. Of course, the car made it back to the starting point and was found to have no fuel at all in the tank, and just a dribble in the pipes.

And then there was the Land Rover expedition to the top of Mount Tongue in Scotland. Had it rained, I never would have made it, but it didn't. So I did. And then there was the other race, between the Aston Martin DB9 and the new fast trains through France. Of course, I won that too, with moments to spare. And talking of moments to spare, I tried to drive a Jaguar S-Type diesel round the Nürburgring in under ten minutes. Needless to say, on my very last attempt, I managed it in nine minutes and fifty-nine seconds.

If anyone ever asks what two things have made *Top Gear* such a success in recent years, I'd have to say it's a) the producer Andy Wilman and b) my phenomenal personal luck.

One day, though, the fortune fairy will find another pair of shoulders on which to hang out. One day, we'll film something that doesn't work. And then we'll be left with nothing. A story where the car doesn't make it up the mountain, where it runs out of fuel in Watford, where it gets beaten by the plane. And then what?

All of this occurred to me on that extraordinary drive in

the 612. When James called to say he and Richard had landed in Switzerland and were boarding a train, I had just gone past a sign saying 'Dijon 180km'. And the correct address for Dijon is 'Dijon. Nowhere near Switzerland. France'.

A spot of mental arithmetic resulted in some alarming news. They were 250 miles ahead and, with the best will in the world, the best luck and 540hp, that looked like an unjumpable gap.

This meant I was faced with the prospect of losing and that, in turn, meant I had to start thinking about a meaningful and worthwhile conclusion for the piece. Some snappy little piece to camera, which would make the car escape from its defeat with some dignity, and give the viewer a sense that they hadn't just wasted twenty minutes. That seemed like an even bigger task than winning.

It was on the motorway, just outside Besançon that the solution began to spawn. If those guys got to Verbier before me, I'd just keep right on going. I'd just drive and drive until the tyres burst and my Visa card exploded. This, I reckon, would have happened somewhere in Jordan.

I'd then climb out and claim I'd been having so much fun, I really didn't want the journey to end. This would have made their victory hollow and, as an added bonus, it would've stuck to the central principal of journalism. It would have been true. Because that 612 is something else.

I'd actually campaigned long and hard to use something else for the trip. I made enquiries about getting hold of a Ford Lightning pickup, or a Bentley Arnage; something with a bit of character, something I could get excited about.

The Ferrari, on paper, didn't blow my frock up. It costs £70,000 more than a Continental and, on the face of it, it's hard to see why. They have the same number of doors and seats, they have the same performance and they have big name badges.

What's more, in photographs, the 612 really looks like a butchered ape. Its eyes are too piggy and what are those scallops doing down the side? It looks like a mess. And then the rattle started. It turned out that some dozy ha'porth had bent one of its wiper arms, which was responding by buzzing whenever the speed went past 'X' mph, which it would have to do if I wanted to win.

And on top of all this, it's a Ferrari, which was all right in the days when they went wrong all the time and waved their arms around. But now they're so reliable, and so complete, it's like driving the love child of Pete Sampras and Michael Schumacher. In essence, modern Ferraris are boring.

That said, on those long, car-free motorways in northern France, this dullness was something to be welcomed. The 612 cruised effortlessly and, apart from the buzzing wiper, in sepulchral silence. The ride was good, the seat was comfortable and the driving position, just so. Only when pulling away from toll booths or petrol stations did it behave like a supercar. There was a muted roar and a definite sense that this was one quick car.

When I got to the Alps, however, the whole thing turned round completely. It became a very quick car, that feels that it could do motorway cruising as well. On that switchback road, with ice on the inside of every bend and sheer drops on the outside, it became the fastest and most exciting four-seater I've ever driven.

I began to feel I couldn't lose. If I won, I was going to prove that public transport was useless. And if I lost, I was going to keep on going. All the way to . . . I fancied Petra, to be honest.

This is one of those cars that sneaks up on you. It leaves you cold until you've become properly acquainted. Then, I suspect, nothing else would do.

I feel lucky to have spent so much time with it. Furthermore, I have the sense that I've driven a car that gets very close to motoring perfection.

March 2005

Mollycoddling

News from the land of the free and the home of the brave. Parents can now buy off-the-shelf computer technology that allows them to monitor how their children are driving and, if necessary, remotely shut down the car.

But before we all burst out laughing, I should explain that this snippet came to my attention on a day when 400 schools in Britain were closed. When asked why by a television news reporter, one headmistress said, 'It's a health and safety issue. It's very icy and we don't want children falling over.'

Later that day, three boys were suspended from their school because they'd been throwing snowballs. And, as we know from recent health and safety advice on how to play conkers, you can't just go around lobbing snow at one another unless you're wearing goggles, and some kind of helmet.

On the same lines, we now have a water fountain in the Top Gear office, but we are not allowed to fit a new bottle when the old one becomes empty because water bottles are . . . wait for it . . . heavy!

So we must call for a porter who has been trained on how bottles may be lifted safely.

And then there's the bothersome business of actually filming the programme. If there is the slightest chance, at all, of anyone being injured then we cannot go ahead. It's that simple. We even have to assess the risk of an airliner crashing into our heads, and what precautions should be taken if the earth were to open up suddenly.

Of course, we're old and intelligent enough to ignore the stupid, interfering, safety police, but it's a different story for children, who must now stay at home whenever it's too hot or too cold, or if there's a mobile phone mast within 200 miles.

My son, who's a strapping nine-year-old, likes to play rugby for the local town on a Sunday morning. Obviously, I'm not allowed to video the games in case the tape falls into the hands of a paedophile, but then there'd be no point because it's not rugby as you'd recognize it.

The scrum, for instance, is just six boys leaning on one another. And any player doing something remotely dangerous has to do twenty press-ups.

Then they're clipped into their anti-submarine seats in a four-wheel-drive tank and ferried home to spend the rest of the day trying to get round the parental controls on their dad's computer.

As a result of all this mollycoddling, our kids are growing up with no concept of danger. So, when my boy climbs into one of our off-road go-karts, he drives like the devil, refusing to slow for corners on the basis that someone in a hi-vis jacket will have smoothed out the surface before he gets there.

Inevitably, one day he rolled it and this hurt. It wasn't the pain, however, that caused the tears. It was the amazement that an adult had allowed him to get into a situation where pain might be possible.

We saw the same sort of thing the other night while he was watching a programme about Ellen MacArthur's truly astonishing record-breaking trip around the world. 'I want to break a world record,' said the boy. 'But I don't want to sail round the world. I want to see how many Smarties I can eat with chopsticks in under a minute.'

What kind of an ambition is that?

Of course, I don't want him to be hurt, and when he starts to drive, I don't want him to have an accident. So will I fit his car with computer software that allows me to kill the engine from the comfort of my own sofa?

Tricky one, isn't it? You buy your kid a car to give him some freedom, some sense that he's approaching adulthood, and because you can't be bothered to take him to parties any more.

And then you explain that it's fitted with an RS-1000 teen driving device.

This feeds real-time information about his driving via email, a website or your mobile phone, using kits that cost up to £260. It will even sound a warning at home if the car's driven recklessly.

And then later, a card can be removed from the onboard black box, which lets parents see just how fast 'junior' was going during his journey.

Now obviously, he's going to be damn glad you bought him a car. He's going to love you for that. But how long do you think that gratefulness will last if his engine dies every time he puts his foot down? And how deep into your chest will he plunge a carving knife if, when he gets home, you remove the card and explain that his gear-changing was a little sloppy.

There's another, more worrying issue too. Because the technology already exists to monitor every car on the road, I'm amazed His Toniness hasn't got involved. He's already decided we all need ID cards so he can monitor our pupil dilation, and I bet he would just love to be able to keep tabs on us in our cars too.

The only thing stopping him is a fear of the public back-lash. But if lots of parents demonstrate they like the idea, he'll introduce it like a shot. And then get his health and safety Nazis to send us fines every time we do 31mph.

So, let me give you a very good reason why you should not fit your kid's car with a spy in the cab.

You see, when I passed my driving test, only thirty-seven hours elapsed before I careered off the road and into a herd of sheep. Had my mum been alerted to the speed I was going prior to the accident, she would have hit the kill switch imme-diately and the sheep would have been saved. As indeed would my ego, and the entire underside of the car.

But that accident had a profound effect on my driving. Because when the examiner told me the previous day that I had passed my test, what I actually heard was, 'Congratula-tions, Jeremy. You are, without any shadow of a doubt, the single best driver I've ever seen.'

I felt invincible, and the crash blatantly proved I was not. As a result of this, and I'm touching a lot of wood here, I have not had a single accident on the public roads since.

This, then, is the dilemma. Had my mother killed the car's engine, I'd have hated her on a cellular level for trying to pre-vent something that I knew, with total certainty, was not going to happen. And then I would never have been shaken into realizing that I needed to take more care. So I might very well have had another, much more serious crash later.

I really do believe that all new drivers should have a big one as soon as possible after passing their test. Because the aftershock of such an event will act as a giant psychological traction control system until full maturity is reached. In men, this is around forty-five years later.

There's another reason too. With no danger in life, there are no thrills. And with no risk, there'll be no more Ellen MacArthurs, no more world championships for our rugby team and no real point in being alive any more.

May 2005

Communism

I've spent the last week or so hammering around in a new BMW M5 and I have many things to say on the subject, starting with this: was Communism such a bad idea?

Obviously the citizens of Soviet Russia weren't allowed to vote, but they were allowed to do pretty well everything else: smoke in bars, drink a very great deal of vodka, hunt bears and walk their dogs.

Best of all, though, they didn't have to worry about choosing the wrong sort of trousers or the wrong home-cinema equipment. Which brings me neatly on to the perils of living in Mr Blair's Britain.

This is a country where we're so content and so happy with our lot that the government is bored. You'd imagine they would have many important things to do, but somehow they find the time to draw up precise rules about when and where you are allowed to take your dog for a walk. And how you can kill a fox. And how many wheels should be driven on a school-run car. It's pathetic.

They're even bored with the concept of democracy, so now a focus group tells Mr Blair it might be a good idea to worry about dog walking, the prime minister's office approves it, the cabinet rubber stamps it and then it goes before the 650 MPs who moo a lot and do what the whips tell them. Honestly, I'd rather have Stalin.

Meanwhile, out on the streets, we've taken to worrying about the most ludicrous things. Like what sort of coffee we should have, for instance. When I was growing up, coffee was powdered, made by Maxwell House and delicious . . . because we knew no better.

Now, there are people making a very good living from selling two million different varieties.

And then there's the question of music. I wrote last month about the iPod and, already, it's yesterday's news. Now you need a billion songs stored on your mobile telephone, and it had better be the right phone or you'll be ostracized by your friends, shut out from society.

How has this happened? How, in thirty years, have we gone from a society where everyone had a bog in the garden and Dad had a diseased lung, to a society that worries about its choice of mobile phone? I stayed in a hotel recently where guests were offered a choice of two types of bog roll.

Someone had a meeting about that. Someone said, 'Have we thought of everything?' and someone else piped up with a forehead-slapping, 'Christ. What if someone doesn't want to wipe their arse on embossed paper. We'd better get some plain in too.'

If your life's that empty, it's time to take up fishing or embroidery or hair styling. Because next thing you know, you'll be worried about global warming and your next-door neighbour's Land Cruiser. Or whether people should be allowed to walk their dogs on the common. Or the plight of that urban rat known as the fox.

Plainly, there are similar problems over in Germany too, because BMW fitted the new M5 with a gearbox and then someone said, 'Hang on, is five ratios enough? Wouldn't we be better off offering six?' And then someone else chimed in with, 'Nah. Let's give it seven'.

This opened the floodgates, because on the new M5 you're able to choose how much ferocity you want from the gear changes. There are, in fact, a whopping five settings for this, as well as three settings for the electronic diff. You're even asked, before you set off, how much horsepower you'd like from the V10 engine: 400 or the full 507.

There's even one sub-menu in a sub-sub-menu on the iDrive computer that allows the owner to select how long their headlamps should stay on after the engine has been switched off. Now that's bonkers enough, but to make it window-lickingly mad, the choice is infinite. Anything from one second to one light year.

Why? How can it make a difference whether they stay on for thirty-three seconds or thirty-four? How empty is your life to have thought of such a thing? And how empty do they think mine is that I will have enough time to make the choice?

There is only one feature in the M5's electronic armoury that's good; it's a little button marked with an M on the steering wheel. Quite what M might stand for, I have no idea. Motorsport? Mohawk? Mombasa? I like to think it might be M********** because that's the effect it has.

Naturally, you can programme what effect you would like this button to have, but I'm delighted to report that someone far cleverer than I am had already set it up to loosen the diff, unleash all the horsepowers, savagerize the gear change, firm up the suspension, and change the head-up display to show a rev counter. In other words, turn the boring, ugly and annoying 400bhp 5 Series into what you thought you'd bought. An M5.

In M********** mode, this car is pretty hard to describe. But 'perfect' will do for the moment. The engine, which sounds like a diesel when you start it up, is transformed into a machine of unparalleled brilliance, churning out such a prodigious amount of power that there is simply no let up in the speedo's rate of climb. Even as it gets close to the 155mph limiter, there's no slowdown, and then it just surges past. I saw 168 before the nanny stepped in. Apparently, if you have her disconnected altogether, 204 is achievable.

Then there's the handling and, again, I just don't know where to start. On one run, I found myself in convoy with a rather well-driven M3 and, eventually, I had to let him go by because we were reaching the sort of speeds you read about in the *News of the World*. And he was beginning to look edgy. I wasn't, though. The M5 can go round any corner at any speed that takes your fancy.

I wish it had fewer badges. I wish there were fewer spoiler add-ons, too, and I wish the four exhausts were better hidden. The whole point of an M5 is that no one knows about the power. But this one shouts a bit too loudly. It's a bit too Beckham for my liking.

Mind you, this pales into insignificance alongside my gripes with all the electronic brouhaha. I mean, why could they not just sell the damn thing already set-up, for all of time, in M********** mode? And with lights that stay on for forty seconds. Why make it all so bloody complicated?

Only a month ago, I stepped out of the Ferrari 430 and thought that maybe in 200 years, someone, somewhere, using materials that don't currently exist, will make something better. But in fact I only had to wait four weeks. The M5 is that good.

Except when it's being a complicated pain in the arse. What this car needs, badly, is a dose of Stalinism. A bit of dictatorship. It needs to be less of a village fête with some-thing for everyone and more of a *fait accompli*. A car that does only one thing, very well, for those in the know.

The M5, I think, may very well be my next car. I absolutely love it.

August 2005

Noisy motorcycles

As you may have heard, there are proposals to cut the noise that a motorcycle can make from 3,400 decibels, at which point human heads have been known to explode, to 74 decibels, which is around the same as a hairdryer.

What's more, it would not only be illegal for a manufacturer to sell a noisy bike, it would also be against the law to tamper with the exhaust and then ride a noisy motorcycle. Under the scheme, offenders would have their bikes confiscated.

It was predictable, of course, that Richard Hammond would convulse in spasms of righteous indignation at the news, because he's the sort of biker who wears green and white Power Ranger romper suits and enjoys riding around on those bikes where the handlebars are all droopy and there are many vivid decals on the petrol tank.

James May is different. He rides around very carefully, refusing to overtake even the slowest moving bus. He indicates with his arms, wears Kenneth More goggles and refuses to deviate from a perfectly perpendicular riding position. It's almost as though he thinks he has an imaginary sidecar alongside. So I assumed that he'd approve of the cut. But no. He was just as vehement as Hamster.

It's therefore up to me to be the voice of reason. You see, I live near to one of those Cotswold roads which, whenever the sun comes out, plays host to approximately half a million city boys on their PQRSTTTs. So, apart from a brief break at lunchtime when they all go to the pub for some bitter lemon and exaggeration, you absolutely cannot hear your-self think.

Some days, when the weather is really good, the only way of keeping my sanity is by dreaming up new and imaginative ways to pay these people back. Yesterday, I thought I'd turn Richard Hammond into a sort of mushy pulp and hose him through an offender's letter box, as an example.

Or maybe I could just follow one of them home – not hard, bikes are pretty damn slow on the twisty roads up here – and indulge in my passion for Seventies prog rock with a powerful boom box at four in the morning outside the culprit's house.

It's weird this, because normally I do believe that it's vital to live and let live. If someone wants to be a Pakistani, and live in Bradford, then that's fine by me. Why should I care if he supports the Pakistani team when they play England at cricket?

It's the same story with bird watchers. I think it's pretty idiotic to sit in a bush, listening to your hair grow, in the hope you'll see a bird that you know is there anyway. And I have similar views on those who like to be tied up and whipped.

Generally speaking, I don't even mind when someone else's passion is a mild irritant for other people. Microlight-ing, for instance. In anything above a light breeze, these airborne lawnmowers hang in the sky, making no headway at all for about six hours at a time, ruining the peace for every-one within 50 miles. But their pleasure, I suspect, far outweighs the pain the drone causes other people.

I don't even get cross when people use their mobile phones on the train. Usually because I'm miles away, in a car. But even when I am on a train and they're sitting next to me, it's really not the end of the world. One side of someone else's conversation can often be quite entertaining. Once I even got a share tip that worked out. And it's better than listening to the clatter of steel on steel.

There are exceptions to this, however. I'm talking about behaviour so antisocial that it can drive even Patience McPatience into a flurry of rock-throwing rage. Environmentalism, for a kick-off. The idea that the world should spend more averting climate control, over which we may – or may not – have any control, than we spend providing drinking water for the starving and diseased of Africa. That kind of thing really pisses me off.

And then there's campanology. Those who think it is perfectly acceptable to climb a church tower six nights a week and allow everyone within five miles to hear them 'practising' for an event that no one goes to anyway. i.e. church. Why can't they take up the piano instead. Then we wouldn't have to listen to them getting it all wrong.

It's a tradition, they say. Yes, it is. Like burning witches and persecuting Catholics. Two other traditional church pastimes that have been dropped.

Biking falls into the same category as bell ringing. You can still wear your leather romper suit. You can still accelerate from 60–150 in minus 1.3 seconds. You can still crash and die so that someone in need of a spleen may live. But you absolutely do not need to deafen everyone in the process.

Hammond says that this is part of the appeal of biking, the sense that you're being a bit rebellious, and yes, even a bit frightening. I think he likes to think he's something of a Hell's Angel, but it's hard to be scared of a man whose feet don't touch the ground when he's on his Yamuki Davidson.

And it's hard to conceive any situation that would make James scary. Even if he leapt out of a forest on a dark night, brandishing a blood spattered axe and going 'grrrrrrrrr', he'd still be good, old affable James.

I'm sorry. I'm not scared of bikers at all. If they crash into my car, they crumple and I go home and have supper. And if they were to chase me on foot I'd get away, because it's hard to run when you're encased in leather. That's why cows are so slow.

At this point, I'm sure, some of you will be accusing me of hypocrisy because I've spent the last fifteen years enthusing about loud cars. This is true. I love the sound of an American V8 or an Italian V12. I love the way cars bark and bellow and wail.

And sure, Hammond and May like the sound of a massively amplified mosquito. They probably like burglar alarms, too. And drum 'n' bass. Or bass 'n' drum as Hammond called it the other day.

But here's the thing. Most of the noise that comes from a modern car is made by the tyres. And that is now being addressed by dimpled road surfaces that collect the sound and absorb it into the earth. Only a very few cars are truly noisy, and they're owned by people who would never dream of accelerating high enough into the rev band for that little valve in the exhaust to work its acoustic magic. I'd like to bet that the majority of people reading this have never heard a Ferrari or an Aston at full chat.

Whereas everyone, except for a handful of sheep farmers on Dartmoor, knows exactly what a bike sounds like at speed. Because all bikes are noisy, there are thousands of them and they're bought specifically to be thrill machines. I say again: they can be just that, without pissing everyone else off.

If Hammond and May want to try and be frightening and rebellious that is, of course, fine. I don't care if they go to the woods every night and drink one another's blood; they can sacrifice as many goats as takes their collective fancy. But what they're being at the moment, with their loud exhaust pipes, is annoying. And that's not cool.

October 2005

Taking the scenic route

This month, I have mostly been picking bits of banana pie from out of my nose, but there has also been time to drive down the Pacific Coast Highway in one of the new Pontiac Solstice two-seater rag tops.

The car was ghastly, as you'd expect from a country that hasn't produced a sports car since the Crosley Hot Shot in 1952. But the road was something else. Even by the standards set by the Stelvio Pass in Italy, the mountain road in the Isle of Man, that beach blast in New Zealand and Highway One in Iceland, Route One in California is pretty special. But not for the reasons you might be thinking.

Built in 1919 by the locals, including one John Steinbeck, and prison labour – they actually moved three jails to California to ensure there were enough men – it goes all the way from Mexico to the Canadian Border. But the bit I'm talking about here is the 139-mile stretch from Monterey to Morro Bay.

With the Pacific Ocean to your right and fog-topped hills to your left, you could hammer along at 100mph, with your tyres scribbling for grip on the corners and your engine wailing. You could sit there, reading the road ahead and dealing with the twitches and shimmies when you've misinterpreted what's next. It really is an exceptional drive.

You don't even mind when you come up behind a recreational vehicle and are forced to drop from 35mph, the traditional US cruising speed, to something not far removed from walking pace.

Occasionally, if you're going slowly enough, you can catch a glimpse of the northern Californian hinterland. It's train-set country really, with white picket fences, lollipop trees and a velvety texture to the hills. It is stunningly, hand-bitingly, breathtakingly beautiful.

Then you get to the Bixby Creek Rainbow Bridge at Big Sur and you'll almost certainly want to drop to 4mph, then to a complete standstill. It's far from the most sophisticated bridge in the world, since it's built from wood and concrete, and it's not the most beautiful either. But when it spears off into the fog, and all you can hear are the bark of the sea lions below, well, it's a moment you don't want to waste by passing through at 120 with your hair on fire.

The next day, I had a similar sort of feeling while cruising down the waterfront in San Francisco. I felt sure the speed limit here is 30mph, but that's way too fast. I did about three, so I could spend more time drinking in the smells from the sea and gawping at the Bay Bridge. Peering up those concrete canyons, I saw the funfair road system that had launched Steve McQueen and his Mustang 30 feet into the air, and into the consciousness of small boys everywhere.

Counter to this, I recall driving once through a eucalyptus forest in Portugal and because there wasn't much to look at, I went nuts, squealing my tyres on every corner and generally being quite loony. Quite an achievement in a Toyota Starlet.

Had the Banana Girl who filled my face with pie this month seen me being so reckless, she would have dropped a large boulder on my foot. Or maybe shot me in the heart with an organic gun.

And she'd have been similarly mad if she'd caught me in Alice Springs, having driven at an average speed of 130mph on dirt roads from some massive ranch about three million miles away.

This brings me on to the Buttertubs Pass in North Yorkshire. Travelling from Thirsk at the eastern end, the temptation is to drive very quickly because it's a great road and, unless you like sheep, there are few visual distractions. But at the top, you just have to slow down. This is because there's a very steep drop to your left and the barrier is nothing more than a length of B&Q hosepipe. But also because the view is just epic.

I could go on, but to summarize, here is a list of places where I tend to drive fast and recklessly:

- Lincolnshire
- Germany
- Holland
- Australia
- The middle of Spain
- The west coast of Barbados

And this is a list of places where I tend to drive quite slowly:

- The Cotswolds
- Italy
- Southern France
- Iceland
- New Zealand
- Corsica
- The Costa Blanca
- The east coast of Barbados

In other words, I'm a lout in places that have the topography of blotting paper and the colour of wallpaper paste. And I'm also what James May calls a 'Christian motorist' in places that are usually spectacular and bright.

And I think I'm not alone. Ever wondered why people go so slowly through 'The Cut' on the M40 near Stokenchurch? Could it be because the view of Oxfordshire from here is the view featured in the title sequence of *The Vicar of Dibley* and is just so captivating?

And if it is, then could it be that I've stumbled on a rather wondrous new road safety idea: when building roads, ensure they go through the prettiest scenery possible?

Certainly, while watching the recent BBC series of *Coast*, I was startled to find how little of our magnificent shoreline is lined with a road. There are thousands of miles of wondrous views which can only be enjoyed while on foot, not from a car.

Take north Wales as a prime example. At present, people wishing to get to Anglesey from Aberystwyth must trundle up the A487 and the A496, which have to be rigorously patrolled with speed cameras in a bid to stop all those bored drivers from going too fast.

If there were to be a proper road that hugged the seaside, everyone would dawdle along looking at the waves and the bird-life. The act of driving, which is inherently dull, would be enhanced by visual stimulation and consequently there'd be no need to stimulate the limbic system of your brain with high-speed thrills. And as a result, there'd be fewer crashes, fewer distraught parents and orphaned children.

Best of all, such a scheme would blow a fuse in the head of the girl who mashed my face into a pie this month. Because everyone would be going so much more slowly, there'd be fewer fumes to spoil her precious environment. But to achieve this goal, several hundred diggers would need to chew up the natural beauty of Britain's prettiest bits.

What's it going to be, Banana Girl?

November 2005

The British road system

Ever wondered why so many people from countries that don't have proper facilities want to come and live in Britain? State handouts? Our multicultural capital city? Or maybe it's because you can learn English here, which is useful for when you move to America? I think not.

When you move to another country, it's good to have reminders of home. And the fact is, in many ways, Britain is the same as Bulgaria was in 1955.

Yesterday, I came here from France on the mole train, and as I emerged into the daylight, I thought I may have been on a time machine. It was like moving backwards 200 years. Very quickly, for instance, you find out why Kent is called the Garden of England: it's because driving up the M20 is like driving over someone's rockery.

It is staggeringly rough, with potholes and craters big enough to swallow a small car, and ridges big enough to launch even a heavy truck into orbit . . . if it were going fast enough. And it is made from concrete, which is fine if you're building a block of flats in Uzbekistan or wishing to bury a business rival in New York. But using concrete to surface a motorway is idiotic because it's so damn noisy.

Pretty soon, I needed some petrol and a pee (and some ear plugs), so I pulled off at Maidstone Services – it was like refuelling in Cuba. The pump had the sort of readout that was amazing in 1974 and the lavatories looked like they could double up as a KGB torture chamber. Bog roll? Forget it.

Even the Polish truckers I found in there were standing with their hands on their hips, wondering how the country they learned about at school had become so filthy and broken. Especially as most had arrived from France, where things are a little different.

The fuel over there is delivered from pumps that McLaren would consider to be fast. Whoomph and you're full. The lavatories come with baby-changing facilities, and I do think they mean just that. They're so clean you could indeed perform major surgery on even the most brittle of newborns.

What's more, in France you can buy sandwiches that you might actually want to put in your mouth and coffee that is delicious. All I found to eat in Maidstone was fat or lard. So I paid for the fuel, made a mental note to get a tetanus jab and skidded back to the car on a river of spilled diesel.

Pretty soon, I was on the link road from the M20 to the M25, which, presumably to save money, was built along the lines of a Lake District back road. And it was full of people sitting far too close to the wheel, in awful mini MPVs, in the wrong lane.

Not once in France was I held up for a second by inattentive or bigoted driving. But in Britain that's the norm. Move over? For someone in a big, fast, loud car with white stripes on the bonnet? No chance. That might imply that he's better than me ... And to think, James May calls the French communists.

Stuck resolutely behind some bitter and twisted failure in an N-reg Peugeot of some kind, I hit the roadworks on the western fringes of the M25. We're getting used to them now, of course, but if you stop and think for a moment, how can it take two years to build 14 miles of road? The Romans could do ten times better than that 2,400 years ago.

And when, in the nineteenth century, the Great Western Railway was converted from a seven-foot gauge to four foot ten inches, do you want to hazard a guess how long it took? I'm talking about lifting up a length of rail all the way from Bristol to London, moving it exactly two foot two inches and then attaching it to the sleepers again, without the benefit of any cranes or mechanical devices? Well, I'll tell you. They did it in one night.

Mind you, they weren't stuck with a herd of health and safety officials, which is the problem today. No one you see working on the M25 these days is actually working. They're just walking around backwards in hi-vis jackets, making sure that all the other health and safety officers don't fall over.

In France, earlier in the day, I'd seen a pretty big crash. A small Toyota had plainly hit the central reservation and then buried itself underneath a large articulated lorry. Here, the road would have been shut for two hours while men in hi-vis made sure the surface and the barrier were fine, whereas over there, there was a sign asking drivers to slow down a bit and that was that. They hadn't even closed a lane.

And then there's the business of speeding. The French are having a crackdown, for sure, but when you're caught, the police don't act like you've just anally raped President Chirac. They just take 100 euros from your wallet and that's that.

Here, it's a very different story. On the M25, each gantry was showing a different limit. One minute it was 60, then 40 and then 50, and woe betide anyone who failed to comply because there were cameras every 500 yards. You can't help thinking that the variable limit varies this much simply to confuse everyone. So they trip the light fantastic.

The cameras, we're told, are to keep speeds down and save lives, but we all know this is horse shit. In France, they put up a blacked-out human silhouette at the site of every fatal crash. And let me tell you that's scary. After I passed the fifth in 50 kilometres, I realized I was going too quickly and slowed down.

Of course, you pay lots for the privilege of using a French autoroute – getting from Millau to Paris the previous day had cost £30 – but you get the impression the money is actually being spent on the road, which is smooth, clear and well serviced with amenities.

I mean, have you seen that epic new motorway from Montpellier to Clermont-Ferrand? And the bridge they've built at Millau, the one so tall you could get Canary Wharf underneath it?

Did you know that one in four people in Britain today is employed by the state? The government employs more people than live in Sheffield. And despite promises to cut the civil service, the only redundancies so far have come from the forces.

This is why our infrastructure is so dreadful. It's why the M20 is as rough as the surface of the moon and why the roadworks on the M25 take so long. Because government agencies don't work.

And that's the bitter irony of today's immigration problem. You have thousands of people coming here from behind what was once the iron curtain, only to find that behind Mr Blair's smile lies half a million Bolsheviks. And that rather than moving to Britain, what they've actually done is moved back in time.

That's why immigration doesn't worry me at all. Because one day, when we've got enough Polish plumbers and Bulgarian car mechanics, we might get rid of the grinning jug-eared ape. And replace him with a road system that works.

December 2005

CAR OF THE YEAR: RENAULT CLIO

2006

TOP 5 BESTSELLING SINGLES
SONG TITLE – ARTIST

1 I don't feel like Dancin' –
   Scissor Sisters
2 Chasing Cars – Snow Patrol
3 Crazy – Gnarls Barkley
4 America – Razorlight
5 Rehab – Amy Winehouse

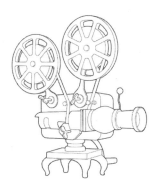

TOP 5 BOX OFFICE MOVIES

1 Pirates of the Caribbean: Dead
   Man's Chest
2 Night at the Museum
3 Cars
4 X-Men: The Last Stand
5 The Da Vinci Code

The Bugatti Veyron

Sometimes, I wish I was James May. Obviously, I don't want his jumpers, his hair or his collection of Bach records. Nor do I want his house, his cars, his accent, his ability to mend motorcycles or the leather ballet boots he bought recently.

But sometimes I do wish I had his regimented, organized mind, because that would make my life as a columnist so much easier. Take Richard Littlejohn for example. Present him with a news story and you know exactly what he's going to make of it. And it was the same with the late Auberon Waugh. When you read in his autobiography that he was three when he learned to hate the working classes, you know what his take's going to be on everything from the French riots to *Big Brother*.

James is the same. James likes his beer to be brown and his house to be beige. I therefore know what James will think of a new car long before he actually drives it. Poncy, usually. And I know he'll continue to call it poncy until the day he dies.

I'm rubbish at this. I change my mind six or seven times before I get out of bed. One minute, I think the only way to deal with disaffected Muslim youths is to drop a bomb on them. The next I think the solution is to drop a bomb on America.

I try on opinions like I try on clothes, standing in front of a mirror and wondering if they suit me. Sometimes, I take them home and realize I made a bad choice, so I throw them away and get new ones.

This gets me into all sorts of trouble because I can have a definite, firmly held view on, say, a new Peugeot and then, when I drive it again, I can't remember what on earth that view might have been. People sometimes stop me in the street and are alarmed to find I sing the praises of something I destroyed in print just two weeks earlier.

Take the McLaren F1. When it came out, I said it was a stupid car because it had a stupid price tag. You'd have needed to win the premium bond jackpot twice to have bought such a thing, and then there'd have been nothing left over for shoes, or supper. 'Why dream', I asked, 'about something there's no point dreaming about?'

On this basis, I'd be similarly dismissive of the Bugatti Veyron. I mean, it's on sale now at £840,000. And for that money you could buy a house.

If there were any consistency in my life, if I had even a shred of Jamesishness, I would have refused a test drive. Why bother? It's too expensive. I'm not going to dangle such a thing under the noses of the readers knowing full well their chances of having enough money to buy one are about the same as being gnawed to death by a platoon of woodlice.

I didn't though. I packed my little suitcase and went to Italy, where I was presented with quite the most stunning piece of automotive engineering ever created. (This opinion may change at some future date, but I'm sticking with it for now.)

I mean, take the flappy-paddle, seven-speed gearbox. I spoke to the man who headed up the project at Ricardo and he said he'd never done anything so difficult. Quite an admission from someone whose products are used by F1 teams.

'Oh, F1 is nothing,' he said. 'They don't have anything like the power of a Bugatti and only have to last two hours. The one in the Veyron has to work for ten or twenty years.' Small wonder it took fifty people five years to make the damn thing work.

It wasn't just the gearbox, either. It was the engine too, that massive quad turbo W16, and the aerodynamics as well. The team had been given the shape of the body and told there could be no alterations. They'd been told too that it must do 400kph and must produce 1,000bhp.

They weren't fighting to beat Mercedes or BMW. These guys were fighting to beat heat and friction and lift. They were fighting nature. And how did motoring commentators react? Instead of cheering them on and offering support, we laughed at the many and very public setbacks.

Well, the laugh's on us now because they've made it work. When that massive rear spoiler begins to rise on specially cooled hydraulic rams, you can feel the back of the car being pressed into the road.

It's not that it can do 252mph, it's the way it manages to do 252 so effortlessly that impresses me most. At high speed, a McLaren F1 feels like the Bell X-1 – a mass of vibrations and terror. At high speed, the Bugatti feels like an Airbus – solid, planted, safe.

You may not like the look of the thing, or the gaudiness of the interior. You may think Ferdinand Piëch a mentalist for ordering such a car be made, and to hell with the shareholders. But you have to love the engineering. You just have to.

It isn't even a straight-line rocket ship, either. On that twisting dual carriageway that comes back down to the ionosphere from the Mont Blanc tunnel, I had it in handling mode, and it's hard to put into words how much grip there is.

Foot down and with 800bhp hitting the front wheels, you get a dollop of power understeer, but it's not like any power understeer I've ever felt because there's still 200bhp going to the back wheels . . . and that's a number that's growing by the moment. It feels odd at first, but then it feels spectacular.

Nearly as spectacular as the hammer-blow power delivery when the corner's over, or the chuckability when you get to the next. I could describe this car as the Lotus Elise's big brother. So I will. It's that good.

And now I've changed my mind. It's not 'that good' at all. It's better, because I drove this car for twelve hours and emerged in London with no aches. You can't do that in an Elise, and not only because after twelve hours, you'd still have twelve to go.

At a stroke then, the Veyron has rendered everything I've ever said about any other car obsolete. It's rewritten the rule book, moved the goalposts and, in the process, given Mother Nature a bloody nose.

Of course, I don't mind changing my opinions about Ferrari and so on. I'm used to it. I spend half my life apologizing, and I don't mind finishing up here with another. I'm sorry I laughed at the Bugatti Veyron's gestation. I didn't realize quite what a project it was.

James too is bowled over by the scale of what's been achieved – I knew he would be – but sadly, the praise is not universal. I've read a couple of reports where commentators are still sneering about the problems of making it, and the supposed soulless nature of the finished product. Come on, chaps, admit it. You were wrong and the Veyron makes you look like a twat.

I know how you feel. The McLaren F1 did much the same thing to me.

January 2006

Top Gear

May I begin by wishing you all a very happy new year. I certainly hope you enjoy reading *Top Gear* magazine over the next twelve months, because the way things are going, the programme of the same name isn't going to be making much of an appearance.

Thanks to Wimbledon, the BBC's strange obsession with covering snooker, which is like billiards for poor people, and the World Cup, which is a competition in which people on vast salaries run around a field, there simply isn't enough space left for the sort of television programme normal people might actually want to watch. I think there will be one episode of *Top Gear* in 2006, on a Thursday, in August, while you're at the beach.

This might be a disappointment for the huge numbers of teenage girls that tune in to to see Richard Hammond's new teeth every week, but for those who actually work on the show, it'll be nothing short of a blessed relief.

In the olden days, making *Top Gear* was easy. You drove round a few corners, put some suitcases in the boot of whatever you were testing and then, back at the edit, the director would cover up the gaps with lots of pounding Seventies' rock music. It took about fifteen minutes.

Not any more, because the show has become a monster. You may have noticed that the credits at the end of a normal programme roll for about six seconds, whereas the ones at the end of *Top Gear* give the impression you've been watching *Ben Hur*.

So what, you may be wondering, do we all do? Well, obviously, a lot of the time we stare at Sophia and Rachel, our production co-ordinators, but then we have to get down to it.

Take the Bugatti race from Alba to London. Someone had to find a Bugatti that was available for six days. Then someone had to get two crews out to Italy and someone else had to find a four-minute hole in Richard Hammond's diary so he could come too. While all this was going on, I was chained to my phone, talking to the engineer at Volkswagen who'd designed the car. And then I wrote the script. But, finally, we're all ready to go.

A lot of people ask how we film these races and whether they're fixed. Well, let me say here and now, in print, they're not. I follow a Range Rover tracking car, and we really don't pull over for anything except fuel. In the drive to Oslo, the cameraman spent twenty-four hours in the boot and had to relieve himself in a bottle because there was no time to stop.

Meanwhile, James and Richard are doing all they can to beat me. We take it very seriously.

But not half as seriously as the director who, when the race is over, has to retrace our steps, adding to the miles of tracking shots he took in the race with many more miles of arty 'ups and passes'. This usually takes three days. And then he edits the film.

And to edit the thirty-two-minute Bugatti race took a staggering thirty-three sixteen-hour days. That's not even a minute a day, and no one spends that much time (or money) on a commercial. It's the main reason why *Top Gear* doesn't look like any other show on television. Because everyone on it works so bloody hard. And because we have the best production manager in the whole of the BBC.

We also have the best executive producer. Unlike most executive producers, who are paid to have a lot of lunch, Andy Wilman spends all day in the office, swearing at anyone who walks past, and then when everyone's gone home, he goes to the edit suite in central London to swear at everyone there. In the last run, he never got home before one in the morning.

He's so busy, in fact, that he doesn't even stare at Sophia and Rachel all that much. Then he announced he was firing everyone in the office who was a first-born child, 'to keep the faith'.

Eventually, all the films are made, and edited, and normally everyone would go home to relax. But on *Top Gear*, we then go into production. We record on a Wednesday in the old hangar where they used to paint Harrier Jump Jets, and that means that on a Tuesday, the presenters have to rock up at the office.

Richard spends the day flossing or talking to his dentist, James looks at Rachel a bit, and then looks at the prices of old motorcycles on eBay, but I have to write the show and prepare the guest interview.

On the Wednesday, we read through the script I've written to make sure it's not in French. Then we do a quick rehearsal in the freezing, or boiling, studio. Then James has a full three-course lunch, as it's been a while since his full three-course breakfast. And it'll be at least six before he sits down to a three-course dinner. Richard doesn't eat as it dulls the whitener.

Then it's time to get ready. This means we have to break out the ironing board and do our shirts – when you've spent thirty-three days editing one film, there's no money left over for wardrobe girls. Or cars to whisk us to the studio. Or even a green room.

What we do have is a Portakabin. This is the beating heart of the operation. It has no heating, no broadband, no chairs, and nowhere for the guest's entourage to relax. We like it that way.

In summer, we sit on the grass looking at the airfield where WW2 fighters used to take off and imagine we're in the RAF, waiting for the signal to scramble.

This comes at around 2.30 p.m., when the audience is herded in and the gates shut. At around 2.28 p.m. a bird normally flies into the Portakabin and craps on James. Or he decides he's hungry and needs another course, or that he needs a shit. So just as I'm saying, 'Please welcome James May,' I see him going to the bogs with the *Daily Telegraph*.

Currently, there are 190,000 people on the waiting list for tickets to see *Top Gear*. And with space for only 500 a week, it would take nineteen years to accommodate them all. So we know it's a big deal and have a tea break, so Richard, James and I can stand around having our pictures taken on people's telephones. This baffles James a lot, partly because he doesn't understand camera phones, but mostly because he can't work out why anyone might want a picture of someone who's spent most of the day having a crap. But I love Wednesdays and the buzz of a studio, standing there wondering why no one's laughing at your jokes and speculating on how big the laugh will be when it's dubbed on afterwards.

I love the sheer volume of Red Bull we get through, the vast quantities of cigarettes we smoke. And just how often we can call Hammond gay. I love the energy, the buzz and the way people react when you show them the films you worked so hard to make. It'll be hard to get that same buzz from watching two men play snooker.

February 2006

Rover

And so, with the hysteria over Rover now reduced to a few bits of tumbleweed, and most of the workforce settled into new jobs, it's time to turn our attention to the plight of those customers who kept Britain's sick old dog going for so long.

I often wondered what it was that caused someone to buy a Rover in the autumn of the company's life. Technology? I rather think not since the bestselling models in the range were based on the Honda Civic. And not the current one, either, or even the one before that. But the one before the one before the one that was pulled along by an ox.

Style perhaps? Well, there's no denying the 25 was a pretty little thing, but the 45 wasn't and the 75? That was an automotive incarnation of Austin Reed. It was a theme pub and the theme in question was bingo. And to make matters worse, it was sold latterly in a range of snazzy colours, which always put me in mind of a Day-Glo danny mac and a lime-green shopping trolley.

It should have been sold in that extraordinary colour that doesn't exist in any chart or on any spectrometer, existing in the tailoring department of shops frequented by those in their eighties. It's not green, brown or grey, but a sort of sludgy blend of all three. A colour that's called simply 'old'.

So, if it wasn't style or technology that drew people to the Rover brand, and it certainly wasn't power, economy, space or comfort, then what was it? Well, I've thought long and hard about this and the only thing I can come up with is that they perceived the brand to be 'British'.

Why? If it was the British workforce that the customer was trying to support, then why not buy a Nissan or a Toyota or a Honda? If it wasn't the workforce, perhaps it was the designers. So why not buy a Ford or a Renault or an Audi or indeed anything that takes your fancy, because just about every car firm in the world employs a Brit somewhere in the styling department.

It can only have been some sense that Rover was British owned. Well, yes, but if you were to buy shares in Ford tomorrow, then Ford would be British owned, in part at least. If you bought shares in GM as well, and DaimlerChrysler, Renault, PSA, and VW, then Britain would have a stake in just about every car firm in the world. So now you can see how daft the concept of buying a Rover was.

It can only have been done because the Britishness of the brand gave the customers a sense of pride. And that's just plain weird. The notion that someone in a retirement home in Bournemouth should have anything in common with a Midlands car worker is laughable. Politically, these Rule Britannia types have more in common with American neo-cons. Geographically, they're nearer to the French and biologically, they are a gnat's genome away from a fossilized bat.

I like being British because it gives me someone to shout at in the World Cup. I also like being British because I think we have a reasonably honourable history. But neither of these reasons would have caused me to buy a sub-standard product just because it was emblazoned with the Union flag.

Apart from anything else, I think of myself as European these days, and please don't trot out the age old question:

would I rather be governed by a bunch of German bankers? What? Instead of Tony Bloody Blair? Too damn right I would.

Not that even my pro-EU stance would cause me to buy a European car. In fact, my Ford GT comes from pretty well everyone's idea of hell. America. And the car I'm most looking forward to in the next few months is the new Nissan Skyline. Oh wait. Under the Rover customer rules, that's actually French. But the Ford GT has an Aston Vanquish steering rack. So does that make it British? Maybe so.

All this is by the by, because Rover is now Chinese, the dealers are all gone and Britain's barmy army of Rover drivers is now in urgent need of a replacement. Morgan would be the obvious answer, but many, I suspect, would find the Plus 8 a bit too Welsh.

Some will drift to where they should have been in the first place. Honda. They'll love the reliability, the space, the lightness of touch and the way other road users part when they drive by. We're not parting of course; we're running for our lives, because we know the Honda driver is deaf, mad and blind.

Some, however, will not buy a Honda because of a perceived war crime committed by Tojo in Burma.

These are the really dangerous ones. The sort of people who can't forgive and forget even after sixty years. That makes them old and vindictive. And if they've been a Rover driver, stupid as well. There are creatures with big teeth in our nightmares that are less terrifying. Even Bill Oddie doesn't match up.

This lot, then, have an unusual set of requirements for their next set of wheels. They need to demonstrate that they are not remotely interested in cars, and that they simply want the cheapest most anti-car money can buy. A Fiat Panda, then? Oh crikey, no, because who can forget Mussolini? Well all of us, actually, but not Sid and Doris.

So we must find a car made by a country with whom Britain has never had a fight. Er . . . Finland then? Oh wait, we did have a scrap with them in 1940 – the only time two democracies have declared war on one another, incidentally. Um, Ethiopia? Yes, but it's not big on car manufacturing. And it's the same story with Chile, Uzbekistan and Bhutan.

France is out, as is Germany, of course. Then there were the Spanish, who sent an armada; the Dutch, who sank our entire fleet in the Medway; there have been endless problems with the entire Middle East; and we can't simply gloss over the American War of Independence either. Bunch of ingrates. Then you have Argentina, Iceland, China, Japan, Malaysia and Korea. Even the damn Swedes have had a pop, although this was back in 1810. Or, as Sid and Doris like to call it, yesterday.

A solution is to be found in the shape of Ford's Galaxy. All MPVs are horrid, but this is one of the worst, with uncomfortable seats, no bootspace at all, and an image that could have come directly from the Argos catalogue. I'm using one this week and on every bend, down every straight and over every surface it never fails to disappoint and horrify. It even manages to make the kids sick, so therefore it is perfect for the motorists who loved Rover. The sort of people who buy a bad car on purpose so they can really show the world their anti-car zeal.

But d'you know the best thing about it? It's built in one of the few countries anywhere on planet Earth that has never had a war with Britain. Portugal.

March 2006

The fuel crisis

And so, Porsche has turbocharged the new 911, Ferrari has introduced an 800bhp Enzo, Aston is beavering away with its new DBS and, imminently, Mercedes is expected to announce plans for a new collaboration with McLaren.

The message is clear. As fast as politicians wrap the motor industry up with noise, emission and safety red tape, car designers are unravelling the constraints with more and more power.

No really. We already have a 240bhp Golf. That's twice as much as we were given twenty years ago, and if that rate of change keeps going, people learning to drive today will finish their career in a family hatchback with 1,000bhp under the bonnet. Nice.

We've already got family saloons with 500bhp to play with. That's 100 more than Jackie Stewart had when he won the F1 Championship in 1973. What's more, Mitsubishi can sell you a car that develops 200bhp per litre. And it's only twenty years since Daihatsu became the first car maker to sell a car with half that. We're on a roll, boys. And I'm loving it.

However, some say this is nothing more than a last hurrah before the oil runs out, that the engineers are having one last party with their outdated nineteenth-century toy box before they're forced by circumstance to put down their petrol and pick up some potato peelings instead.

The most recent scare story suggests that the world's supply of oil, gas and coal will be exhausted in about thirty years' time. And if that's true, then there's no doubt the big car makers are being completely irresponsible. Gorging on the fat of the land now when they know full well a famine is just around the corner. Only an imbecile would do that.

There's plenty of evidence to suggest it's true. At present, people in the Third World use around half a gigajoule of energy a year, compared to the average American, who gets through 300 gigajoules. And forty burgers. But as we keep being told, it's not the 'Third World' any more. It's the 'developing world', and that's where the problems lie.

If China and India increase their consumption to just a tenth of the US average, they could suck Arabia dry in about fifteen minutes. This would plunge the world into the Dark Ages. Or worse. Sociologists tell us that when the oil starts to go, nation will fight nation for the last few drops, and the social order will disintegrate.

They may have a point. When we had that trivial fuel shortage eighteen months ago, people formed disorderly queues outside garages, waiting with fists clenched and blood vessels fit to burst as the chap in front filled his tank, and then his washer bottle, and then his trousers pockets with petrol.

Imagine that on a global scale. Imagine if there were no trucks to deliver food to the supermarket and you knew that your neighbour had 300 tins of baked beans stashed away in his basement. Would you watch your children starve or would you pop round and shoot him in the face?

Same goes with power. You'll have your nose pressed to the gates at Sellafield begging for a cup of electricity to run your kid's iron lung. But they won't be able to help because, back in 2005, all the eco-mentalists told them that nuclear energy wasn't green.

Eventually, when every candle had been burned, and every tin of baked beans consumed, we'd be back in 1550, using beads to buy chickens. And dying three times a day from diphtheria and rabies. Death, famine and disease all topped off with a light sprinkling of nuclear holocaust. And it's all Porsche's fault for turbocharging the 911.

Unfortunately, the people who tell us these things tend to be card-carrying lunatics with an agenda. They're the ones who were chained to the fence outside Greenham Common, saying that atomic war with Russia was inevitable, and that if the Earth's climate changes – something it has done constantly since the dawn of time – we'll all drown.

They're the ones who see only bad in the world. The ones who lie in fields of gold on glorious summer days, complaining about the distant hum of traffic, the ones who see a corporate conspiracy at the bottom of every packet of crisps.

Life has usually dealt them a handful of low clubs and diamonds. How many good-looking women did you see at Greenham? And because everything turned out so badly, they want to change the system. That's why they want us to cycle to work and adopt a fox – because it brings us down to their level, not because the oil's running out. Because it isn't.

In the 1920s, Germany developed a system for extracting oil from coal. In the war (which we won, by the way), it was used to propel tanks and trucks. In Brazil, they run cars on oil from chrysanthemums. And I used to power my old Land Cruiser on chip fat.

But all this is by the by because, with a barrel of conventional oil costing around $35, it is now economically viable to go after unconventional oil. The black gold that's held in sand, for instance, under Canada. How long will this last? Well, according to scientists, centuries.

Even if half of China decides that it wants to go to work every day in a Jet Ranger, and India becomes the biggest market in the world for Lamborghini Diablos, Neil Young and Donald Sutherland will provide the juice to keep them going.

Oh, and don't worry about the carbon dioxide either because, apparently, this can now be extracted from coal gasification plants and then pumped deep into the earth, where it increases pressure, forcing more oil and gas to the surface. Brilliant. The eco-mentalists will have to go and worry about something else. Horses, perhaps.

In fact, don't worry about anything because, when the chips are down, man always finds a way. With no power tools at all, we survived the last ice age. Without the benefit of aspirin, we came through the great plague. And since then we've conquered space and developed the Rice Krispie.

You think bird flu's going to wipe us out? Well, I wouldn't count on it because somewhere, right now, a nerd with a white coat and pipette is figuring out how it can be beaten. And it'll be another nerd, a few centuries from now, who finds a way to power cars using the sun's ultraviolet light.

And when the sun runs out, we'll get on a space ship and go somewhere else. Or build another one.

The message, then, really is clear. If you want a 911 turbo, and I must say it does look rather good, buy one. In fact, you can buy whatever car you want. Not an Audi Q7, though. I drove one in Norway recently and it seemed to be rubbish. And a rubbish car is, I'm afraid, a waste of petrol.

April 2006

American muscle

The phone chirps. It's a text message from a footballist, who's been offered a Mustang GT500E Super Snake for two hundred and eleven billion dollars. And he wants to know if it's a good buy.

No, obviously. It'd be a terrible buy. Mustangs are like those blondes with hair and breast extensions who hang around in clubs hoping to snare some poor chap who's just been evicted from Celebrity Who Wants to Get Thrown out of the Brother.

He knows he shouldn't. He knows she has the *News of the World*'s number on speed dial and that he'll be reading about how he performed before he's actually finished performing. But she's so cute. And she wants to bring her friend along. The dilemma.

I have toyed with the idea of a Mustang ever since I was old enough not to need reins while out shopping. I like the way they look, and the way they sound. I like Steve McQueen's car in *Bullitt* especially.

But every time I drive one, I'm left with an abiding sensation that I'm in a dustbin lorry. It has a Seddon Atkinson-quality feel and it handles like it's towing a fully laden skip. And this is true: I do have a weird feeling that if I buy something American, I'm in some way supporting George Bush.

So no, then. No Mustang. And yet I still want one. Or a Charger. Or a 'Vette. I'm not bothered. Just so long as it's a car with a big set of muscles.

I'm not alone either, it seems. Quite apart from the footballist, there are plenty of others in the same boat. Plenty of others who've grown up with Beemers and Benzes and now want something orange. With a Confederate flag on the bonnet and exhausts big enough to sleep in.

I know this because the value of anything loud 'n' proud is accelerating faster than the stock market. Three years ago, a 1971 Plymouth Hemi Cuda would have fetched a million. Last year, according to CNN, they were changing hands for twice that.

Of course, the Hemi Cuda is an exception – only eleven were made – but lesser, more common stuff is out-performing the stars from Ferrari and Maserati in the auction houses. Just the other day, a boggo Mustang 500 convertible went for $550,000. Why?

Well, of course, in the olden days, glamour came from the race tracks and every small boy grew up wanting a Ferrari or a Maserati. Ferris Bueller's dad had a Ferrari. Ferris Bueller would have no clue why.

I understand that. When I was growing up, Hollywood and TV was where we went for a spot of escapism, not Monza. And what we saw there didn't wear a prancing horse or a trident. It wore a big, lazy V8 snarl. It was an American muscle car.

What's more, a Ferrari is built primarily to go round corners. That five-way traction control and e-diff combo in an F430 is designed specifically to provide a simply staggering amount of grip, way, way more than any normal driver would ever have the balls to explore.

An American muscle car, on the other hand, is built primarily not to go round corners. So, its abilities are on a par with those of our own. This makes us feel heroic and manly as we wrestle to keep the back end in shape. While doing a safe 4mph.

Then, when we get to a straight bit of road, we can bury the throttle, rejoice in the intake sizzle, revel in the roar and hang on for dear life as two gallons of juice catapult us to the horizon. Muscle cars, in short, are not as clever as Ferraris. But they're just as exciting. And they're simpler, which, in a world of convenience food and remote control TV sets, is a good thing.

I haven't finished yet. A friend recently sold his DB9, and though he's probably the worst driver in the world, he replaced it with a Ferrari 360. Within a week, he knew he'd done the equivalent of passing his cycling proficiency test and then attempting to mountain bike down Everest.

So what's he going to buy now? In the past, there were countless alternatives from AC to Gordon Keeble via Frazer Nash and Humber. Now there aren't. There's Maserati, Merc and, at a pinch, the new Jag XK.

In essence, the world's millionaires are starved of choice. They struggle to find a single car that lets them stand out from the crowd. I know someone who bought a Maybach knowing it was terrible . . . and as a result, no one else would have one.

People like this often eat in a restaurant in Barnes. It's called Riva, and opposite there's an American car dealership. It's full of tempting alternatives: 'Vettes, Hummers, Thunderbirds and the new Mustang. But none of them quite does it somehow.

The Hummer is nothing but a GMC Tahoe in a Power Ranger suit. The current Mustang is pretty but wet. The Thunderbird is gay and the 'Vette, though lovely to drive, has lost some of its family tree's sparkle.

So, here we have a group of wealthy, middle-aged men who've never watched motor racing and therefore don't want a Ferrari. They can't drive very well, either, so don't care about slip angles. And they don't want a modern car because their mates will have one too.

Result: my footballer friend is sending texts wanting to know about a Mustang Super Snake. And I'm on the Internet seeing what the bloody hell he's on about.

Holy Cow. What a car. It isn't what you'd call 'lovingly restored and authentic in every detail'. But then this is America, remember, where an 'authentic' Elizabethan house could have been built yesterday.

To explain. There was only ever one Super Snake Mustang and now it tours the country, amusing people called Bud and Skip. The new Super Snake is made by a 'legendary' company – probably formed in the last two weeks – called Unique Performance.

What it's done is take an old Mustang and bring it up to date using products I've never heard of. It has, for instance, a Currie 31 Spline 9' Posi-Traction Trac-Locker Differential.

And that's before we get to the Chris Alston Chassisworks Power Steering Rack and Baer Tracker Bump Steer Adjustable Tie Rods. Or the Baer 13' x 1.1' Track System, PBR aluminium front brakes.

But it's under the bonnet that things get really interesting because there's a 427-cubic-inch (large) V8, which produces 525bhp (a shit load). And if you like, they'll fit a supercharger, which takes that up to 725bhp. And you don't need that translating. 725bhp renders all the suspension stuff irrelevant because it doesn't matter if it corners at 2mph. With that level of grunt up front, you'll make up time on the straights.

However, the best thing about this car is the way it looks.

At first, it appears to be a normal '67 Mustang with huge tyres and a bulge on its bonnet. But if you look closely, you can see it's been modernized. It looks fabulous, and that's probably why there's only one left.

So what I've done is told my mate that it's rubbish. And I'm giving serious thought to buying it myself.

June 2006

Idiots

She's sitting on a sofa, a fag in one hand and an overflowing ashtray perched on one knee. Her stomach is huge. And in the next room we see her mother, smoking a little smack and telling reporters that she's very proud. No dear, that's the wrong word. You're not proud. You're a stupid waste of the world's resources.

And she's not alone. In fact, I am becoming increasingly concerned with the sheer number of properly idiotic people who call Britain home.

Last year, towards the end of an all-weekend open-air gig, I went to the portable lavatories in the VIP enclosure. You know the sort. Blue water, a dead flower and lots of powder on all the shelving. Anyway, they were immaculate.

This was not the case with the bogs provided outside the VIP enclosure. They were in a total state. Piss on the floor, shit on the walls, entire bog rolls unravelled and stuffed down the pan. Now come on. How hard is it to use a lavatory? And how thick do you have to be to get it wrong?

You see this kind of thing at motorway service stations as well. I had cause to visit one the other day and it was extraordinary. Even the Polish lorry drivers in there were standing, hands on hips, wondering exactly how anyone had managed to get crap on the ceiling. Not even cows can do that.

These were people who had grown up under the hammer of communism. They'd had to queue for bread, knowing that just a few hundred miles away in the west, people were buying Hovis to feed to the birds. I wonder how they would have felt if they had known we couldn't go for a piss without getting it in someone's eye.

And here's the thing. All these people – mothers of pregnant eleven-year olds, van drivers who are confused by plumbing – are all eligible to do jury service.

I spoke yesterday to a friend who had sat through the trial of a chap who had come from Lagos with a suitcase full of cocaine. He'd told police that he had no idea what was in the bag, only that he had been asked to deliver it to a house in central London – a house that turned out, surprise, surprise, to be empty when it was raided.

Plainly, the man was guilty. Anyone with half a brain could see that. But unfortunately, half the jury didn't have half a brain. Most, apparently, didn't have a brain at all. Two couldn't read the card saying they understood what was going on, one woman said that no matter what, she couldn't find a fellow black person guilty of anything, and another two said they weren't that bothered which way the vote went, so long as they could go home. To piss all over the bathroom floor, probably.

As a result, the drug smuggler walked free.

Now, as I understand it, there are certain conditions that have to be met before you can do jury service. One of them is that you must have a sound mind. This was included in the rules to prevent window lickers from turning up in jock straps and army boots and making dolphin noises throughout the proceedings.

You can't have someone decide your fate if he thinks he's a Cylon from *Battlestar Gallactica*. Fine. Good. But can you have your fate decided by someone who's proud of her chain-smoking, pregnant, eleven-year-old daughter? Or someone who is confused by lavatory paper?

I spoke the other day with someone who said he didn't like fish. What, all fish? Fish in batter? Fish with chips? Prawns, cod, sea bass, trout, smoked salmon? What he means is, I have never tried fish. Because my parents were too stupid to buy it.

And get this. On a Radio Two quiz the other day, a contestant was asked what happens to water at 32 on the Fahrenheit scale. After much umming and aahing, she said confidently, 'It melts.'

Now here's a woman who's allowed to do jury service, to have a say in who runs the country, and she thinks water melts when it gets a bit nippy.

We've all encountered gormlessness on an industrial scale, people who fill up with fuel while smoking, people who drop litter, people who breathe through their mouths and drag their knuckles on the ground. People who could out-Forrest Forrest Gump. And here's what I've been thinking. Are they as intelligent as the average dog?

You can teach a dog where and how to go to the lavatory. You can teach a dog not to drop litter and not to play with fire when refuelling a car. What's more, I've never met a dog that doesn't like fish.

So would you let a dog drive a car?

Of course you wouldn't. While they're bright enough to sniff out foxes, sit still for long periods of time and not smoke when pregnant, you wouldn't ask a spaniel to pop into town for your groceries.

So why do we let stupid people have driving licences? Seriously, if you can't be trusted to get your faeces into a bowl that's at least fifty times bigger than your anus, then why should you be allowed to try and steer a six-foot-wide car at 60 or 70mph, just inches from other people?

I want you to think about this. The latest figures suggest that 18 per cent of fatalities on the roads in 2004 were caused by drink driving. And that 34 per cent were caused as a result of excessive speed. This means that 58 per cent were caused by people who were stone-cold sober and travelling well within both their limits and those of the car.

The only conclusion we can draw from this is that the drivers in question were as stupid as a field full of bees, as daft as a brush. Perhaps they couldn't remember in the heat of the moment which pedal did what, or which way the wheel should be turned, or even that killing people is wrong.

I think, then, that if daft people are removed from the road it will cut the number of accidents dramatically. Furthermore, because they will have to take their working-class rust-buckets with them, there will be fewer fumes, and what's more, we will cut congestion at a stroke as well.

How much we cut congestion will be determined by how stupid people are identified. I favour an IQ test, which must be passed before anyone's allowed a provisional licence. But where do we set the limit? Technically, anyone with an IQ of less than fifty is an idiot, but I think 100 sounds like a nice number.

I reckon this would probably get somewhere between 90 and 95 per cent of all cars off the road. In some ways, that's rather depressing. In others, it's not depressing at all.

August 2006

Americans

We have an image of the American motorist, his big flobbery stomach, flobbering from state to state in a big flobbery car with big flobbery suspension at a flobbery 55mph.

For many years, I've argued that the heart of the average American motorist beats approximately once every fifteen minutes. Technically, they're in a coma.

But, sadly, this is wrong. Nowadays, the American motorist drives at the same speed we do, 80 or 85. And he's the most aggressive creature on earth.

If you wish to change lanes on the freeway, because, say, your turn-off is approaching, you can indicate all you like, but no one will slow down to let you in. They won't speed up, either. They'll just sit there until you remember you're in a rental car and make the move anyway. Then you'll get a selection of hand gestures that you never knew existed.

I know of no country in the world where motorists are so intolerant of one another. The slightest mistake causes at the very least a great deal of horn-blowing and, at worst, a three-second burst from some kind of powerful automatic weapon.

Then we have the question of tailgating. Of course, this happens elsewhere – I've actually been nudged by a nun in Italy – but there's nowhere it happens as often as on the American freeway. Everyone sits, as a matter of course, about three feet from your rear end. Which, when you're being followed by a Kenworth truck, and you're doing 80, and he has an M16 carbine, and you need to turn left, and the person on your inside won't let you in, can be a bit unnerving.

It isn't how they drive that's changed, either. It's what they drive. Now, for every nondescript Kojak-style saloon, you'll see two Evos or Subarus. And almost every car has been modded in some way.

My favourite was an orange Lotus Exige parked at the pumps in the middle of Death Valley. 'Yeah,' said the rather serious-looking driver when I approached, 'I've given it two degrees more camber on the back, fitted a 25 per cent softer compound on the front, uprated the supercharger . . .'

'So,' I said after I'd had enough, 'you've ruined it'.

He was genuinely taken aback. I believe there's a sense over there that car makers are pretty incompetent. And that if GM, Chrysler and Ford can't make a car properly, then what chance do those funny little trolls in Europe have? Never mind the l'il yella fellas from under the rising sun.

I tried to explain to our American friend that the Exige was put on sale after much development work and that if a two-degree shift in rear camber would make it handle better, then he could be assured that it'd be sold that way in the first place. But he was having none of it, launching instead into a long list of things he'd done to make the Toyota engine run cleaner and better than Tojo had managed.

If you want to know what these measures are, he'll almost certainly still be there. It's the only garage in Baker. You can't miss it. Anyway, the thing is that, thanks to the new-found fondness for modding and pimping, and the more aggressive driving style, there are a great many modded and pimped cars on the market. Most of which seem to be based on the new Ford Mustang.

That's no bad thing. With its see-saw damping and damp dishcloth V8, the standard product is like one of those 'girls next door' you see featured in *FHM*. You sense that with a bit of lighting here and a bit of eye shadow there, you could turn the pasty-faced teenager from Pontefract into the next Claudia Schiffer.

Shelby's given it a bash with mixed results. There's lots of power – 475bhp – but the handling, steering and brakes remain untouched. Which means you're paying extra simply to have a bigger accident.

Roush is different. Roush currently fields, I think, five of forty-three Winston Cup Nascar racers, which makes the company a bit like Ferrari, McLaren and half of Williams rolled into one. Roush is also responsible for the alarm/ tracker on my GT, so that's not so good. But I don't allow personal issues to cloud my judgement.

Actually, I do allow personal issues to cloud my judgement – it's why I punched Piers Morgan – but on this occasion, I'm going to play it straight and say, the Stage III Roush Mustang is a delightful way of going fast for not much money.

This opinion rather baffled the salesman. 'But it's $43,000,' he said incredulously. Precisely, that makes it £23,800, and that, for a supercharged V8 muscle car, is amazing really.

'Yes,' said our man, 'but our car only produces 415bhp, which is a lot less than you get from Shelby or Saleen.' To his astonishment, I wasn't bothered.

415bhp endows the Roush 'Stang with a 0–60 time of 4.9 seconds and a top speed of something or other. No one's tested it. But I can tell you the speedo only reads to 140. So in a straight line, it's not that epic. It is, however, when you get to a corner, because it's lowered, firmed up and injected with a bit of beef. It's 15 per cent stiffer than normal and, to be honest, so was I.

There's no finesse, it's not like a BMW in any way, but for sticking the tail out and keeping it there using nothing but the throttle, it's in the same league as that other colonial upstart, the Monaro VXR.

This begs a question, then. Would it be possible to import such a car to Britain? I'm not talking about the technicalities because, of course, you simply put it on a ship, pay some tax and within a few weeks it'll be outside your house, ready and road legal.

No, I'm talking about the sociological issues. Would it be possible to import this car . . . without causing all your friends to die laughing. At you.

Tell someone you drive a Mustang and no matter what it is, you'll come across as a bit of a local DJ. We think of it in terms of *Bullitt*. Everyone else thinks we look like we may be married to our sister. And do you really want a car with two stripes down the bonnet? And exhausts that sound like Katrina?

In America, this works. But that's because they are so much more aggressive than we are. They gave the world KFC. We gave the world the cream tea. And I suspect driving a Roush Mustang here would be like dipping a chicken drumstick into strawberry jam.

And then there's the politics. This car means you are aligning yourself with US policies. You're driving around saying you support the war in Iraq and the strategy in Afghanistan. Maybe you do. But I don't.

So why, you may be wondering, do I own a Ford GT? That's simple. The body is British, the gearbox is British, the steering rack is from an Aston, the chassis was set up by a couple of guys from Lotus, the wheels are German and the brakes are Italian. The power is American, yes, but it's tamed and sophisticated by Europeans. It's a metaphor, in other words, for the perfect world.

September 2006

Quad bikes

Last year I met a chap called Ralph who has Tarzan's hair and is officially the best-looking man on Earth. And he said I should go to Botswana, where he runs a safari company, because I'd love it.

It turned out, however, that Ralph's idea of a safari is not what you'd imagine. Oh, he can do the elephant and giraffe stuff, but mostly he's based at a place called Jack's Camp, miles from anywhere on the edge of the Makgadikgadi, the biggest salt flats in the world.

You've probably seen photos of the salty wastelands in America or Australia, but the Makgadikgadi is nothing like that. It's vast on a scale that simply boggles the mind. I'm talking about an area the size of Portugal, which contains absolutely nothing at all. Go to the centre, get in a Ferrari Enzo, put on a blindfold and set off in any direction that takes your fancy. And flat out, at 200mph, it'd be over an hour before you even felt a ripple through the wheel.

There's just one problem. You can't actually drive an Enzo over these salt flats because they have all the structural rigidity of a crème brûlée. There's a seemingly firm outer casing of ice-white salt, but it's not that thick and underneath you have about a hundred and eleventy four billion dead sea creatures which, over five million years, have turned into slime.

Way back when, the rift valley was formed and created the largest inland sea in the world. And then the planet started to heat up – I have no idea how because the Range Rover hadn't been invented at this point. Anyway, the water started to evaporate until one day it was gone, leaving all the creatures dead and covered with a thin sprinkling of salt. That's what you have today and the only way of getting across it is on a quad bike.

Now, the quad bike has had a fair degree of bad press in recent years. First of all, we had Rik Mayall damn nearly killing himself when his turned over and then, more recently, poor old Ozzy Osbourne breaking what's left of his body in two when his pulled a wheelie, throwing him off the back.

If you want to kill your children, there's no quicker way that I can see than buying them one of those 50cc jobbies you sometimes see at garden centres. My son went on one the other day and, in less than two minutes, he and it were in the swimming pool.

And yet there I was, on the edge of the Makgadikgadi, on a bitterly cold pre-dawn morning in August, with my wife, my three children and two guides – the ridiculously good-looking Ralph and an 18-foot Zulu called Super. No, I'm not joking. Super is his real name.

Super was going to be tail-end charlie for our 250-mile trek. But first, he had a health-and-safety lecture to deliver, Botswana style. Two weeks later I'm able to quote the whole thing verbatim. It went like this . . .

'Let's go'.

There were no helmets, no high-visibility jackets, no disclaimers to sign, no lectures on what to do if you were to be hit in the face by a giant meteorite and no reason that Super could see why our seven-year-old shouldn't drive her bike the whole way if she wanted to. Which she did, very much.

An hour into the journey we stopped at random and began to poke about in the salt. Pretty soon, we'd found several early-iron-age pots, and a little while later, a human leg bone. My eldest daughter also found a couple of diamonds.

I turned out to be very bad at archaeology, mainly, I suspect, because my head is very far from the ground. At one point I dropped my iPod and it took me damn nearly half an hour to find it again.

Anyway, I was genuinely surprised to find so much history just lying around and asked Ralph why it hadn't been hoovered up by tourists and thieves.

He was incredulous, pointing out that in the last 5,000 years, no more than a few dozen people have been onto the flats at all. He gave me odds of a billion-to-one that no human had ever stood where I was standing. Slightly weird feeling that.

We set off again and, after another hour, the view was incredible. Because there was nothing in it. Nothing. Can you imagine that? Utterly, absolutely flat white ground and an utterly absolutely flat blue sky. No clouds. No distant hills. Nothing. Except a bad smell.

This, it turned out, was coming from a dead aardvark, which had been drawn onto the pans by the heat haze, which he'd mistaken for water. Then he'd fallen through the salt and got stuck. Which is pretty much what we did, next to his rotting corpse.

Wisely, Ralph had provided us with Yamaha Bear Trackers, a light, two-wheel-drive machine that, in theory, glides over the surface, leaving almost no clue that it's ever been there. Unfortunately, when you do break through, you must rely on the rear tyres alone to get you out. And they can't.

So then you must get off, sink up to your knees in pulverized frogs and push. This is very tiring.

Soon, however, we reached firmer ground, climbed back on board, opened the taps and . . . aaaaaaaaargh.

Now there was a spray coming off the front tyres directly onto my shins. It looked like water but was, in fact, a highly saline liquid, which is the opposite of acid. But, Christ, it burns.

'No problem,' said Super, 'so long as you get it off within three days. After that, it'll eat through the skin'. Great. Our safari was scheduled to take . . . three days.

Luckily, soon we were stuck again, and I found that a million rotting trout will cure alkaline burns.

By this stage it was nearing noon and the temperature had rocketed to 35 degrees. Out there, in the big white, with no helmet, doing 30mph into the wind, my face was beginning to ripen badly. Super tossed me a ko koi, which is a sheet of material, like a tablecloth, that, if you know what you're doing can be fashioned into a hat-cum-face cover. I made a mess of this, and ended up with what looked like a table-cloth-cum-tablecloth draped over my head.

In the course of the afternoon, it blew off 7,000 times. Eventually, I decided I'd rather have a burned face. And then I got a puncture. I knew this because suddenly the bike veered to the left.

Sadly we had no jack. But we did have an 18-foot Zulu, which is the next best thing. And he was useful again when neither Ralph nor I could see far enough over the horizon to spot our overnight rest-halt; a granite island covered in baobab trees that pokes through the salt. Thankfully, Super could.

As we made it back to base, burned and knackered three days later, we realized it had actually been a genuine voyage of discovery. I loved it more than any journey I've ever made. You can drive something amazing and that'll enliven your life. But if you drive somewhere amazing, that's even better.

An Enzo across Belgium or a quad bike across Botswana? No contest. No contest at all . . .

November 2006

Spending money

Because he's eight, James May likes to invent games he can play when he's not in the bath, mending motorcycles or being made to practice the piano by his mother.

One of these games is called 'Airport Departure Lounge Dare'. It involves trailing through the shops, trying to make a friend or colleague buy stuff the poor gullible fool neither likes nor needs. Apparently, Richard Hammond is a complete sucker and now has a house full of compass cufflinks, digital cameras, currency converters, inflatable pillows, half a hundredweight of shortbread and God knows how many very expensive orange watches.

Me, though, I'm a lost cause. It doesn't matter how much James stands over my shoulder, soothingly explaining that I look great – 'very sexy' – in a pink Hermès tie, I will not buy it because I have a tie already. I also have some cufflinks, some shortbread and a watch. And I do not need a currency converter because I have a head instead.

Hammond and May spend 86 per cent of their lives looking at old cars, and bits of old cars for sale on the Internet, 10 per cent playing 'Airport Departure Lounge Dare' with one another and the remaining 4 per cent, saying, 'Right. I'll show you.' And getting their cheque books out.

If you paid them in meat, they'd eat it, so because they're paid in money, they spend it. It's why Hammond has ten cars, including a rubbish old Land Rover and a nasty Vauxhall

Firenza. And it's why May has 400 old motorbikes, all of which look like they ought to have a sidecar.

But I'm allergic to spending money. I don't mind blowing it on someone else – that's why I bought May a pair of pink aviators – but I cannot buy something if I have an example of it already. It's why I have one tie, one hat, one coat, one pair of shoes and, most importantly of all, one car. May sees this as a challenge. So, the other day, after he'd tidied his room and fed his pet cat, he started trying to talk me into a Gallardo Spyder.

'It's very you,' he said. 'Lambos are very now. And you can't very well spend your entire professional life extolling the virtues of the supercar if you don't have one.'

I should have put my fingers in my ears and sung at the top of my voice. But I really do like the baby Lambo, so he was pushing against an open door. And as a result, I got into the car with him, and Hammond, and went to the nearest Lamborghini showroom.

When we arrived, May availed himself of the colour chart and suggested, in soothing, gravelly, hypnotic tones, that I should have sky-blue paintwork, an orange roof, a lime-green interior and purple wheels. This from a man whose Porsche is brown and whose house is beige, with a hint of more beige.

I ignored him and, to get out of there, made a casual deal with the salesman that I'd love to buy a Gallardo Spyder and that I'd be in touch soon to go through the options list. Yet again then, it seemed like May's idiotic attempt to sucker me into his world of 'Airport Departure Lounge Dare' had failed.

But then Hammond went upside down and in the mess that followed I clean forgot to tell the salesman I wasn't serious. In fact, I forgot all about our trip to the dealership, until a few days ago, when I received an email saying my car was about to be built and they wanted to know what colour to paint it. Eek.

My word has always been my bond and I had said I'd buy one. So that was that. I was back in the showroom with the options list, speccing up a car that's not quite as nice to drive as a Ferrari F430. No really, it isn't. Both cars are as exciting to drive as being on fire and then putting yourself out by jumping over Niagara Falls. But in the Ferrari you feel like you're in flame retardant clothes and that you have a parachute. You feel in control; you feel connected.

Yes, of course, it's all fake. Computers choose the noise made by the exhaust and what the diff does in each bend. But, my God, it works. The F430 is as delicate as the snare drum work on Radar Love.

The Lambo is more smash and grab, more mechanical, more like the drumming you get from Frank Beard on *Sharp Dressed Man*.

It's also a lot more expensive, for reasons I don't understand. You have a sense with the Ferrari that every nut, and every bolt and every gigajoule of computing power is designed specifically for that car and to be as good as current technology allows.

So I began chomping through that options list like it was a maize field and my youngest daughter was lost and in great danger on the other side. Yes, I want a TV. Yes, I want a trip computer. And yes, of course I want a hydraulic nose that lifts itself up when it's presented with a speed hump. I kept going so long in fact that the poor girl who'd been despatched to make a cup of tea, made it all the way to Bombay and back with the leaves. And now, all I have to do is wait for the Italians to build it.

The thing is; he won't be quite as pleased as me, because although the European Car of the Year judges have awarded the top prize in 2006 to the Ford S-Max, and *Top Gear* magazine has gone – for good sensible reasons – for the Jaguar XK, we telly boys think that the best, most fun car to emerge all year was Lambo's new soft-top. And I'll have one. And James May won't.

Apparently, it'll be finished and on its way this month. James May will be beside himself. This will be his greatest ever result in 'Airport Departure Lounge Dare'. It's one thing convincing Hammond that novelty socks are all the rage and that he should have a pair, but quite another talking someone into the orange interior of a £150,000 supercar.

December 2006

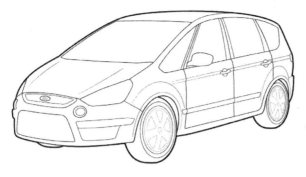

CAR OF THE YEAR: FORD S-MAX

2007

TOP 5 BESTSELLING SINGLES
SONG TITLE – ARTIST

1. Umbrella – Rihanna
2. Valerie – Mark Ronson featuring Amy Winehouse
3. Grace Kelly – Mika
4. Ruby – Kaiser Chiefs
5. Bleeding Love – Leona Lewis

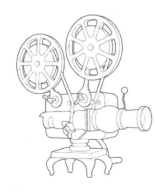

TOP 5 BOX OFFICE MOVIES

1. Spider-Man 3
2. Shrek the Third
3. Transformers
4. Pirates of the Caribbean: At World's End
5. Harry Potter and the Order of the Phoenix

The Germans

I know that there are enough scare stories coming out of North Korea and southern Afghanistan right now to frighten us all to death. And I don't want to pour petrol on the flames, but has anyone had a look at what's going on in Germany?

Yes, I know. In a world of easy global travel, Internet access, the United Nations and rolling twenty-four-hour news programmes, it's inconceivable that a Western power could get uppity without any of its neighbours noticing.

But then it was inconceivable in 1918 that just twenty years later Germany would be ready to take on the world again. And let's not forget, the Fatherland has been as good as gold now for sixty-one years. That's the longest period of peace in their history. Statistically, they are well overdue for a bit of fisticuffs.

And with the world looking under rocks for Korean nukes and Saudi terrorists, now would be as good a time as any for Germany to re-arm and try for Moscow once more.

Of course, you may say that they are reducing the number of Eurofighters they initially ordered, and that's true. You may also note that they have no nuclear weapons, a smaller navy than us and a constitution that actively prevents them from going abroad in a tank.

What's more, if you go to Germany, you find them in bars, singing along to peculiar oompah music, and slapping one another on the back. All appears to be fine. But is it? I only ask because DaimlerChrysler appears to be behaving very strangely at the moment.

Not that long ago, the only four-wheel-drive car they made was the G-Wagen, a rough-and-tumble sort of Bosch Land Rover for the German army. And they're still making it, even though they now also do the ML-Class, the R-Class and the GL-Class as well. And I haven't even counted in this lot all the Jeeps and wotnot made under the Chrysler banner.

Why do they need to make all these different types of off-road car? Especially now as the global warming debate, er, heats up. Where can they be going with them? I'll tell you what. If I were Polish, I'd be giving up my plumbing job in Wakefield, going home and putting some cans of baked beans in the cellar.

Of course, you might argue that this is nonsense, and that DaimlerChrysler needs all these different models because the world is very demanding. We're no longer happy with a cup of instant. We want a skinny latte with extra water and a dash of espresso.

Hmm.

The thing is, I can sort of see why you might want a G-Wagen. It is because you have to drive round London selling drugs and guns. And I can see why you might want an R-Class. It's because you are stupid and can't see that the Volvo XC90 is much cheaper, much more practical and much better.

That brings us to the ML-Class. It's a good car. I'd have one like a shot if I woke one morning to discover I'd suddenly become allergic to the Range Rover. But I'm afraid, when it comes to the GL, I'm stumped. I can see no reason why anyone, mental or otherwise, would choose to spend upwards of £50k on a car that seems at face value to be just like its brothers, only less wieldy, more expensive and uglier.

Plainly, I had to find out, so I rang Merc and asked for a test drive. One day later it was nosing through my gates, and a week after that, the rear end arrived as well. My word, it's big. 5.3m big. And wide with it.

Later, I was on the Earls Court Road in London and thought, for no particular reason, that I should get into the left lane. So, I did all the right things. I checked my mirror, I indicated and, after I'd established all was well, I moved over – BANG – straight into the kerb.

It turned out I was already in the left lane. And the centre lane. And the right lane, all at the same time. What's more, the nose of the car was outside the restaurant where I was having lunch, while the rear was coming out of the BBC's car park. In Birmingham.

It felt like I was navigating the Shropshire Union Canal in the *USS Dwight D. Eisenhower*.

I think this is a car designed for use mostly in America. It certainly looks that way, with all sorts of unnecessary styling details and chromed bits and bobs – the sort of stuff simple people and children like.

Inside, you'd expect more seats than you'd find in a bendy bus. But no. There are in fact, just seven.

I'm not a hysterical man. There are many things that annoy me – church bells, for example – but there are only a handful of things I'd actually want to ban. Church bells are one. The Mercedes GL is another.

It seems to me that while the aviation industry is attracting much of the socialists' ire at the moment, the car is still teetering on something of a brink. Any perceived arrogance from the motor industry and it could have a dramatic effect on government policy.

Already we're seeing celebrities queuing up to appear green. Nearly every Hollywood actor claims to have a Prius and here, things are equally bleak. Davina Whatsername from *Big Brother* says that while she wants a Range Rover, she feels guilty about the damage she might do to the sky. And the gorgeous Fiona Bruce is thinking of selling her XC90.

People are starting to fall for the spin. That's why Land Rover is planning on making the next Range Rover weigh half what the current model does. It's why Toyota is making hybrids. It's why BP won't shut up about trees. So why is Merc introducing the GL, which is so wasteful and stupid it annoys even me?

I don't mind if you want to buy a 4x4, I really don't. I think you're a bit of a loony if you have one in central London, but would I stop you? No. Because it's no skin off my nose, and even if it is true that you're making the world hotter, good frankly. I like it when it's warm. This summer was lovely and if the world's petrolheads and school-run mums helped create that, I think we should pat ourselves on the back.

That said, however, I damn nearly got out and shot myself the other day as I tried to reverse the GL into a parking space. As I inched forwards and back in a blizzard of beeps from the infernal parking sensors, I was holding up half of the world. And when I finally decided it really wouldn't fit, I had to try and get it out again. By the time I'd done that, I was holding up the other half of the world too.

Sure, that night, the GL rode through a flood that its big V8 engine had apparently caused, and it was a smooth and quiet companion on the rush-hour drive to Oxfordshire.

But I'm sorry, it serves no purpose and I give fair warning now: if ever I find myself sitting next to someone at a dinner party who has one, I shall stab him in the eye with my fork.

In the meantime, I would urge MI6 to have a quick look under the Bundestag. It might be nothing, but when it comes to Jerry, you can't be too careful . . .

January 2007

The Porsche GT3

I can't quite remember how we left Hannibal Lecter in the last 'Silence of the Sheep' film. As I recall, he'd sawn the top off Ray Liotta's head, lost his hand and was on a plane, offering brain paté and crackers to all and sundry.

Or was he being eaten by a pig? Or was he setting fire to a man in a wheelchair?

The fact is that Lecter creator Thomas Harris only ever gave Hannibal a very small role in his first book on the subject of mass murder, but since the movie boys moved in, he's been turned into one of the biggest baddies in cinema history. Which is another way of saying 'milked to death'.

But even so, I understand there's to be a new Lecter film next year in which we see the cannibal as a young man, growing up in Eastern Europe. I daresay he will eat his mother and feed his father to the dog. And then he'll splash on a bit of exotic aftershave, and generally make a nuisance of himself in various set-pieces designed to get the audience vomiting.

We see this with James Bond too. I'm the hugest fan of 007 and know most of the films off by heart, but even I will admit that while *Moonraker* produced the best Bond villain of them all – Michael Lonsdale – it was such a stupid story that the only way to go afterwards was backwards.

Today's Bond films, as a result, aren't really Bond films at all. In the early days, we had long scene-setting sequences – the carnival in Rio and the funeral in New Orleans, for instance. They were impossibly glamorous and set the films apart from other home-grown movies, which mostly featured Robin Askwith peering through windows in places no more exotic than Wakefield and Plaistow.

Today, though, we can go to Hong Kong for 300 quid. We can see the carnival in Rio on a web cam. We can ski and scuba dive and do all that Bondy stuff whenever the mood takes us. Bond, thanks to Ryanair and the Internet, lost his glamour.

And now, in Casino Royale, he's lost his gadgets too. Because why give him a watch that can undo a bra strap when the world is awash with Vin Diesel and Arnie and a host of other secret agents whose watches can be used to get stones out of horses' hooves?

So what are we left with? A bloke with a biggish packet and a triangular torso in a film that everyone agrees is pretty good. But would it have made the grade were it not for *Thunderball* and *For Your Eyes Only*? Would *Casino Royale* work without the history? This, of course, brings me to the new Porsche GT3 – the latest offering from the 911 franchise.

In essence, it's a stripped-out, ready-to-race version of the Carrera 2. So you get a roll cage instead of back seats and a massive fuel tank instead of a boot. You also get tyres that are nigh on slick, a spoiler big enough to serve as a landing strip for small aircraft and a ride quality with all the give and compliance of a Chechen terrorist.

This car, then, is exactly what you don't want to find in the car park of your London flat when you have the worst hangover in the world and you need to be in the middle of Gloucestershire for 8.30 a.m.

As I rode down to the basement in the lift, holding on to

the walls with one hand to stop myself falling over, and my head with the other to stop it coming off, I didn't know what sort of car my wife had left down there. Fondly, I imagined it might be a Rolls-Royce Phantom. Or maybe a bright grey Honda Legend. Or anything with wallowmatic suspension, excellent air-conditioning and an engine that made no noise at all.

The GT3 was wrong in every way. And to compound the issue, it is, of course, a 911 – a car I've never liked. My relationship with this brainchild of Hitler is curious. I've always enjoyed driving them, apart from the 1992 RS, which was horrid – and purple, if memory serves – and I've always admired the quality. But they've all failed to put their hands down my trousers and give me a squeeze. I find them as emotionless as limestone and, as a result, I would never even think of buying one.

No matter. In his review in *The Sunday Times* recently, esteemed writer Andrew Frankel said that the GT3 is a car you cannot drive slowly. Well, I'm sorry, but at 7 o'clock in the morning, in a horrid wet London rush hour, when you have a pile-driver in your head, trust me on this, you can. And I did. And, boy, was that car nasty.

Uncomfortable, noisy and fitted with a gearbox that wouldn't ever go into gear, along with a pair of front tyres that had been fitted with minds of their own. You can do what you like with the steering wheel, but if those Michelins snout a bit of camber that takes their fancy, forget it. You're going where they want to go. I'm not joking. If a snow plough had left one of those little grooves in the road, I would now be writing this from the snow plough base. Because that's where I'd have ended up.

Later in the day, when the hangover had been blitzed, then, yes, of course, the GT3 shone. It was an exciting companion on the road, as good as any Ferrari and, at a whisker under £80,000, good value too. I liked very much the way it soared to nearly 8,500rpm before I needed to change gear, and the huge traction afforded by those fat back tyres and the flat-six engine on top of them.

I even quite liked – in a 'shit, I'm going to die' sort of way – the moments when they lost traction and the car wiggled its hips while it decided whether to kill me or not. All this seat-of-the-pants, thrill-a-minute stuff was in keeping with the ice-white paint and the shouty styling. So, make no mistake, on the right road this GT3 is what engineers call 'a right old laugh'.

So yes, it works without the history: if this had been the first 911, we'd love it so much we'd all want to lick its private parts. But is it better than the last GT3? Or the GT2? Or the GT3 RS? Maybe, on a track, some decimal points could split them; maybe there, among the marshals and the red and white kerb stones, the spoilers and the roll cage would look less ridiculous. But on the road, I'm buggered if I can tell the difference – any more than I can tell the difference between an Evo 8 and 9.

It is, in this respect, a bit like a Bond film. The same basic formula endlessly tweaked and fiddled with to make it 'different'. But the fact is that, with its camber-hunting tyres and no boot, and a chin spoiler that's defeated by even the smallest sleeping policeman, it's a bit of a *Moonraker*. So if I were going to buy a 911, I'd stick with the basic Carrera 2 *Thunderball* or the turbo *Goldfinger*.

Look at it this way: in the whole of cinema history, the

sequels that have been better than the originals can be counted on one hand. There was *French Connection II*, *Mad Max 2: The Road Warrior* and The Godfather: Part II. And that's it. And the best Hannibal Lecter film was *Manhunter* – the Michael Mann original.

February 2007

4x4s

If you're a dizzy bird who's just read something in the hairdresser's about how your big SUV is murdering polar bears, then it's really not difficult to find a smaller, less bear-killing alternative.

The Range Rover you have now is, in essence, a five-seat estate car, so you could have a BMW 5-Series, an Audi A6, an Audi A4, a BMW 3 Series, a Mercedes C-Class, a Mercedes E-Class, a Ford Mondeo, a Vauxhall Astra, a Vauxhall Vectra, a Ford Focus, or any one of about a million Nissans, Toyotas, Skodas, VWs, Citroëns or Fiats. Or, if you are really worried about bears, an Oyster card.

Yes, I know you live in Surrey where the roads are sometimes covered in twigs or frost, but trust me, you'll be able to manage without four-wheel drive. No, really, you will. Cross my heart and hope to die.

We heard recently that sales of four-wheel-drive cars dipped by 15 per cent in November, and most industry analysts reckon there will be similar falls in 2007. So eventually, I presume, the car makers will get the idea and stop making them altogether. That's bad news for the Army.

Replacing our boys' Land Rovers with Renault Espaces is a bit like replacing their boots with flip flops. It won't really work.

I've just been reading a book about the history of Britain's special forces – well, it beats the crap out the book my wife is reading, which is called *Cloud Atlas* – and I learned something intriguing. Contrary to popular myth, the SAS was not born from the Long Range Desert Group. It was born from the commandos and simply used the LRDG as a taxi service.

And here's something even more intriguing. To get around the desert, the boys had to use ordinary 2WD trucks. This, they say now, was jolly tricky.

I should say so. Have you ever tried to drive in a desert? If you try to keep the revs low, and use low-end torque to pull you along, you will sink into the sand. If you keep the revs high and the wheels spinning you will sink into the sand. And if you do anything in between, you will also sink into the sand.

Driving over sand in a two-wheel drive car is like trying to marshal air with a dustpan and brush. It cannot be done. And yet, somehow, those boys did it. Digging and heaving and shoving and pushing their trucks over the softer stuff, and then blasting over the shale in the hope they'd have enough momentum to climb the next dune.

But not so much momentum that they'd reach the top of the dune with too much speed . . . and take off. One heavily laden truck, apparently, was going so fast when it reached the ridge, it flew for 96 feet. And broke the driver's back when it landed.

Many things prompted the SAS to ditch the LRDG, chief amongst which was their capacity for theft. They could steal anything from Army supplies and some of the things they stole were a handful of new-fangled American Jeeps.

They fitted them with two twin machine guns, fore and aft, and would whizz about the desert blowing up more Italian and German planes on the ground than even the best fighter ace could manage in the air. Put very simply, four-wheel-drive helped Britain win the war in North Africa. And today it's still being used in the fight against the Taliban and the insurgents in Iraq.

Unfortunately, while the Americans have replaced their Jeeps with Humvees and moved on, Britain is using a car that's based on a WW2 relic. The Land Rover Defender.

I had the honour of being allowed to drive an Army Land Rover when I was in Basra last year, and honestly, it was like stepping back through a 200-year time portal. I've seen trees grow faster. And it was more top-heavy than a mushroom.

Much to the amusement of the Americans, they're called Snatch Vehicles and they're supposed to get troops into and out of a battlefield quickly. Yeah, right. If you try to do anything quickly they fall over, and the only reason they don't is because they're fitted with the smallest engines in the world.

They put me in the driver's seat and feigned an attack on my 'wing man'. I screeched to a halt, the soldiers in the back leaped out, the 'injured' from the other vehicle were brought on board, a grenade was lobbed into the other vehicle to stop it falling into enemy hands and then, as the back door on my car slammed shut, the sergeant shouted, in that Army, boomy way, 'Go, go, go!'

I tried. Really, I did try. But we set off at a speed even Jane Austen would call pedestrian. And yet, despite the slowness, as I swung us round to get us away from the 'trouble', I thought we were going to roll over and crush the men who were poking out of turrets on the roof, giving what they call top cover.

We are told that Britain is getting its arse kicked in southern Iraq and I'm not surprised. Never mind better housing, better vests and better hospitals—all of which are important—what our troops need is better, faster, less top-heavy transport.

I keep thinking of the Bowler Wildcat, fitted with flame-throwers and machine guns. That's what the SAS would have chosen if it were 1943 and they were up against Rommel.

Then there's my Land Rover, which has a 3.9-litre V8. That's what the Army would have been given when Britain was an empire run by an empress, or even a kingdom ruled by a king. But of course today we're a country run by a, er, man, so it won't happen.

The plan at present is to replace the Land Rovers with a vehicle called the Panther. It looks like a mini Humvee, and is designed specifically for the military, so it paints a low radar image, goes pretty fast and can be fitted with whatever level of armour the commanders see fit.

Great, but it's made by Iveco, which is owned by Fiat, and that of course is fine ... for now. But Fiat is not in rude health at the moment, so in the future it may well be bought.

And that's where things get tricky. Bought by whom? The Chinese? The Libyans? The North Koreans? Who may decide the best sort of armour plating, actually, is cardboard.

Really and truly, British troops should use British equipment. They should use Land Rovers, and Land Rover should be working on a new Defender now, with that in mind. But instead, they're working out how to survive in a world where bear-obsessed dizzy women no longer want Range Rovers. This means our troops will soon be asked to defend our nation from the seat of a North Korean Fiat Uno. So, there we are then. It seems we're in a race. Whether we kill the polar bears before they have a chance to kill us.

March 2007

Top Gear content

As Top Gear finished its much-delayed run a few weeks ago, the cheery continuity announcer said that the show would be back in the summer. Well, I'm sorry, love, but it won't be. Not unless someone from the Greenwich Observatory suddenly decides that we need a new month between May and June.

The fact is that it takes four months to film enough material for a run of *Top Gear*. And then another couple of months to turn the miles of tape we generate into something you might actually want to watch. So trust me on this, no one has a clue when Top Gear will be back.

But assuming we do come back to BBC2 at some point in the future – October, if we're lucky – our problems will be far from over. Because as I write, no one has much of a clue what the programme should look like. I'd therefore like your help.

Here's the problem. When Richard Hammond went upside down last September, we had pretty much finished filming everything we needed for a nine-week run leading up to Christmas. Oh, there were a few loose ends to finish off: the limos, for instance, had been bought and converted, but not tested at the track nor used to deliver celebrities to a glittering gala do.

Then came the accident, the postponement and the news that only six programmes could be shoehorned into the slot we eventually used in January and February. We had material for nine shows. But only six to show it. So what to leave in? What to leave out?

Economics won the day. It is hugely expensive to make triple-header events like the America run, the farming story and the limousine test. And it's fairly cheap to drive a manufacturer's test car round some corners on a quiet country road or on our track.

So if we were going to ditch anything, it'd be the cheaper stuff: the road tests. And if we were going to show anything, it'd be the big films featuring James, Richard and me. The ones that need three crews, a few days on location and countless late nights at the edit.

As a result, and quite by accident, the series that's just finished was full of us three cocking about, and almost completely devoid of anything you might fairly call 'a road test'. You had us growing petrol, getting stuck in Fulham, being hounded out of Alabama and resurfacing roads. And about two seconds of a Porsche going round corners in Lincolnshire.

This has gone down very badly with the people in Internet land. After every show, they dived into their forums and moaned like Nigel Mansell stuck in a jet engine that their beloved car show had become an entertainment show for the terminally childish. They're right too. Perhaps we should have changed the name to Last of the Summer Petrol.

All these people want to know why there aren't two or three proper car tests a week. And not car tests where I drive around shouting 'poweeeeer', but proper ones done by James where every nut, bolt and torque is taken out and examined.

What they want, secretly, is Chris Goffey back. And I'd love to oblige. I'd love to spend the day hooning around in a

599 or a lightweight Gallardo. I'd love to make those cars live for you on the screen. It'd be great.

I'd even love to take that little Fiat Panda 100hp for a spin and wonder out loud how many Nurofens you'd need to take before the headache it generated went away. And whether that many Nurofens will actually kill you.

But galloping like a huge, shit-stained horse over the horizon comes the problem: is that what the vast majority of the viewers want? Not you. Not your mates in cyberland. But the vast swathe of people who just want to flop down on a Sunday night and watch entertaining telly. I suspect the answer is a Thatcheresque, 'No. No. No.'

We always knew that when Richard Hammond made his triumphant return to the programme, the viewing figures would be enormous. And they were. We even beat the final of *Big Brother* into a cocked pig. And then we sort of thought they'd tail off again, when people realized the Hamster wasn't going to suddenly fall to the floor and start dribbling.

But they haven't. Apart from a slight blip for the America special, the figures climbed like an F-15 on combat power, until we finished with 8.6 million people watching the end of the final show. To put that in perspective, it's pretty much twice what a very successful programme could dream of getting on BBC2 or Channel 4. It puts us on level terms with *EastEnders*. It means we are, give or take, the most watched show on the BBC. And that's just in Britain. Factor in the rest of the world and *TG* is effing massive.

Great. Secretly, the producer and I take these figures to the pub and, having read them, pour champagne into one another's underpants. We are very proud. But what do we do when the next series begins?

Do we go back to the old days, driving round corners in saloon cars to the accompaniment of Bad Company and 'His Mobiness'? Or do we keep on annoying the Internet dweebs from Norway and North Carolina by continuing to cock about?

I desperately want to make a film comparing the Audi RS4 Avant, the BMW M5 Touring and the Mercedes E63 estate. I want to show those of a 4x4 disposition that there's a life in a stratum below where they normally live. A more fun-filled, oversteery sort of life, where you get home more quickly and with a bigger smile on your face, and (because hippies and Communists only care about four-wheel drive) with less egg on your windscreen as well.

I want to test that new Punto Abarth Fiat is talking about. I want to wring its neck round our track and drive it all over Wales. Then there's the new M3. That versus the new V8 Lexus would surely be one of the great twin tests of the modern age. Which is fastest? Which generates the most g through the Hammerhead?

Who knows? And who cares? I suspect the majority of the audience would rather we loaded both cars into a large plane, flew over the Arizona desert and then pushed them out to see which hit the ground first.

You may say that, as a public service broadcaster, we shouldn't care about viewing figures; and it's true, we shouldn't. We can take them to the lavatory for a little moment of pleasure, but we can't skew programmes to make them as big as possible or we'd end up with Jade Goody and the Hamiltons being loaded into the cars before they were pushed out of the transport plane . . .

Anyway, although we won't chase figures, we still have to give the audience something you want and like. Which means we should make *Top Gear* an entertainment show featuring cars, rather than a car show, which isn't as boring as your wife and kids feared.

Or have I got that all wrong? I'm stuck on this one and would love to hear your views. Obviously, you can write to us here at the magazine, or you can go to our website and do a blog, or whatever it is you do on websites when you're not masturbating.

May 2007

Classic cars

Last month, James May explained to us all that his entire collection of old cars and motorcycles never works.

Well, of course it doesn't. Nothing works when it's old. People, trees, machines, even planets, fall victim to old age. One day, the sun will breathe its last, so why should the same not be true of a Honda CB250?

Even donkeys don't last for donkey's years. I know this because, earlier in the year, one of my donkeys, who was called Geoff, suddenly decided he'd been around for eight years and that was enough. So he died. And this morning, his wife, Kristin Scott Donkey followed suit. Aged ten.

But, of course, there's no point explaining any of this to James and others of his ilk, because they actively want a collection of non-functioning motorcycles. It gives them a chance to get their fingernails dirty and to spend time in their sheds, which they prefer to their wives, obviously.

I don't understand this, but then neither do I understand the appeal of riding a motorcycle with brakes from the time of Chuck Berry's ding-a-ling. And steering from when British cinema comprised entirely of Robin Askwith hiding in a wardrobe so the vicar wouldn't see him in his underpants.

Surely, this is the same as buying a television from the Seventies. Why would you do that? Because you prefer the fuzziness of the picture to the high-def plasma you could have had? Because you like getting out of your chair to change the channel? Or is it because you wanted something that sets fire to your house if you leave it on for more than an hour or two?

Everything made now is better than everything made yesterday. That is a simple, inescapable fact. A digital camera is better than one of those boxes that illuminated the subject by blowing up a light bulb. An iPod is better than a wax cylinder. And James's Fiat Panda is better than all the old motorcycles in the world put together.

And yet . . .

We watch those F1 cars piling into the first corner, and we know that whoever comes out of it in the lead will almost certainly win the race. Because one thing's for sure. His car will not be leaving the track in a cloud of smoke, steam, fire and brimstone. And that, dare I say it, is a little bit boring.

I've just spent eight days at the incredible Ascari track in southern Spain, filming every single supercar that money can buy. It was a punishing schedule, pounding round and round in savage, face-melting heat day after day. And, predictably, all but two of the cars suffered some kind of problem.

You want to guess which two? Go on. I bet you a million pounds you are wrong.

Nope. Not even close. It was, in fact, the two Lamborghinis: the Murciélago Roadster and the Gallardo Spyder. While the others cooked their brakes, boiled their power steering fluids, ate their water pumps and shattered their clutches, the Lambos just powered on and on like a brace of Energizer Bunnies. It made them feel invincible, reliable . . . German. And is that what you want from a Lambo?

Yes, obviously. But, at the same time, no. Not really.

Let me explain. As you are probably aware, I recently drove to the North Pole with James May, who may (or may not) snore. It's hard to say for sure because the farting is so incessant and so loud that you can hear nothing else. He is a sinus and an arsehole.

Anyway, we drove a Toyota Hilux, which had been modified by an outfit called Arctic Trucks in Iceland. It was a brilliant machine: tough, powerful and capable of functioning when everything else – the cameras, the sound equipment, the cookers and my iPod – had been killed by the cold. It was also utterly reliable and, as a result, I never bonded with it at all. Now let's compare that with the Camaro Z28 I bought for the trip across the southern states of America last year. It had very little clutch, the power steering was broken, the radio would only play gospel, there was a dead body in the boot and six gallons of cow juice in the passenger footwell. On top of this, it broke down on a fairly regular basis. And yet, despite all of the above, I loved it.

The fact is that a car which works all the time is displaying what Charles Babbage called the unerring certainty of machinery. But a car that breaks down, overheats and coughs when asked to move is displaying some peculiarly human qualities.

Of course, I don't want a car that coughs, overheats and breaks down when I'm trying to get to London for a meeting. But nor do I want a Toyota Corolla, which is built to function without fault.

And I think the answer to the problem is to be found at the Lucknam Park Hotel, just outside Bath.

I used to go there a lot, and it was heavenly. It's Georgian, of course, it's made from honey-coloured stone and is exactly the sort of place that would cause Jilly Cooper to fall to her knees and weep. Why? Because it's old, so therefore it's full of character. But unlike one of James's old motorbikes, it works. You don't have to wait six hours for the water to arrive, and when it does arrive, it's not grey. When you flush the loo, there isn't a banging noise from the basement that causes any wildlife within 15 miles to run for its life. And all the windows shut properly.

In other words, what we have here is a charismatic building with bang up-to-date innards. Hot and cold running plasma, jus, and a swimming pool that's a bit hotter than the centre of the sun.

I believe the car industry should learn from this and immediately start to make the cars they used to make forty years ago. Only better.

Recently, I drove a Ferrari 275 GTS from the mid-Sixties, and it was much as you'd expect. Terrible. The grip ran out at 40, it accelerated like a Greek afternoon, and I'm willing to bet its spark plugs stop working whenever there's an idiot in Number 10.

But my God, what a looker. What character. What human flaw in the design and the detailing. I mean, who thought it was a good idea to put sixth gear exactly where your passenger's crotch would be?

It has, in other words, all the qualities we look for in a car, all the little foibles that mean we have to tailor our driving style to get the best out of it.

I realize, of course, that there are many companies which can fit old cars with modern components. But what I'm talking about here is Jaguar making an inch-perfect replica of the old girl, using all the things they have learned about car production since. Imagine that.

Imagine, too, James's CB250 with a modern frame, a modern engine, a modern gearbox, a modern electrical system, modern lighting and modern bodywork. He'd have the style he's after. And he would never need to get his fingernails dirty. I even have a name for such a contraption. Trigger's Broom.

October 2007

Risk taking

Spent some of my summer holiday on a small Caribbean island. Created by a volcanic burp at some point in our ever-changing world's past, it was what most people would consider to be paradise.

Surrounded entirely by the sort of sea you normally find in airbrushed travel brochures, it was ringed by an uninterrupted sliver of perfectly white, perfectly deserted beach and, further out, a tropical reef blah blah Jacques Cousteau blah blah etc.

There were no hotels and the only other house I could see from ours belonged to Bruce Willis. Hopefully, you have a mental picture of the scene because now we move onto the meat and potatoes. You see, the island in question was only a few miles long and a few miles wide. So how do you get about?

It's too far to walk from the one shop to the little dock where people keep their boats, but it would be ridiculous to drive. And so, while there is one pickup truck – used to pull boats out of the water when a hurricane is coming – the residents move around in a collection of communal golf buggies. It's all very communist. You help yourself to a cart and then, if you're the last to use it at night, you have to plug it into the mains and charge it up.

Brilliant. No noise, no fumes, no pollution, no jams, no sense that Bruce's golf cart is bigger than mine and I must respond. And, of course, absolutely no chance of anyone being even slightly killed . . . You'd think. But that ain't necessarily so because, you see, sticking its oar into this Liberal Democrat's idea of heaven comes something called youthful exuberance. Mix that with a T-junction and someone's going to need the flying doctor.

If the golf buggy had had an engine, the person going the other way would have heard it coming. But it didn't. So he came round the bush, and bang. Of course, you may argue that a golf buggy can only do 15mph and that no harm can come to a driver at this speed. True enough. But when it has a head-on with another buggy, also travelling at 15mph, you have a 30mph impact. Doesn't sound like much? Really? Well try running face first into a wall and then send me an email explaining how things turned out.

Did the accident bring everyone to their senses? Yes . . . we thought. But wait, what's this? Why, it's a teenager attempting to do a donut in his buggy. And over there, there's an eleven-year-old trying to jump his over an iguana. This is the problem, the concept that our friends in the yellow and green parties just can't seem to understand. That, for some, taking risks is fun.

Of course, they'll say that the people I'm talking about are yobs. They'll point to someone called Darren in a Nova, doing handbrake turns in a Tesco car park. But me? Well I'll point to Steve Fossett.

As I write, the American adventurer is missing in the Nevada desert. There are fears that he's crashed his plane and that he's dead. It'll be a terrible shame if it's true, because Steve, to me, is what the baby Jesus is to the Archbishop of Canterbury.

I met him once many years ago and he didn't really fit the profile. I knew, from reading his biography, that he'd made a fortune on Wall Street and since retiring had raced at Le Mans, swum the Channel and beaten the world speed record for crossing the Pacific in a sail boat. So I was expecting him to be a cross between Gordon Gekko, Thomas Crown and the Terminator. I was expecting him to break every bone in my fingers when we shook hands and for him to slap me on the back with such force that my spine was shattered.

This turned out to be wrong. 'Can you tell me where Steve Fossett is?' I said to a man in tatty combat trousers, sweeping the floor in a big aeroplane hanger. 'That's me,' he said quietly.

He was a rubbish interview, stammering and not quite being able to enunciate what drove him. But when the cameras were off and we were just chatting, he was funny, extremely kind and driven by a quest for adventure so powerful that if you took out his soul, it could be used to light the world.

Since our meeting, he's gone properly berserk, setting twenty-three world sailing records and nine distance race records. And when he breaks a record, he doesn't do things by halves: when he crossed the Atlantic in 113 hours, he shattered the previous record by nearly two days.

Most people would have had their work cut out keeping ahead of the game in the world of sailing. But not Steve. Because during this time, he set a new record for crossing America in a non-military jet. His average speed was 726mph. And then he turned round, went back to the West coast and set a Transcontinental record for turbo props. Then he broke the record for crossing Australia. And then he broke one for flying round the world. Of seven world records for fixed-wing aircraft, Steve has three.

On top of this, he's broken ten of the twenty-one world

records for gliding. He's gone further than anyone else and he's been higher – 50,727 feet. And then, just last year, he got back into a powered plane and flew round the world again, without refuelling, in seventy-six hours and forty-five minutes. The longest flight in history.

I have nowhere near finished. He has competed in several triathlons, is one of only eight men to have done all of the world's ten toughest ski races, he has done the 1,165-mile Iditarod Trail Sled Dog Race in Alaska and he has piloted an airship at 71.5mph. Another absolute world record.

And I haven't even got to the ballooning yet. He was the first to cross the Pacific in a balloon and, after six attempts, the first to go all the way round the world. You get the impression he's circumnavigated the globe more often than most 747 pilots. Oh, and he's climbed six of the world's seven highest mountains.

He disappeared while on a flight looking for somewhere in Nevada where he could break the land-speed record. He had the car – 47 feet long and powered by an afterburning jet engine from a Phantom F4 – he just needed somewhere to drive it.

A menace? A one-man carbon snowshoe? I don't think so. I dislike using the word 'hero' because I think it should be mainly reserved for soldiers. Or at the very least people who risk their lives to help others. But in a way that's exactly what Steve Fossett did. He risked his life to show that there's still some hope in the Liberal Democrat's stupid vision of a perfect golf-buggy-and-cotton-wool world.

At the very least, that makes him an inspiration.

November 2007

Attraction

Right now, I'm looking out of my window at the new Subaru Impreza WRX, and I'm sorry, but there's no getting away from the big, all-consuming, overpowering fact that, despite a number of outstanding features, no one in their right mind will buy such a thing. Because it looks like it's been hosed down with a massive and sustained burst of fire from the ugly gun.

There is no excuse for this. There are designers at Subaru who can create a pretty car. You only need cast an appreciative eye over the Legacy shooting brake to know that. But Subaru obviously felt that when it came to the Impreza, the badge alone would be enough to carry the day. And therefore allowed the styling to be done by the boss's dog.

They are wrong. No one will buy an ugly sofa, no matter how comfortable or cheap it might be. And while women harbour the Austenesque notion that men find kindness, a good heart and a sense of humour important when looking for a spouse, the fact is that what we really want is tits like the Alps, legs like the Silk Road and a face like Kiera Knightley's.

I like a painting. But I will not buy one, no matter how deft the brushwork, or how well the artist captures the natural light, if the subject matter is James May's scrotum. Because I would not find that attractive.

And look at animals. If I told you the Dobsonfly – the ugliest creature ever to walk the earth – was in danger of extinction, you'd be glad. If, on the other hand, I showed you a picture of some cute little tiger cub that was about to be chopped up by a Chinaman who wanted its bones to make his penis bigger, you'd be on the first plane to Beijing, full of hate and righteous indignation.

No one gave much of a damn when the hideous dodo went West. But when Al Gore says baby polar bears are all drowning (they're not, by the way), half the bloody world puts its patio heaters on eBay.

I'll give you a simple fact. When it comes to cars, looks are everything. What first catches a person's attention is not the reaction time of the sequential 'box or the size of the boot. It is the styling.

You might imagine, if you've seen the clothes I wear, or the hairstyle I choose, that I wouldn't be able to tell the difference between a good-looking car and an ugly one, even if my life depended on it. But look at the cars I've owned over the years: a Mark 1 VW Scirocco, a BMW 3.0 CSL, a 1500cc Honda CRX, an Alfa Romeo GTV6, a Ford Escort Cosworth, a Ferrari 355, a Mercedes SL and SLK and a Lamborghini Gallardo Spyder. Not a minger among them, you'll note.

And it's the same with everyone. You hanker after a Ford Mustang or a Corvette, not because of the noise or the power, and certainly not because the interior is so tasteful and well-appointed. No. It's because of the way they look. It's why you want a supercar. It's why you never wanted a Pontiac Aztec or a Bristol. It's why I have the Lambo now and not a 430. Because, and this isn't a matter of opinion, it is much, much prettier.

What made the Vauxhall Nova such a hit among the nation's youth? Because it was such fun to drive? Because it was so well-made? Because it was cheap to run and cheap to insure? Nope. It's because it had flared wheelarches.

And it's exactly the same story with that all-in-one crumple zone known as the Citroën AX. It won the hearts of every lout and yobbo in the country because, despite the Algerian carrier bag build-quality, it looked great.

I could go on giving you examples from now until the end of time, but I think the case is proven beyond reasonable doubt. Looks matter, whether you're a person, a table, a dog, the crockery in a restaurant or a gun. And they really, really matter when it comes to cars.

Which brings me back to the Subaru and a big question. Why aren't all cars good-looking?

Did the boss of Subaru look at the clay model of the Impreza and say, 'Yes, I especially like the droopy arse and the way it doesn't in any way match the front. Oh, and I see you've put a life-size model of the Sydney Opera House on the bonnet. Well done.'

No, he didn't. He must have known it was even more ugly than David Abrahams, and yet he gave it the green light. And now millions of Subaru fans will have to buy something else instead.

This brings us to the long-wheelbase Mitsubishi Shogun. What's that all about? Who thought that rear-window arrangement would work? And the BMW 1 Series, and the Chevrolet Tacuma, and the Chrysler PT Cruiser, and its sister the Crossfire Crapping Dog.

And the Fiat Doblo, and the Citroën Picasso, and the Morgan Aeromax, and the Mitsubishi i, and the Peugeot 307, and the Toyota Avensis and its ridiculous mutant cousin the Prius.

I haven't finished yet. There's the Seat Toledo, the Renault Mégane, the Jaguar S-Type, the Mazda 5, the Kia Sedona and that Hyundai whose name I can't be bothered to remember.

Why were these cars made? We know it's possible to make a pretty car, so why employ a stylist who cannot? It doesn't make any sense.

I think the problem is simple though. Today, everyone is too polite. When Jenkins comes in with his ideas for the new car, the bosses are slightly in awe of his polo-necked jumper and his thin glasses. What's more, they know he's been toiling away for months on the project, and they don't want to reward him by saying, 'That's terrible.'

It'd be like saying to a new mother whose just shown you her baby, 'Jesus Christ. I think I'm going to be sick.'

I think, however, that since looks and style are the most important part of a car, the board of directors is going to have to gird its loins, follow the example of *The X Factor*'s Simon Cowell and speak its mind.

This brings me neatly on to a friend of mine, who, while staying in Bermuda recently, was invited to a swingers' party. His wife was unwilling to go but, being a decent sort, said that she wouldn't mind if he went on his own.

Sadly, this wasn't possible. The invite said, 'Couples only'. So he spent two whole days trawling the local bars and night-clubs looking for someone – anyone – who was willing to accompany him.

By his own admission, the girl he eventually found was not what you'd call a looker. But since it was a swingers' party, he felt it wouldn't matter.

It did. He arrived at the address, where a burly bouncer with a curly-wurly, FBI-style earpiece pointed at the girl and said, 'That won't do.' And shut the door.

You feel sorry for the 'that'. I should imagine it was very hurtful. But who knows. Maybe it was just the impetus she needed to go home and do something about her appearance.

I choose my final words on the Impreza carefully, then – that won't do.

December 2007

CAR OF THE YEAR: FIAT 500

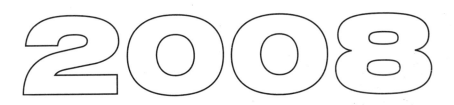

TOP 5 BESTSELLING SINGLES
SONG TITLE – ARTIST

1 Hallelujah – Alexandra Burke
2 Hero – X Factor Finalists
3 Mercy – Duffy
4 I Kissed A Girl – Katy Perry
5 Rockstar – Nickelback

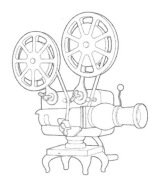

TOP 5 BOX OFFICE MOVIES

1 The Dark Knight
2. Iron Man
3 Indiana Jones and the Kingdom of the Crystal Skull
4 Hancock
5 WALL-E

Motor racing

You may not understand the appeal of motor racing. You may not like it. But me? I have never understood how it is technically possible. Think about it. If you are in the lead, you take the fastest line through the corner, which means the chap behind has to be on a slower line. This means he cannot get past. It is impossible.

And how do you outbrake someone into a bend? The chap in front will brake at the last possible moment, which means you have to brake beyond the last possible moment. And to make matters worse, you have to brake more because you'll be going faster, and you'll be off line.

Any attempt, therefore, to make an overtaking manoeuvre in motor racing can only result in one thing: your untimely and extremely painful death.

This is one of the reasons why I have always found it easy to say no when someone has offered me 'a drive'. There are other reasons though. I look stupid in racing overalls. My head is too large and misshapen to fit in a helmet. And for some extraordinary reason, I'm always busy doing something else when the invites arrive. 'Oh, I'm sorry. I'd love to, but I've just looked in my diary and I'm planning on laying an egg that day.'

Once, however, I gave in. It was for a charity of some sort, and though it would be held in front of a Silverstone Grand Prix crowd, we'd all be driving measly Honda Civics. Better still, I wouldn't be up against lantern-jawed superheroes called Clint Thrust. It was a field full of people like John Alderton and Jeremy Irons.

At Stowe, on lap one, I put my theory about the impossibility of overtaking to the test and found it flawed. I did get past. But I don't know how, because I had my eyes shut from the moment I stamped on the brake pedal.

It was so frightening I began to hyperventilate, which caused my visor to steam up. And as a result, the chap I'd got past retook the place immediately.

The next lap, I realized I was catching him again and that, if I wasn't careful, I'd be in a position to overtake once more at Stowe. Since I'd tried it once, and had found the experience to be less enjoyable than catching genital warts, I lifted my foot ever so slightly from the floor.

No one was any the wiser and it meant I didn't have to do any silly hero plunges into the corners. Everyone was happy and I came third. Feeling a bit sick and vowing that I'd never do it again.

So I don't quite know how I ended up back at Silverstone for last year's Britcar 24hrs. But I do know this. I loved it. And that makes me very angry.

Over the years, I've tried my hand at all sorts of things that you might call hobbies. I collected stamps as a boy. I had a train set. I've attempted to put up shelves, gardening, reading, chess, jigsaws, golf, tennis, painting, bird spotting, and looking at pornography on the Internet. And I've been extremely bad at all of them.

And then, at the age of forty-seven, when it's far too late, I discover something that I can not only do, but which, more importantly, I absolutely adore. Endurance motor racing. At face value, it looks like normal motor racing.

There are motorhomes and laptops and people in branded

shirts rushing about, pretending to be Bernie Ecclestone. But there is one difference . . .

For the first half of the race, everyone is keen to do as many hours as possible. And for the second half, everyone wants to finish. This means that when you want to overtake someone, they get out of your way. There's none of that scrabbling around that you get in a sprint race.

And what made this doubly enjoyable was that our little BMW diesel, which we'd bought from the classifieds for £11,000, was such a joyful car to drive. Even with a revised engine management system, it wasn't what you'd call fast. In fact, it was what you'd call slow. But with lower, stiffer suspension, slick tyres and bigger brakes it cornered and gripped like no car I'd ever driven before.

All the way from Stowe to the pit straight, it was an easy match for everything up to, and including, the 911s. On one occasion I made a lunge for the supercharged works Jag and, even though I'd started from a long way back, I damn nearly made it.

Lesser stuff: Golfs and so on? They were a breeze. Our car could outbrake them easily and outgrip them as well. Often, the stuff that comes out of the *Top Gear* technology centre is a bit of a disaster. But that BMW? Jesus. It was astonishing.

Truth be told, though, you never really compete out there against other cars. When you come across a pair of tail lights in the night, you don't know what it is, what class it's in, whether it's 200 laps ahead or 300 behind. So, it's not really racing.

Honestly then, what you do is spend most of your time competing against your team mates. Trying to go faster than they did. Sadly, in my case, this was a waste of time. There was no way I could be as fast as the Stig, even if I'd fitted warp drive. And, without wishing to be too disloyal, May and Hammond were a bit pedestrian.

I therefore spent most of the time competing against myself. Trying to make each lap a little bit faster, and a little bit smoother, and a little bit kinder to the tyres than the one that went before. I found this more satisfying than almost anything I've ever done. Certainly, it was more successful than my shelves. Or my golf.

And for the first time I began to understand all that motor-racing chit-chat I'd heard over the years. When the tyres go off, you really can feel the grip going. And when we lost the front splitter, which I'd only attached because it looked good, we also lost four seconds a lap. Yes. One bit of plywood makes you four seconds a lap faster. But it was the night-time I enjoyed most. Aiming for a corner you can't see and then feeling the inside tyres kissing the rumble strips was so wondrous that sometimes I think I may have even been nursing a semi. Conversely, aiming for a corner you can't see and then finding it's not there because you're on the other side of the track is so alarming that your blood boils and your teeth move about.

As a result of this massive range of emotions, you never feel tired. Not even when the tyres are shot or the tank is empty and you have to pull in for a break. You sit there, in the garage, with everyone telling you to get some rest, but you can't because your blood is fizzing like champagne and you are just so excited.

Strangely, however, I never felt like I was in any danger. Everyone assumes motor racing is only one stepping stone from the Pearly Gates, but at Silverstone, in a diesel BMW, it felt no more perilous than sunbathing. Mainly because the barriers are all so far away I would have died of old age before I hit them.

It's not a cheap thrill this. Quite apart from the cost of the car, and the modifications, our tyre bill at the end was £6,000. Money, though, should concern no one engaged in a pursuit of happiness. It was invented for spending. And I can think of nothing I'd rather spend it on.

Oh, and just in case you think these are the ramblings of a senile old man who thinks he could have been Michael Schumacher if he'd been given the chance, consider this: James May, aka Captain Slow, agrees with every word. Next year, I suspect we may be back.

February 2008

Old saloons

Last year, I trawled through all the large executive cars on the market today and concluded that they're all rubbish. Oh, they have things that swivel, and buttons that summon air support, and the LS600h is glorious for cocking a snook at our whisky-sodden Mayor of London, as it glides immunely past the congestion-charge cameras while using a gallon of carbon-juicy fuel every three inches.

But all large cars are as cool as a crusty French loaf. And they're all grey. Turn up anywhere in any one of them and you will immediately be marked down as a Rotarian. A businessman. A bore. Someone who thinks the 19th hole is on a golf course and the 20th is in his wife.

You ever wondered when you see a 5 Series cruise by, or an Audi, or a Jag or an E-Class or a Lexus, why there's only one person inside? It's because no one likes him very much.

And this is a problem for me because, truth be told, I've known for some time that I need a saloon car. The Lambo, the Merc and my wife's Aston are lovely, but whenever we want to go anywhere with the children, we have to use the school-run Volvo. Which is like clattering around in a diesel-powered wardrobe. Or the Land Rover which, because it's a Land Rover with a TVR engine, works only when there's a wolf in the month.

The solution, of course, is a Range Rover. I love them. Every time I drive one I get all sticky with affection. You know when you try on a jacket you can always tell straight away that it suits you. Well, that's how I feel when I'm in a Range Rover. That I'm the teapot and it's the comfy woollen cosy.

The trouble is that we live in a country full of vegetablists, communists, hippies, social workers and various other lunatics who've got it into their thick heads that people in Range Rovers are somehow causing people to have soggy sofas in Tewkesbury. So they glower and leave rude messages under the windscreen wipers. This is very annoying. It makes me cold-prickly when what I want from a big comfy car is to feel warm-fuzzy. The upshot? Well, as a family, we tend to stay at home most of the time playing computer games because I don't like driving the Volvo, the Land Rover's throttle cable has broken and everything else in the yard only has two seats.

But then I had a brainwave. Car makers may not have the ability to make an interesting, cool, non-businessman saloon today. But that wasn't the case in the past. So I have bought a Mercedes 600 Grosser. This is the car used by Lewis Winthorpe in the film *Trading Places*. It was also used by Idi Amin, Mao Tse Tung, Leonid Brezhnev and Elvis Presley.

From 1963–1981, this was the most expensive, most advanced and most governmental car in the world. When I have fitted flags to the front wings – black eagles on a red background – I shall feel like Mussolini.

Mine is thirty-eight years old, 38 feet long and, because it uses hydraulics rather than electric motors to move the seats, the bootlid, the doors and the windows, I shouldn't be surprised to find it weighs 38 tons. It is a piece of dark-green metallic magnificence.

Or it would be if it would move. Sometimes, the starter

whirrs enthusiastically, but having been unrewarded by either a spark or a supply of petrol, it loses interest and fades to an asthmatic wheeze.

Other times, it just clicks – signifying that, for some reason, the battery has forgotten what it is, and is hanging around in the engine bay imagining that it might be a hammer, or a fighter plane. I therefore called an expert on the 600 and asked him to check out the points. That made me sound like I knew what I was talking about. I also asked him to check the carburettors. That made me look like I didn't, because the 600 is fuel-injected. Anyway, since he didn't need to check the carbs, he had some spare time, so I asked him to give the car a once-over to make sure it's mechanically sound.

In my mind, I knew it would be. You can always tell just from looking at an old car whether it's been cared for, or whether the undersides are being held together by friction and bits of dried-up fox that it's run over. Mine was kosher. I knew it.

And I was right. The expert has had a chance to plug it into various machines and agrees that while the bodywork is a bit pitted here and there, the mechanical components are in good order. Apart from one or two little issues, which he has detailed in a short, 800-page document.

Let's kick off with the brakes. They are good except the fluid condition is low, the offside front disc is marked and will judder, the nearside front disc is smeared with oil and may need a new caliper, which costs £3,000.

The front pads are worn and will need replacing at around £500 a pop, both rear brake discs are rusty and marked, the offside rear anti-dive pivot is worn, the nearside pivots have slight play and the nearside rear anti-dive gaiter is perished and split. This means I won't be stopping in a hurry. But it doesn't matter because, chances are, I won't be going anywhere anyway.

The list of what's wrong under the bonnet is so long, it's easier to list what's good: the compression. Everything else is split, worn, broken, bent, leaking, flat, incorrectly fitted, backwards, upside down, rusty, empty or loose.

I called the man to talk through the issues and as I sat, for several days, listening to the tale of woe, I wished, for the first time in my life, I was James May. Someone who understands what's broken. Instead, I just made a selection of what I thought might be appropriate noises at various intervals.

Then we got to the V-belts. There are seven in a 600 and, combined, they take 50 of the engine's 300bhp. And guess what? They are not loose, leaking, broken or empty. But they are noisy. 'Well,' I said, 'if they are being noisy and using all my power, let's just take them off.'

This isn't possible it seems, as without them the car will either not run, or will run briefly before exploding. I think the man on the other end of the phone thought I might be a lunatic.

Anyway, it seems that the propshaft coupling is good. The wiper arms may be bent, the rear bellows cracked and split, the front exhaust pipe bouncing on the road, the fuel tank dented and the fuel pump even noisier than the V-belts. But joy of joys. The propshaft coupling is good.

'Well, yes,' said the man. 'It's good. But the bolts holding it are incorrectly fitted.' Of course they are. Wouldn't have expected anything less. And what makes this litany such a face-reddening, bowel-loosening experience is that this car comes from when Merc didn't make its cars out of diamonds, because they were too weak. The exhaust system, for instance, is welded together. With myrrh probably.

That makes a replacement not only expensive to buy but also eye-wateringly expensive to fit. Then you have the four electric window switches. Take a guess? Go mad. Let your mind run free.

Nope. You're wrong. They are £5,000. Not including labour. Or VAT.

The thing is, though, even if I buy a whole trolley full of electric window switches, and several spare exhaust pipes, the Grosser will still have cost me less than Johnny Rotarian's 540i. And when it's working, gliding from place to place on its air suspension, I tell you this: it will be the coolest car on the roads today.

March 2008

Electricity

Thirty years ago in South Africa, there was white power. Then there was black power. And now there is no power.

No really. There isn't. The electricity-generating company over there has just announced that the power stations are not capable of meeting demand and that there will be outages for two, three or six hours a day for at least the next seven years.

So far as I can see, no one is asking why this has happened. Everyone suspects it's because the power company, since it took over the reins from De Boer Pik Racist, has been operating a policy of only employing black people. So the whites, the ones who know how to run a power station, have left the job of generating electricity to a bunch of guys who don't know how to.

No one's actually saying that of course. It's a political potato so hot that you're going to get your fingers burned if you even whisper such a thing. And anyway, working out why the country's run out of juice is nowhere near as important as working out what the bloody hell you can do about it.

I'm old enough to remember the power cuts we had in Britain when Ted Heath went to war with Johnny Miner. They were great. You had newspaper clippings on the wall telling you when the lights would go out, so you could plan your supper accordingly. And when they did go out, all you really lost was the television, which only ever showed grown-up crap like *Panorama* anyway.

This meant your parents were forced to play Monopoly with you by candlelight, and as a child that was epic. Sitting huddled round a coal fire, warm and comfortable, with the undivided attention of your mum and dad. I get a warm, melted-toffee tummy just thinking about the joy of it all. And I still remember the sadness I felt when Heath gave in and the lights came on again.

Today, however, things are extremely different, and not just because I'm an adult. Because when you lose power today, you don't just lose a 40-watt bulb and Robin Day in a black-and-white beehive. You lose absolutely everything.

I was in South Africa last month when the lights in my hotel room flickered and died. So did the TV and so did the aircon. And so did the phones. And so did the wall sockets that were being used to charge my laptop. And so did my mobile. If I'd had an iron lung, that would have gone too.

But I don't have an iron lung, so I toddled off into the city to do a bit of shopping.

Nope. Because today, most city-centre shops are in windowless malls, so when the lights go out, you have no clue what you're getting. I wanted a rather nice framed butterfly, but fearful that I might actually be buying a washing machine, I felt my way back out of the shop again and gave up.

Not that I could have bought anything anyway, because the tills were down, and so were the remote credit-card readers. Seriously, you have no idea what paralysis a power cut brings these days. Not even the stock exchange was working properly. And if you want a generator, you'd better have nice tits and loose morals because, frankly, that's the only way you're going to get one.

I found myself wondering, as I skipped up the darkened streets, past the gridlocked traffic, hemmed in and going nowhere because the traffic lights weren't working, what on earth Britain would look like should such scenes be repeated there. Chaos, I don't think, is a big enough word.

I'd lose my computer, my PlayStation, my iPod, my coffee machine, my kettle and even the ability to get into my gun safe so I could shoot the looter who'd just come through the front door. The only good news is that all those sanctimonious fools who'd bought a G-Wiz would be stuck at home, unable to fill their stupid little car with juice.

You might think it won't happen here, but if you look at what's happened in Denmark, you'll change your mind. Like good communists, the government has jumped on the eco bandwagon and carpet-bombed the nation with 6,000 wind turbines.

But together, they produce only 19 per cent of the nation's power needs. And this is Denmark we're talking about, which has a population of seven, a Lurpak factory and two blokes called Bang & Olufsen making everyone's stereo thinner.

What's more, not a single one of Denmark's normal power stations has been closed down since the windmills were built. In fact, they are running at full capacity, twenty-four hours a day because Mr Bang and Mr Lurpak don't want to be faced with darkness every time the wind drops. Which it does. Often, and without warning.

Of course, here in Britain, the government has sensibly decided to go down the nuclear route. But trust me on this, by the time the public enquiries are over, and they've dragged Swampy and his mates out of all the trees, America will have invaded Iran, buggering up the oil supply, the Russians will have turned off the gas, and we'll be back in the Seventies, playing Monopoly.

The only possible way all this can be averted is by rounding up everyone who opposes nuclear power and shooting them. Unless, in the meantime, Honda comes to the rescue.

You may have read about the fuel-cell car they are running in California. Uncharacteristically, we even sang its praises on *Top Gear*. Unless that bit was edited out for not being funny. I can't recall.

Anyway, the idea is that a company somewhere, possibly in Iceland where you only have to drill a hole in the ground and free electricity floods out, makes hydrogen. This is then stored. And then you, the motorist, buy a card and insert it in your car. Once there, witchcraft happens and the car moves.

I do not even begin to understand how hydrogen is used to make electricity and how that electricity is used to propel one ton of car, but I do know this: all that comes out of the back is water. Pure, clean, drink-it-when-you're-thirsty liquid silver. I also know that hydrogen is the most abundant entity in the universe.

Of course, you might think that this is all terribly dreary, that no matter how the electricity is produced, it's still an electric car. That when all is said and done you're still going to work every morning in a glorified G-Wiz.

Aha. But here's the really good bit. You see the Honda they're testing in America produces 100 kilowatts, which is a lot. And if the starting point for this technology is a nice round ton, you can only begin to imagine how much Porsche and Ferrari will be producing in the next ten or twenty years. By 2028, you'll be doing 200mph again.

Of course, you might think this has absolutely nothing to do with the complex business of providing power for your PlayStation and your iPod. But here's the thing: even if I were to turn on every light in my house, and every appliance and every gadget, I'd barely use 10 kilowatts.

So the car, with its silent engine, could simply be plugged in to your meter cupboard, and Bob's your uncle. Even the Honda we have now could generate enough of a zap to power the whole street. And forget having to stock up on Evian and Perrier. Simply attach a hose to the exhaust and sip from the fountain of Honda's genius.

Back at the beginning of the twentieth century, the motor car saved the world from the disease and pestilence brought on by having so much horse shit in the streets. Today, at the beginning of the twenty-first century, it's about to save it again.

April 2008

Porsche

I don't want a Porsche Boxster. There are several reasons for this. First of all, while it's beautifully made and beautifully balanced, it's a bit cramped for fully grown men, the clutch is a bit of a faff and the styling's a bit backwards. Most of all, though, I don't want a Porsche Boxster because James May has one. And there is, quite literally, nothing in his life that I covet. Not his postcode, not his old motorcycles, not his hoopy jumpers. Not even his swish new Vickers Velos aeroplane.

However, parked outside my house right now is a limited-edition Porsche Boxster called the RS60 Spyder. I've been using it for the last seven days, and I've decided I don't want one of these either.

Partly this is because it isn't a limited edition at all. It's just a normal Boxster S with a button that makes the exhaust a bit louder and an interior finished in what they call Carrera Red. Oh, and it has a 'unique' front spoiler designed primarily to make a hideous graunching noise on every single one of Oxford's 2.5 billion speed humps.

Of course, the RS60 Spyder name is designed to stick its hand down the trousers of every Porsche enthusiast in the world and remind them, with a warm squeeze, of some long-forgotten racing car that Fortesque Major took to victory in the Mille Florio of 1903. But it doesn't. What this car does – what every Boxster does – is sit outside your house reminding you that you couldn't quite afford a 911.

I don't want a 911 either. And no, this has nothing to do with Richard Hammond. Yes, he does have a 911, and that's bad – I mean, look what it's done to his hair – but then he also has one of every other car in the world, so abandoning the 911 just because some fridge magnet in the Welsh borders has one wedged between his cross-eyed Morgan and his Vauxhall Firenza is silly.

I wish I did want a 911. I love the way they drive. I love the way they look. I love the way they are built. In my life, right now, a two-wheel-drive 911S would be absolutely perfect. So why did I buy the souped-up SLK55 Hitler-mobile instead?

Maybe you think I'm heading towards the Cayenne. Nope. Things I'd rather have include ebola, six elbows and an unquenchable desire to goose the Pope. It's brilliant. Tougher than you could imagine and properly fast. But it simply doesn't float my boat.

This is odd. We are all aware that there is a chemistry between people. You meet someone, and before they've even drawn breath to speak, you know you hate every fibre of their being, and would like to hit them over the head with a shovel. Certainly, I felt this way when I first met Piers Morgan.

But how is it possible to have a chemical reaction to a ton and a half of wiring, glass, steel and oil? Why do I now want a Mercedes SL65, which is a pointless car that has so much torque it will only accelerate downwards, through the centre of the Earth, and not a Porsche turbo, which is excellent?

I understand, of course, why some people deliberately buy awful cars.

Take the Citroën Picasso. This is a car for people who drive everywhere at 40. On the motorway. On the A44 when I'm in a rush. Through villages. In garden centres. Everywhere. Styled to be non-threatening, it manages, by trying not to be offensive to anyone, to be offensive to everyone. So why does anyone buy such a thing when there are so many alternatives? A wheelbarrow, for instance, or a holiday in Guantanamo Bay, or gout. I'll tell you why. Because the Citroën is cheap.

It's cheapness that causes people to buy a 4WD Kia. They need something to pull their caravan up a muddy field, and while they'd like a Range Rover, it's too expensive. That makes perfect sense to me. If I were a caravannist, with a family to feed and a modest income, I'd probably buy a Kia.

No, come to think of it, I wouldn't. If I were a caravannist, with a family to feed and a modest income, what I'd actually do is kill myself.

What I'm bothered about, though, is what happens when you take value for money out of the equation. When you are making a purchasing decision in which dealer service, fuel economy, carbon dioxide and government tax bands are not an issue. In short: what I'm bothered about is why don't I want a Porsche.

It's not the badge. Speak this quietly, but I was the only person in the world who wanted a 924. I knew that it had an engine from a Volkswagen van and that it took six years to get from 0–60mph and that it cost a million pounds and you were only paying for the badge. But it had pinstripe velour seats, and I liked that.

And then they fitted flared wheel arches and a new four-cylinder 2.5-litre engine to create the 944. I wanted one of those so much I ached. In fact, if I were to draw up a list of the ten best cars I've ever driven, the 944 turbo would certainly be included. You can buy them these days for five grand.

By rights, I should hate the 928. It was the first press test car I ever crashed. And I used one to go and see my dad the day before he died. I also disliked the dreadful ride quality in later models. And yet, even today, when one grumbles by, my head does the full Linda Blair. It is, I think, one of the best-looking cars ever made.

So what's happened? Why did I used to like Porsches and now I don't?

Image? Well, yes, there was a time when a flat-nosed, guards red 911 with a whale-tail spoiler was an automotive precursor to the imminent arrival of a twat. But since then, the cocks have been through the BMW phase and are now tailgating your arse with big, fast Audis. So what's stopping me?

Happily, I think I have an answer. In the old days, Porsches were flawed and a bit flamboyant. The 944 had flared arches. The 924 had a van engine. The 928 had chequered flag seating. In brown. You got the impression they were designed by people who understood the whole business of cars. Not just how to make them go round corners.

Today, though, I have the impression that Porsches are built by people who have an enormous collection of small screwdrivers. They really like choosing the exact composition of the tyres and the precise calibration of the fuel injectors. This is why the engine bay of a 911 looks like the back of a washing machine. It's because it was developed by engineers, possibly the best in the business, and they don't really care about aesthetics. They only want to build an equation, a formula that will go round the Nürburgring as quickly as possible.

So, when you buy a modern Porsche, you are demonstrating to the world that you are very interested in driving. And being 'very interested in driving' means that, for you, it's a hobby.

This is bad. Hobbies are for people who were caught masturbating as a child. They were told by their mothers that it'd drop off unless they got out of bed and did something useful. So they did. They built model planes and collected stamps. Some may have taken up ornithology. This will have made them very unpopular with their peers, who could think of many more exciting things to do with bushes and birds. Show me someone in a 911, and I'll show you someone who was bullied at school.

I have no statistics to hand, but I bet a great many golfists drive 911s. It's because of what their mums told them. That they must have a way of filling their time that doesn't include shuffling off to the loo with *Asian Babes*. They are not wankers, then. And that, weirdly, is exactly the problem.

August 2008

Idiots (part 2)

As we know, Royal Ascot is a place where the great minds of Britain dust down their top hats and gather in the presence of Her Majesty the Queen to watch some of the world's finest equine breeding stock compete for glory on a course steeped in pomp, circumstance and history.

Oh no, hang on a minute. I seem to be stuck in the wrong century. Because now the whole event has been hijacked by a bunch of overpaid Audi-driving chavs with rented fancy dress costumes and flammable wives, who think we'll mistake them for great-minded philanthropists simply because they are there, smoking parvenu cigars, drinking the wrong champagne and being terrified that they are all holding the picnic cutlery incorrectly. As if a great mind could give two shits.

This month, I sat at a party next to someone who had tickets for this hateful glimpse into everything that's wrong with *Heat*-obsessed Britain, and she had about her person a letter instructing her on the dress code.

Now let me make one thing absolutely plain. Dress codes are for the terminally stupid. Telling your guests what to wear implies that a) you are a megalomaniac or that b) you've invited such a bunch of witless fools, they'd all turn up in bearskin hats if left to their own devices. I simply will not go to any establishment that requires me to wear a suit, or a tie. And even if my bestest friend were to celebrate his fortieth birthday with a fancy dress party, he'd be doing so without me.

Anyway, the dress code required for Ascot was even more

barmy than I could have imagined because it said tans must not be streaky and that knickers must be worn. What kind of halfwit cares about how the chavs paint themselves orange? And surely, if the whole place is going to be full of spivs, the only upside is that we get to see some arse every time there's a gust of wind.

What puzzled me most, though, is who gets the job of checking? 'Can I see your ticket, miss? And now if you'd like to stand on that mirror . . .' Actually, I'm thinking of introducing a similar policy for the *Top Gear* studio audience. Speaking of which . . . I understand that it's very difficult to get tickets for our studio days. People stop me in the streets all the time, saying they've been trying for years and then, just last month, a story appeared in the papers saying the waiting list, even as it stands now, will take eighteen years to clear.

You would imagine then that those who do get tickets are mustard-keen fans, eager to be a part of the moment when we stitch all the films together. We certainly hope so, because without audience laughter and a bit of banter, it's a flat day for us, and we end up with a useless, dull-sounding show.

Mostly, the audiences are great. But recently – I won't say when, for fear of upsetting any good guys who were there – we found ourselves faced with 700 zoo animals. You could have cracked the funniest joke in the world and all you'd have got in return was a face full of tumbleweed. It was horrid, and it made me very cross to think there were thousands of people sitting at work that day, who hadn't got tickets because they'd all been sent instead to the cages of the Cotswold Wildlife Park.

This has made me think. You know how foreigners coming to Britain are soon to be faced with a 'citizenship' test before they are allowed to live here? They'll have to say they know what a wee wee is and that it's considered bad manners to rape your hostess at a dinner party.

Well, surely such a test could be implemented at Ascot. 'Do you have an Audi RS4?' If yes, you are a cock and you can't come in. And we could adopt it at our studio too. 'What is a Mercedes?' If you think it is a type of grain, or the top of a carrot, you are barred, just as surely as if you turn up wearing knickers.

September 2008

Mopeds

Sometimes, you just want to run around the fields, screaming. We've got the Green Party hosting its annual conference in the School of Oriental and African Studies in London, not because it's convenient, or because it's an especially eco-friendly building, but because it's got the word 'African' in the title. And the Greens want a law that forces television companies to screen their party political broadcasts. Give me strength. Honestly, I'd rather watch *Hollyoaks* than that lot with their chunky jumpers and their fair-trade teeth.

Then you've got the government. Did you know that since the Labour Party came to power in 1997, it has introduced 3,605 new laws? That's nearly one a day. As a result, you are no longer able to disturb a pack of eggs unless instructed to do so by an authorized officer. Nor may you sell a game bird killed on Christmas Day.

But while they are very good at bossing us about, they plainly don't have the first idea what to do about anything else. Take transport as an example. Gordon Brown wants us all in battery-powered cars by a week on Wednesday, but does he have a clue where all the electricity that will be needed to power these cars will come from? Does he hell.

He's got half the Green Party on top of every power station chimney in the land, and the other half living in trees where he plans to build some more. Nuclear power? Yes, he likes that very much, but sadly, despite his completely mad predecessor claiming that the three most important things in the country are 'education, education and education', nothing's actually been done, so now the number of people in Britain qualified to design and build a nuclear power station is about none.

As a result, we've had to go to the French, who are behaving like those Froggy soldiers in *Monty Python and the Holy Grail*. Sniggering a lot and telling Mr Brown they'd love to help him build his shiny new power stations, but it won't be possible for another 400 years because they're a bit busy at the moment building them for countries they actually like.

And as our politicians dither about, making silly noises, and oil prices continue to scream toward the heavens like they're trying to beat some kind of altitude record, everyone in the country is facing a simple choice. Shall I spend this week's wages on a pint of fuel for the car, or on a pizza for the kids' supper?

Then, last month, some jumped-up little pipsqueak waded into the debate, wondering why demand for expensive organic food is down 19 per cent. Well, let's think . . .

It's because people haven't got any money, you twat. When your house is worthless, food costs more than gold, you are facing redundancy and petrol is a million pounds a gallon, you are hardly likely to spend a hundred quid on some shrivelled-up mushroom just so a polar bear can have a bigger playground.

Happily, the only place I like to see a polar bear is without the meaty bits, in front of my fire. With Cameron Diaz on it.

I don't care about how much carbon dioxide is in the upper atmosphere, I don't care about genetically modified crops, or whether the Olympics will be sustainable or not. I don't care about whales, or Tasmanian tree frogs. Because really, all that matters is getting people to and from work easily, so they can earn money, which they can use to buy food and heating oil. The end . . .

Except it isn't the end, because you join me now in Hanoi, which is the capital of Vietnam. This is the fifty-seventh poorest country in the world. The average wage is £500 a year. People live in one room, with their pigs and a buffalo. It is exactly the sort of place, then, to which stupid do-gooders come to see if they can teach the locals the ways of the West.

Strangely, however, I think we'd be better off seeing if we could learn a thing of two from them.

You see, despite Vietnam having a population of 86 million, a habitable land mass about the size of Luxembourg and very few roads, you never encounter what we'd call a traffic jam. This is because in Vietnam there are almost no cars. But 20 million motorbikes. And that number is growing by 3.6 million a year.

As you know, I am no fan of the motor bicycle. I do not wish to wear a leather romper suit. I do not wish for my spleen to end up in someone I don't know, just because there was a diesel spillage. And I do not wish to do 0–60 in two seconds on a machine that can't stand up by itself and which is utterly bamboozled by a small pothole.

However, the motorbikes in Vietnam are not the R1s and Fireblades we have here. They are small; 125s mostly, with a top speed no one even tries to reach because, when you earn £500 a year, you simply don't have money to blow on a thrill.

No. The motorbike is simply a tool. It is a device that transports you, your family and your cattle to the market. I jest not. You often see people wobbling down the road on a Honda Dream, with a live cow on the back. They are even sold as family saloons, and you see them being used as such with five people on board. Mum, Dad, the two kids you're allowed to have, and Grandad on the back.

They are also delivery trucks. Need a 50-foot length of pipe delivering? Call someone with a Dream. Need a fridge freezer popping down to your chum's gaff? Call someone with a Dream. Over there, nothing is so large that it can't be fixed to the back of a Honda.

It all sounds like mayhem, but it's not a free-for-all. There are rules. If you are over seven, you must wear a crash hat, although it doesn't say what the hat must be. So anything goes. Flower pots. Burberry baseball caps. Kettles. Anything that stops the police pulling you over and demanding a two-dollar fine.

Sadly, because of the headgear issue, the casualties are fairly high. About fifteen people a week get wasted. But despite the sheer number of bikes, the system never jams up.

Here, for instance, is how the Green Cross Code works. You arrive at the pavement and simply set off without looking. So long as you neither speed up nor stop, you will not be hit. The bikes simply flow round you like you are a rock in a mountain brook.

At roundabouts, you pull out when you get there. And if you can't be bothered to drive on the right, don't bother. Use the left. Then, when it rains, which it does for months at a time, and hard, you simply pull a plastic sheet over your Burberry flower pot and keep right on going. Buses? No need to worry, because in the whole country there are about three.

It is very obviously a system that works. Even my twelve-year-old son worked that one out, all by himself. 'It should be like this in London,' he said. Unfortunately, he's twelve and is therefore precluded from becoming Britain's Minister of Transport.

The funny thing is that Vietnam is Communist and has recognized that mass public transport is not really an alternative to private transport. So they are building more factories to build more bikes. We, on the other hand, get bus lanes. And that's because who we've got in power are worse than Communists. They are fools.

November 2008

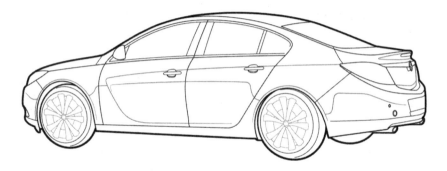

CAR OF THE YEAR: OPEL/VAUXHALL INSIGNIA

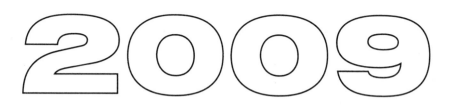

TOP 5 BESTSELLING SINGLES
SONG TITLE – ARTIST

1   I Gotta Feeling – Black Eyed Peas
2   Poker Face – Lady Gaga
3   Just Dance – Colby O'Donis /
     Lady GaGa
4   Boom Boom Pow – Black Eyed Peas
5   Fight For This Love – Cheryl Cole

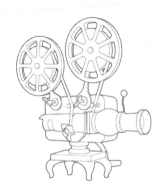

TOP 5 BOX OFFICE MOVIES

1   Avatar
2   Transformers: Revenge of the Fallen
3   Harry Potter and the Half-Blood Prince
4   The Twilight Saga: New Moon
5   Up

Living the dream

You join me backstage during the Birmingham leg of the *Top Gear Live* world tour. It is very noisy because a bus, built on a Nascar chassis and powerplant, is practising its donuts in the arena. It's visually displeasing too, because James is sitting in a massage chair, wobbling like he's been boned and Hammond is completing the misery by playing Westlife songs, endlessly, on the jukebox he insisted we have to while away the down time.

I agreed to do this tour because I thought, aged forty-eight, it would give me a taste of what life might have been like if I'd practised the piano more earnestly and become a rock star. I imagined we'd be zipping from continent to continent in a blizzard of cocaine, naked women and smashed hotel rooms. Sadly, it's not working out quite how I imagined.

Yes, we have invented a new game. It's called Celebrity Escape From Richard Hammond's Bathroom, and the rules are very simple. You go into his bathroom, tuck the end of the loo roll into the back of your trousers and see how far you can get through the hotel before it snaps.

We have also tried this on an aeroplane – and I'd like to apologize to the passengers we woke up – but it works best in a hotel because then, while waiting for your turn, you can go through all the rooms in Hammond's suite, buying pornography on every one of his numerous televisions. This makes him very embarrassed when the time comes to check out, especially if you've kicked the lavatory roll dispenser off the wall because that way you can travel further – often into the lift and down several floors – before the paper breaks.

We have also been very careful to ensure that all sorts of silly things are included in our riders. As a result, all the girls that look after us are over six feet tall and we have many big pots of M&Ms on every flat surface – with all the blue ones taken out. This idea was stolen, apparently, from Bon Jovi. We also have a sit-down PlayStation game loaded with Gran Turismo 5, and all the cars. Not just a handful of useless Hyundais.

Then there's Hammond's jukebox, James's massage chair and my Winnebago, which is very large and extremely ostentatious. I like to sit in it, as I am doing now, looking through the tinted glass at the vast army of 'roadies' who busy themselves between shows repainting damaged cars, recharging the pyro systems and generally ensuring the multi-million-pound extravaganza is ready to roll again in an hour.

In many ways then, this is rock-star living. We finish at night, get drunk, go to bed late, wake up with hangovers and get up the next day ready to do it all over again. I have even taken to calling the show's promoter from time to time to tell him that the loo seat in my 'bago's bathroom is the wrong colour and that the space invader game he's provided doesn't have asteroids on it. Silly things. Spoilt child things. He wanted to know what it might have been like to be Harvey Goldsmith in the glory days. So it's sort of my duty to fill him in.

Tonight, we've even arranged to go and get trashed with the lead singer from another band. He's called Tiff Needell from *Fifth Gear,* a million-selling outfit on the Five record label, and he's in Birmingham to do some voiceover work on the new album, which is released every Tuesday night at eight. In a beehive.

And yet, despite all the trappings, our life on the road feels about as rock 'n' roll as a Pam Ayres poetry reading. Because the fact is that, at forty-eight, it's very tiring. And I don't like the noise of the Nascar bus. And I loathe my Winnebago, because it's full of furnishings even a sink-estate benefit cheat would call 'tacky'. And now, instead of snorting drugs from the back of a naked groupie, I'm writing this on a laptop, while wearing reading glasses. The fact is then, I'm just too bloody old. And I'm experiencing much the same sort of thing on the road these days.

When I look in the mirror, I'm always surprised to see the craggy, grey balding head looking back at me. I feel eighteen. I think eighteen. But the body is forty-eight, and no longer enjoys being smashed to bits by suspension systems made from RSJs and bits of oak. I don't want an exhaust system that never shuts up either.

I recently bought a Mercedes CLK. It's the black edition from the skunkworks inside the AMG tuning house. I imagined, having tested it on the programme, that it would be a Fender Stratocaster with windscreen wipers; that in it, I would stride the road network like a rock god, legs apart, face contorted with a mixture of passion and concentration into the sort of shape that would convince ordinary motorists coming the other way that I was sucking on a lemon full of stinging nettles.

It does all this, of course. It feels like it's running on amyl nitrate, and every time you turn it on, the four massive tailpipes shout, 'Hello, London.' It is Bad Company.

Literally. If you try to accelerate, at all, on anything other than a completely dry surface, the back end steps out of line in an instant and you're doing the Spinal Tap. Oh, it may have a limited-slip diff and a wide axle and a weapons-grade traction control system, but there's no getting away from the fact that the team that designed this car are plainly industrial-strength drifting enthusiasts with little or no reason to live. Jesus, it's a tricky bastard.

So tricky that even if there's a hint of moisture in the air, and the traction control is on, it will still kick its arse out. With it off, you will slide sideways, at extremely high speed, and within a mile of your house, into a tree. Only when the road is bone dry and arrow-straight can you unleash all of the 507bhp. And only then do you get the full John Bonham drum solo, because this is a car, make no mistake, that goes all the way up to eleven.

That hurts the fuel consumption, and because it's a normal CLK with a normal CLK petrol tank, you will empty all of it, even if you are gentle with the volume knob, in less than 150 miles.

Then there are the seats. They are deep buckets, which is great, but for some reason the seat-belt anchor point is in the seat itself, so it's the most enormous faff to do it up. Last week, I had to give a lift to a fat woman whose arse was so wide she couldn't put her belt on at all. She had to sit there with the seat-belt delivery device waving the buckle in her face and there was absolutely nothing she could do to make it go away. This made conversation a bit tricky. 'So you're enormous, then . . .'

I love this car with every fibre of my being. And since it's already worth 8p, that's a good thing, because I can't afford to sell it. I love it, in fact, as much as I love being on tour with *Top Gear Live*. It's not what I want it to be, but that's only because I'm not what I want to be, either.

January 2009

The future

Subtlety works in a book. You can go back and re-read a passage to savour all the stuff that isn't there, all the hidden meaning and innuendo. It doesn't work, however, on a crash bang wallop show like *Top Gear*, which is why almost no one seems to have understood the significance of finishing our last run of 2008 with a James May review of the hydrogen-fuelled Honda Clarity.

You might have thought it a bit earnest – you should have seen the forty-five-minute techno explanation James had planned – and you might have wondered why on earth we should finish a show that featured caravan jumps, a history of the crashes in touring car racing, Richard in an ill-fitting hat and me being in love with Will Young with that straight, dry look at the Clarity.

Simple. We were trying to be subtle. We were trying to demonstrate that this is the most important car since the car was invented. That, with one stone, Honda has bagged a left and a right on the big problems facing modern society. It addresses the question of what we will do when the oil runs out, and it shuts up those who would have us believe cars are melting the ice caps. In short, and with all the subtlety removed, the Clarity means we can sleep a lot more easily.

And what's more, since it produces only water from its exhaust, there is no earthly reason why you should not plug it into your house at night and use its motor to power all your electrical items. All of them. Even if you live in a palace. It really is, we think, the solution to everything.

Unfortunately, it's very difficult to make hydrogen. There is currently no infrastructure for either transporting it or selling it. And the Clarity, if we're honest, is only Genesis. We will need to get through Exodus, Deuteronomy, Numbers and the entire Old Testament before you can buy and run such a thing, practically and for a reasonable price in Wakefield.

Ordinarily, all these problems could be solved with money. But the one thing the car industry does not have right now is that. And nor will it have any for the foreseeable future. Other industries? It's hard to think of one. The oil companies are muddling through as I write, their liquid gold selling for just $50 a barrel. And if anyone else feels inclined to invest, they are going to find the banks are not lending. In short, and with no subtlety at all this time, money is the one thing the world does not have.

And so it seems likely the car firms will opt for the easier, cheaper option of making stupid hybrids, like the Prius, which all right-thinking people can tell are nothing more than a complicated way of making people 'feel' like they are making an effort. We know, as readers of a car website, that they are doing no such thing. Hybrids are power-hungry when they are being made, and environmentally devastating when they are being scrapped. And in-between times, they do, at best, 45mpg.

Making a hybrid to stave off disaster is like replacing a broken window pane with a sheet of polythene. Yes, it makes the room feel all snug and warm again, but you're still going to get burgled. You need a replacement for the empty space? You need hydrogen? But that's expensive. And you don't have any money. And you won't have any until people start buying your wares again. Which they can't because they don't have any money either. And if they have, they are not going to spend it, because the *Daily Mail* will say they are smug, and extravagant, and that they will give women breast cancer.

I fear therefore that, for the time being, there will be no great leap forward. There will be no revolution. The hybrids will continue to be bought by misguided fools, the Clarity will continue to dribble about in California, and the car as we know it will soldier on unchanged.

However, I do believe that they will become more boring. In the last few years, we've had a call almost every week from some bloke saying he's made a two-inch-high, £8 million V48 car, and would Stig like to take it round our track.

We've had Aston Martin pricing its cars with a 'think of a number, then double it' technique. We've had Lambo and Porsche working on fantastically expensive four-door super-cars. We've had Mercedes making an SL that costs £250,000, and BMW imagining that what the world needs most of all is the magnificently daft X6. The world has had its snout in the trough, and the car firms have been only too happy to feed us with caviar-infused peacocks. It's been fun, if I'm honest, but now it's over.

This needn't necessarily be a bad thing. I was wandering around London the other day, and strangely all the flash showrooms on Park Lane looked a bit old-fashioned, a bit fat, a bit last-week. Whereas the red and white Fiat dealership on Berkeley Square seemed to be completely right. I wanted almost everything in it. And when they get the 500 Abarth – which I hear will be available with a 200bhp engine in the near future – I might be tempted to actually go inside and do some buying.

This is going to be the trick the car makers must, and will, pull off. They are going to have to take their bread-and-butter Pandas and, with a splash of paint here and a dash of the designer's brush there, make them a lot more desirable.

I'll let you into a little secret. In the real world, away from the wide-open spaces of the *Top Gear* test track, a Fiat 500 is much more fun to drive than a Zonda. A Zonda will pull more men, but on a bumpy B road, you'll be wearing a bigger smile in the Fiat, I promise. Or a Mini. Or if they can zanify the Fiesta, a baby Ford.

In the not-too-distant future, cars like this will become the norm for enthusiastic drivers, in the same way that in the early Eighties people were selling their Gordon-Keebles and Bentleys to buy a Golf GTi. And instead of dreaming of the day when you can have a Gallardo or a Scuderia, you will tone your aspirations down to something like the new BMW Z4.

This, it seems to me, is about as right for today as the X6 is wrong. Twelve months ago, which seems as far away as the nineteenth century, the Z4 was hopeless. People put its small sales down to the curious styling, which is probably true, but I reckon the main reason it didn't sell is because it was too cheap. Customers were walking into the showroom to buy a four and coming out with a six. Because why not?

The new model is as well-proportioned as the old one, though now a lot of the strangeness is gone. It's very handsome. It also has a metal folding roof. And, of course, it's a BMW, which is OK these days, because the cocks are now buying Audi TTs instead.

Strange, isn't it? The changes to the Z4 are welcome but fairly superficial in the big scheme of things. You might even call them subtle. Really, it has stayed the same, and the world has changed. We used to dream about shagging a supermodel, whereas now we've sort of grown up and realized that, actually, we'd be better off dreaming of shagging the girl next door.

Two years ago, we'd have dismissed the Z4 as a bit dull. Now though . . . I'm yearning.

February 2009

The new Focus RS

I'm reliably informed, by my fourteen-year-old daughter, that there are two types of people in the world: Chavs and Sloanes. And there are no prizes for guessing which type will be most interested in the new Focus RS – a car that comes in a choice of three colours: DFS blue, Stiletto white and Bacardi Breezer green.

On the very day production of this new car started in Germany, I took it for a spin up here in the Cotswolds and, frankly, I couldn't find one house outside which it might look even vaguely appropriate. If it were a garden ornament, and it sort of is when it's parked outside your house, then it would be a stone lion and, as a result, I feel fairly sure that if you were to apply the *Top Gear* cool test – would Kristin Scott Thomas like it? – the answer would be, 'No thanks. I'll go on the bus.'

So let's ignore the Sloanes, shall we, and start off by saying, 'Chavs. This one's for you.'

I'm the man for the job, because I'm a sucker for flared wheel arches. I've often said that in the same way a man can never be too rich, his wheel arches can never be too flared. And the RS, to accommodate its wider track, has some whoppers.

There's another reason I'm a man for the job, though. I love fast Fords. My first love was a GT40, my first car was a Cortina 1600E and, back in the Nineties, I ran two Escort

Cosworths. And I've always loved RSes too. From the X pack Capris through the Escort 1600i to the 150mph Sierras.

That's why I was so quick off the mark with the new car. I wanted to see what it was like. And when it arrived at my house, the aural promise of greatness was unmistakable. Its big exhausts, through which the Palestinians of Gaza could smuggle the entire contents of a zoo, make the sort of rumble that rattle even the most beautifully finished sash windows. I honestly thought as it reversed into my yard that my wife was out there in her Aston. It's low loud. Bass loud. Dog-frighteningly loud.

And then came the crushing disappointment. Despite the enormity of Ford's global operation, they had fitted the steering wheel on the wrong side of the car. The man who had brought it tried to argue that in other parts of the world people drive on the wrong side of the road, but obviously he was covering up for some other bloke's massive cock-up. Wrong side of the road? Whatever next?

Assuming that they get this fixed before the car goes on sale, and I'm assured they will, the interior is much as you'd expect. Extra dials (which you can't read), a satnav with a woman who cannot be silenced unless you are Steve Jobs, and excellent bucket seats. If you have a tweed jacket in your wardrobe, you will hate it in there. If you do not, you will find it great.

But what about on the road?

The last Focus RS was a huge disappointment. It looked good – better than this one, in fact – but to tame the engine's not particularly stratospheric power, it had been fitted with a front differential of such monumental hopelessness, it probably thought it was a biscuit. You got a ton of torque steer when you set off, then the steering system would jam and then you'd hit a tree, fly through the windscreen and be killed. Technically, engineers called the system 'shit'.

I was hoping, as the new RS produces 300bhp, it would have four-wheel drive. But no. That would have been too expensive to engineer, so they've stuck with a diff. I'm told it's all new, and softer in its responses. In other words, it's designed for people who like to drive on roads and not be killed.

Does it work? Well, because it has a revo knuckle – and if you know what this is, you are James May – the driveshafts always stay level with something or other. This means you can blast one wheel through a puddle and not have the steering wheel wrenched from your hand. It also means the car doesn't follow the camber of the road with anything like the hopelessness of the previous RS.

I have to say that even when the weather is awful, the grip and the poise are excellent. Better than excellent. I can't imagine that even an Evo X is going to pull away. I know for a fact that on a damp road, it would leave my CLK Black for dead. It's that good, and not once did I encounter any of the dreaded tread shuffle that seems to plague the testers on other magazines.

But there's no getting away from the fact that the torque steer is still there. I suppose it's a consequence of putting 300 horses through a system that also has to deal with the steering. It's physics. Get used to it. It's worth it.

The engine is epic. Yes, it's essentially the same blown 2.5-litre Volvo five-pot from the ST, but it has new pistons, a new blower, a new intercooler, a new inlet manifold and that new, dog-baiting exhaust system. Of course, there's some lag, but from less than 3,000rpm you can feel the shove, you can feel the urgency, you can feel the 324ft-lbs of torque. And unlike most turbo engines, which run out of puff when you get near the red line, this one keeps right on singing. Well, shouting.

Ford says the ST is like a dolphin, and the RS is like a shark. I'd like to laugh at them for this, but they're right. It's a good analogy.

Except the RS is nowhere near as hard as you might imagine. Of course it's firm, but it's not 'Oh Christ. My Teeth!' firm. It's more sort of reassuring.

So let's talk money. The Focus RS costs £24,995, and at that sort of price, this sort of speed and this sort of engineering is unheard of. Especially as it comes with seating for five, a big boot, fold-down rear seats and lots of buttons.

As a result, I wouldn't hesitate for a moment. I'd have a slower but more discreet Golf GTi. But that's because I've moved on. My house is yellow and my wellies are French. But if you haven't moved on. If your hat is still on back to front. If you still think the Boss is God and your collar's still blue, then trust me: life has never been better. The RS glory days, after a momentary blip, are back.

March 2009

Drinking

At home, I have a pair of Sega Rally arcade machines on which two people can race a Lancia Delta Integrale or a Toyota Celica GT4 on a choice of rally circuits. They were very cutting-edge ten years ago, and in various Northern airport terminals, I note they still are.

Obviously, because I have them at home and because it costs nothing to have a go, I am very brilliant. I guarantee I could beat you, even if you are eight, or if you actually designed the coded software that allows the true expert to convert their cars from four- to much faster rear-wheel drive. And in case you don't believe me, my top ten times sit on the memory chip like the grouping on a sharpshooter's target. The top eight are identical. The next two are off by just a thousandth of a second.

Here's the funny thing, though. If I have a go after drinking just one small glass of wine, I can't even get close to my best score. I'm way off, sometimes by as much as two tenths of a second.

It's odd. Drinking one small glass of wine does not make me feel different in any way. I can touch my nose, get all the way through 'Peter Piper' and balance on one foot easily. Even our fanatically bossy government agrees. But the Sega experiment shows that even a pipette of booze affects, noticeably, the reactions of a fully grown, sixteen-stone man.

After two bottles of wine and some sloe vodka, I'm all

over the place. Once, I was so drunk that I was nearly half a second off the pace. And on another occasion, on the forest stage, I actually fell asleep. And so you should be in no doubt – especially as this is a BBC website, and the BBC gets criticized for everything these days – I am not for a moment going to suggest that booze doesn't affect our ability to drive. It does. The end.

However, despite this, I have decided that people should be allowed to drive a car even if they are so completely wasted they have lost control of their bowels.

Here's why. We are human beings, which means we are naturally gregarious. We like the company of other people, and we are nervous of loners. We imagine, correctly, that people who enjoy their own company have a large collection of knives and dream of one day walking into a shop and shooting all the customers.

To quench our thirst for company, the world is awash with places where people might gather to be convivial. Pubs, clubs, restaurants and so on. And because alcohol loosens our inhibitions and our shyness, it is usually served in these places to get us in the mood. A night out with friends. A few drinks. A bit of a laugh. Life simply doesn't get any better.

But then you've got to get home and, sadly, life doesn't get any worse.

Obviously, you cannot use the bus because, if you are in a city, you will have absolutely no idea where it's going, and even if you do manage to board something going vaguely in the right direction, someone will be sick on your trousers and then stab you in the heart for complaining.

If you are not in the city, you can wait as long as you like at the bus stop. But nothing will come by till the morning, by which time you will have died from hypothermia. The upshot, then, is that everyone who attempts to use a bus ends up covered in sick and dead, or just dead.

A cab? Again, there's a split. In the city, there are any number of companies who will take you home, provided you don't mind being raped on the way. In the countryside, there are no cabs at all.

Where I live, near a small market town in the Cotswolds, I could ring for a taxi at 11 p.m. tonight and pretty much guarantee it won't arrive until October. By which time, even if I've had a very heavy night on the sauce, I can pretty much guarantee I'll be sober enough to drive.

So, if you don't want to be raped or murdered, the only way of getting home is in your car. But if you do that, you will either hit a tree and be killed, or you will be stopped by the constabulary. You will then lose your licence and your family, who will leave because you have no job and therefore no money.

The upshot is that you can either stay at home and collect knives, or you can go out and not drink. In which case, you will be boring, your friends won't want to see you any more and, pretty soon, you will be alone, in your attic, downloading pictures of dismembered dogs and dreaming of the day when you can run amok with an AK47.

Many years ago, I developed a solution to the problem; in short, it goes like this. If you have been out and you've had some drinks, you are allowed to drive home, but only if you place a green flashing light on the roof of your car.

And here's the clever bit. If you are driving with the light flashing, then you are limited to a top speed of 10mph.

Think about it. Normal sober people will see you weaving down the road toward them, they will clock the light and they will know, whether they are on foot or in a car, that you are drunk and that they should give you a wide berth.

Because you are going so slowly, they will have plenty of time to make the necessary adjustments, and what's more, even if you do hit a bus shelter or a tree, you will cause very little damage.

Thanks, then, to the green-light system, you would get home without being raped or murdered; what's more, the next day your car would be outside your house, and not 15 miles away outside a country pub.

There is, however, one further feature in my plan. If you are caught drink-driving with no light on the roof, you will be shot, in the head and on the spot by a police executioner. If the government is going to introduce a fair and sensible system for getting you home safely, in your car, the least you can do is play ball. So it's instant death for people who don't.

Likewise, anyone found travelling at more than 10mph with a green light on their roof will have a brown paper bag put over their head and be bludgeoned to a lifeless pulp. If you are sober enough to remember the light and get the key in the ignition, you are sober enough to keep your speed down. There is no excuse.

I believe that if my system were employed, the number of pubs closing down – at the moment, one is shutting for good somewhere in the country every four hours – would be cut dramatically. I also believe more people would be inclined to go out at night, which would make the country a happier, more civilized place. This, in turn, would reduce the chances of there being another Hungerford.

Plainly, then, there are no drawbacks to my idea, but sadly it can never be implemented for three reasons. Firstly, allowing people to do something they were not previously allowed to do is not the government way. Nothing ever gets un-banned. Secondly, with no drink-drive laws, there would be a reduction in fines received by the exchequer. And thirdly, the more people who can be excluded from the roads, the better it is for the government's much-publicized drive to remove the terrifying scourge of carbon dioxide from the upper atmosphere.

Pity.

April 2009

Cheap cars

The ultra budget Tata Nano is being hailed by many as the biggest leap forward since the Model T Ford. So if they're right, it's more important than the Beetle. More important than the Mini. More important than man's conquest of the moon. And, amazingly, more important too than the invention of Sky+.

I don't think they are right, though, because the only thing that makes it stand out is the low, low price. Brilliant. But I could make a cheap car if I built it in a factory made from wattle and mud, paid the workers in rice and motivated them into a twenty-hour day with whips and flame throwers.

Especially if the car in question didn't have to conform to any of the safety requirements that make other cars so much more expensive. Look at it this way. The Nano, on home soil, is £1,700 and that, I'll agree, is impressive. But the model we'll get in Europe will be £4,500. And I'm sorry, but £4,500 for a car with no boot, no top speed, three wheel nuts and a petrol tank under the passenger seat? That's not Sky+. That's not even a laser disc.

It's just a car. The people who've tested it already report that it's much better than the mopeds most people in that neck of the woods drive. Much better than a moped? Give me a break. That's like saying syphilis is much better than Aids.

Of course, I hope a great many Indians buy the Nano. Partly because I want Tata to make lots of money that they can spend on more supercharged Jags, and partly because its success will infuriate the eco-mentalists who like people to be poor and downtrodden. I don't, which is the main reason I want the Nano to succeed. I want it to mobilize all of South East Asia. It's only right and proper that Johnny Cong should be able to afford a car.

But here, in Britain? No thanks. Because what we are getting here is a tool, and a home-brand tool at that. Do you have a Curry's stereo system? Or a Daewoo television? No. Because while such things are cheap, they are not the real deal. You want beans on toast, you go to Heinz.

And it's the same story with cars.

Because what you're buying when you buy a brand-new cheap car is a smell and the latest registration number to impress the neighbours – who won't be impressed because almost no one knows where we are these days with the 57s and the 08s and so on. So it's just the smell. And you can achieve that by buying a second-hand car and some Pledge.

Normally, the second-hand car I'd recommend is an Alfa because, as we've said many times, you cannot be a petrol-head until you've had one. With an Alfa you get the sunshine. But then you get the inevitable thunderstorm. And I'd rather have that than an eternity of Tupperware grey that comes as standard with every budget stack-'em-high Toyota, Kia and Nissan.

This time, however, I'm not going to suggest an Alfa, I'm going to suggest something even more preposterous: a Lancia.

I know that for many of our younger readers, a Lancia is the other car in Sega's first arcade rally game. But that wasn't just a bunch of pixels, you know. That was a Delta Integrale. It existed in real life, had four-wheel drive, a turbo the size of

Sicily and performance every bit as big as Michael Winner's ear lobes. And guess what? A quick check of the *Autotrader* site reveals you can buy one today for less than a Nano.

If you don't fancy a car with left-hand drive – I had an Escort Cosworth because of this very thing – then do not despair because this was simply the last of the great Lancias. Go further back and it's like crawling on your hands and knees through a field full of oiled-up lesbians. After ten minutes you will end up panting with the possibilities.

There's the Fulvia HF, the HPE VX, the Beta coupé – the same car I used to cross Botswana – the Ferrari-engined Thema 8:32 and, perhaps best of all, the mid-engined Monte Carlo. This came with tweed seats, a canvas Targa roof, a transverse engine and no brakes.

No, that's not fair. The early models had brakes, but those at the front would lock up without warning, causing the car to plough into a tree killing everyone inside. Very unusually, the Monte Carlo was taken out of the dealerships and put back on the drawing board, only to emerge about a year later with the problem fixed.

Except it wasn't. All they'd done in the intervening period was have a lot of lunch. And then remove the servo. This meant the front wheels wouldn't lock up any more, or indeed slow down at all unless you had iron thighs and were consequently strong enough to push the brake pedal clean through the floor. Most people didn't, though, and as a result they would hit a tree and be killed. Unless the car had rusted away first. Which it usually had, if it was raining. Or dry. Or hot. Or cold.

This was the other thing about Lancias. They were beautiful to look at and lovely to drive, once. But to keep costs down, they were made from Communistical steel that was so thin you could see the engine through the front wings. I'm told you could even see the pistons going up and down, but I never saw that. Probably because of some catastrophic electrical failure caused by the man who was employed to install the wiring choosing to go for lunch instead.

Make no mistake. Lancias were more tangled than an iPod's earphones, and more troublesome than Robert Mugabe. In every single way, a modern Nano is a better means of getting about. But getting about is only a small part of what a car must do to worm its way into my heart.

It must be pretty, and the Nano isn't. It must have a soul, and the Nano hasn't, and it must excite you, even when it's three in the morning, you're in bed and it's on the hard shoulder of the M42, where you left it, in a cloud of steam. I guarantee the Nano won't do that either.

You will never, I assure you, think of an excuse to go into town in your Nano, whereas if you had a Lancia, you'd deliberately forget the dog biscuits so you could turn round and go back. You'd be like a human yo-yo.

I've decided I must have a Lancia. I've decided that if anything they are even more extreme than Alfas. An Alfa, if you like, is hotel porn. A Lancia is the sort of stuff you can only find at the very edge of the Internet. We're talking dogs here.

I've even decided which model I must have. It's a Stratos, the first car ever designed specifically for rallying. Only 492 were made, it had the engine from a Dino, which was nearly a Ferrari, and it was styled by Marcello Gandini, the man responsible for the Countach, the Diablo, the Alfa Montreal, the Maserati Khamsin, the Bugatti EB110 and the De Tomaso Pantera. It's almost like he was consumed with a never-ending thirst to create the perfect supercar. And I know what fuelled this thirst. In 1972, he'd done the Stratos and he just couldn't match it.

And that's where we'll end. With a simple observation. Gandini did not style the Tata Nano. So far as I can tell, no one did.

June 2009

The system

Back in the winter, when the snows came and the radio reports were telling us that Britain was locked in ice chaos, a forty-year-old man called Simon Lewington decided to tow his son on a sledge behind his pickup truck.

Unfortunately, he towed him right past a police station and so, last month, Mr Lewington appeared in court, where a judge said a custodial sentence was being considered. I'm sorry? Prison? For towing your boy on a sledge? At no more than 8mph? These are indeed strange times.

And there's more. On the very same day I read about Mr Lewington – who I think should be Dad of the Year – I heard that police officers in Bournemouth have been given sophisticated laser guns to catch cyclists speeding on the sea front.

Apparently, they are not allowed to travel at more than 10mph, but cannot be prosecuted if they do since bikes don't have speedometers and therefore there is no way for the individual to know he's breaking the law. Hmm. The purchase of the laser guns does therefore seem like a lot of tax payers' cash down the drain. And that's before we get to the complete waste of police time.

Let me give you another example. Someone I know was recently loading her car with various heavy household items when a traffic warden, or parking attendant as we must call them these days, started to write out a ticket. My friend appealed to the warden's heart explaining that she couldn't possibly carry a fridge freezer to the nearest legal parking space and that she'd only be a moment.

But, of course, wardens don't have hearts, the ticket was written and my friend called her big, fat and the worst word in the world. Fair enough, you might think. We pay the wardens' wages. They are therefore, quite literally our servants, and we are allowed to call them whatever we wish, should their behaviour be unreasonable and stupid.

It seems not. Because later in the day, my friend was visited by two police officers who issued her with an on-the-spot £80 fine for being offensive. But it wasn't offensive. The warden in question was big. She was fat. And if she's going to issue a ticket to someone loading their car with a fridge, then she is also the worst word in the world.

And anyway, how can it be against the law to abuse state officials? At this rate, you would not be allowed to call an idiot who's Scottish and one-eyed a 'one-eyed Scottish idiot'.

I am employed by the BBC and when I say or do something with which you disagree, you are perfectly entitled to write to me saying whatever comes into your head. Indeed, if I rang the police every time someone called me the worst word in the world, I'd get a loyal service carriage clock from British Telecom.

What worries me, then, is that the state is completely out of control. Imposing whatever laws it sees fit, and then hammering anyone who dares to even disagree. I heard recently that they were thinking of making climate-change denial an offence.

The fact is that when I was seventeen, I used to sledge behind cars, and not at 8mph either. Once, some friends and I did it on the M6 at 50mph. And none of us was even slightly killed.

I have also ridden bicycles at enormous speed through Burton on Trent, where many of the locals are drunk on the town's home brew. And to my certain knowledge, neither I nor anyone else died as a result.

In fact, I simply don't have the space here to list all the fun things I did as a kid that simply aren't allowed today. Nicking sulphuric acid from the school labs to spice up water fights, doing 70mph in coned off sections of the motorway, playing conkers, canoeing into the outlet pipes of a power station, lighting fires in the woods, scrumping . . . and not just apples or rhubarb either. Once, I scrumped a nun's habit.

I remember, too, when indoor go-karting first took off. God, it was fun, whizzing about in an old warehouse. And it remained fun right up to the moment when one of the chaps on the other team flipped right in front of us. And then caught fire.

It was a big fire and he was very badly burned, as was the extremely brave chap who attempted to beat out the flames with his bare hands.

Could the accident have been avoided? For sure. The kart could have had a protective strip around its wheels to minimize the chance of a roll. The fuelling system could have featured fewer empty squeezy bottles. The driver could have been forced to wear a Nomex suit, not jeans and a T-shirt.

Or, if you keep going in this vane, the sport could have been banned altogether.

This is the problem. If you do anything at all, you stand the chance, no matter how many precautions you take, of never being able to do anything again. An accident is something which, by its very nature, cannot be prevented.

But no one has got that. Which means that everything now comes with a hand-rail and a luminous jacket and a hard hat and steel-toe-capped boots and a banksman and ear defenders and protective strips and beeps and bongs and warnings and notices and rules, and that means nothing is quite as much fun as it used to be when you could make a buggy from bits of an old pram and see how fast it would go down a steep hill.

Most people blame health and safety for everything that's gone wrong since those glory days when we were free. But, actually, that's like shooting the messenger. Because let's not forget that health-and-safety people, with their clip boards and their adenoids and their horrible shoes, are employed by companies to examine all the risks, and eliminate all the risks, so that the company in question can tell a judge, if someone is injured and they are prosecuted or sued, that they took all possible precautions.

So it's not the company that's to blame. They don't want to cough up every time someone stubs their toe on a paving slab. And it's not the health-and-safety bods, who are simply doing what they were asked to do. No. What's at fault is the system. The whole damn shooting match. The culture that says anyone who's injured must be able to sue someone, and that if they won't the State can step in and make a prosecution. Which will be successful unless the company in the dock can show it employed a man in a high-visibility jacket.

Just last week, while filming for *Top Gear*, the car I was testing suffered a terrible accident. I won't say more than this because you won't have seen it yet and I don't want to spoil the surprise. Whatever, to have continued with the filming would have been stupid. There were jagged bits of metal everywhere and a worrying smell of fuel. Every health-and-safety man in the land would have ordered me to step away from the vehicle and go home.

But if I'd done that, the shoot would have been over, and thousands of pounds worth of licence payers' cash would have been wasted. So in I got and off I set . . . into a world populated only by pain and lashings of blood. I could sue. But I'm not going to. It's not the way of the gentleman. It's not the way of *Top Gear* either.

And if anyone wishes to call me the worst word in the world, feel free. I am to be found in my paddock teaching my ten-year-old daughter how to do a hand-brake turn in her £50 Ford Fiesta.

August 2009

The end of it all

As a reader of *Top Gear* magazine, you are a foot soldier, part of a vast army of people whose Communion wine has an octane rating and whose pew is made from Alcantara by Recaro. Unless of course you are reading this in a dentist's waiting room. In which case you are not a foot soldier. You have toothache, and you have my sympathy.

Let's be clear. I am not speaking now to people with toothache, or to those who have read *Practical Caravanning* and *Dogs Today* and are now ploughing through *Top Gear* magazine because it's that or the instructions on the vomit bag. I am speaking only to the army of genuine car lovers and the news is not good.

Of course, as is the way with all foot soldiers in all armies, you do not know the news is not good. And you will continue to not know until a dirty great missile lands on your car and blows it into the middle of next week. The fact is, though, that you are under attack. And you have no idea.

As a member of the *Top Gear* team, I get to see all the tell-tale signs. I see the press releases from the loony left. I get the Google alerts. I read the complaints sent to the BBC. So I know what's coming. And what's coming is the End of Days.

The number of people who dislike cars is very small. A few ramblers, some bods in Friends of the Earth, various people who run road-safety charities. But they are noisy, and they are motivated. And unlike us who simply worship at the temple of speed, they make it their life's work to bring all that down. To burn our churches. And hang our leaders. And not stop until you, me and everyone we know is going to work on oxen. And what makes it so depressing is that there's absolutely nothing we can do about it.

I honestly can see a time when there are no supercars, and when the hybrid eco electric lentil you are allowed to drive to work every other day is governed by spy satellites to 20mph. And I don't see this coming in 100 years. I see it in less than twenty. Maybe ten.

You may argue that this is nonsense and that Ferrari is in rude health at the moment. Absolutely. So is Bentley and so is Rolls-Royce. But that's because they are selling cars to people in Russia and the Middle East. That won't last.

The fact is that they simply can't stay in business without Europe, which is now fundamentally anti-car, and America, which since the dawn of Barack Obama, is even more green than the lawn outside the White House. He wants to reduce greenhouse gases and, because he's serious about that, the V8 will have to go. Not just in pickup trucks and SUVs, but in Ferraris and Maseratis as well.

Run around all you like, but there is nothing you can do. Yes, a handful of sheikhs may keep Ferrari in business for the next few years, but eventually, without California and Cheshire – and with less dependence on the sheikhs for oil – all they'll be making down there in Maranello is branded aftershave and baseball caps.

It's not just market forces either. Now, if you drive a really expensive car around Britain's cities, you are very often subjected to a torrent of abuse from the hirsute and the stupid. They believe they have right on their side, so they point with their bony, wizened fingers, and spit, and bang on your carbon-fibre roof. Only the other day, a taxi driver, normally the last resting place for the sensible, gave me a ton of what for, for driving a Range Rover. If this kind of thing gets worse, the number of people prepared to stick it out will dwindle to nought.

Seriously. When Henry VIII declared war on the Catholics, some continued to worship Johnny Pope, but after a few burnings, it quickly died out. Car love will go the same way.

And I haven't even got to the biggest problem of them all yet. The mothers of those who've been killed on the roads.

I am able to deal with anyone whose objection to speed and car use is environmental. They are talking utter claptrap and the figures back it up. Similarly, I am able to deal with cyclists. They are jealous. But it is impossible to make a coherent argument for unrestrained car use when you are face-to-face with a mum whose kid has been splattered all over a bus stop by some halfwit in a Corsa.

Boris Johnson, as is often the way, hit the nail rather beautifully on the head when writing in the *Daily Telegraph* recently. He explained that he often receives complaints about the number of traffic lights in London, but says each one is the result of a campaign. And when that campaign has been led by someone whose child has been run over, it is extremely difficult for a local council to turn away and do nothing.

Yes. I can come here now and say that deaths on the road are inevitable and that building a set of traffic lights or a footbridge on the site of each tragedy is utterly preposterous. But you try saying that to someone who is crying.

And so, combine the sobbing mothers, the stupid environmentalists, the jealous and the communistical and you end up with a small but powerful wave, in the face of which we, the army, are powerless to do anything. Don't forget, the Boxing Day tsunami was not tall, but it wiped out everything.

So there you are. One bereaved mum. One man with a beard. A splash of Al Gore and a curious new hatred for the rich, and all I can say is this: get your order in now for the Aston Martin V12 Vantage. Because I can't see its like coming round again.

September 2009

Personalization

You join me in southern Spain, where the women are orange and the men are wanted for questioning. Sadly, though, I am not down here to roast an egg on my stomach or to make sex with a young lady. I'm here to make my annual DVD, which means I'm at the Ascari race track just outside Ronda.

Built as a plaything by a Dutchman, it curls and swoops for five kilometres, and is very excellent in every way. I especially like the pool in which you can cool off after a hot lap. And the waitresses in the bar. And the weather. But most of all, I like the cars we have down here.

Let me make you a bit jealous. Right now, parked outside the pit garage where I'm writing, there is a Murciélago SV, a Gallardo 560, a Jaguar XKR drophead, a Lotus Evora, which is doing its best to put me off by sounding its alarm for no reason every few minutes, a BMW M3, a Vauxhall VXR8 Bathurst, an Aston Martin V12 Vantage, a Ford Focus RS and an Audi R8 V10. All of them are full of fuel. All of them are ready to go. The track is empty. I'm the only driver here. And I have a big pot of keys sitting right in front of me. It's like a bag of sweeties, only better.

Which one would you most like to drive round the track? For me, it'd be the Aston. It's what F1 drivers call pointy and what I call a twitchy little bastard. The short wheelbase and wide track combine to make it extremely precise but extremely waggly-tailed if you forget what you're doing for a moment.

Fun, though. More fun even than the bonkers Vauxhall with the Aussie soundtrack.

Here's the thing, though. For the daily commute from my hotel in Ronda to the track, and for nights out in Romford by the Sea, or Marbella as I believe the Spanish insist on calling it, I have been using the Jag.

Partly, of course, this is because I like the slightly tatty, down-on-his-luck charm of the whole Jag thing. I'm talking about the sort of person who never has a problem with the bank or the leasing company – just a 'misunderstanding'. The sort of person who has a huge house with a swimming pool one minute, but is crashing on your sofa the next because of a 'small problem' with the tax people. Jag people are nice. They're funny. They're mannered. Let's not forget that Arthur Daley always raised his hat to a lady.

The other reason why I use the XKR all the time is because it's just so damn good-looking. Maybe, just maybe, the wind-screen is a tad too vertical, and perhaps the headlights have a whiff of Hyundai, a sense perhaps that they're trying too hard. But worrying about this sort of thing is like worrying about Cindy Crawford's mole.

As a driver's car, of course, it is beaten in all the disciplines by almost all the cars here. The Lambos are more grippy, the Audi is more predictable, the Vantage is way faster and you can be more of a hooligan in either the Vauxhall or the Ford. But if you were looking for one car that combined all these things: grip, power and handling, then you would be using the Jag as well. It can even do hooliganism if you get the nose to turn in and give it a bootful.

Large chunks of my being want to buy an XKR. I abso-lutely love it. Especially the canvas hood, which makes you realize how ungainly the metal alternatives are. Vandalism?

Yes, but not when I come to power, because anyone who messes with another man's wheels will be set on fire. In front of their families.

All in all then, an excellent, five-star, brilliant car. Except for one small thing. It was designed for you. Not me.

You would like the touch-screen control system. I don't. You would like the choice of four screen savers. I think that's silly. You would like the seats. I'm not sure. And so it goes on.

Happily, of course, I've had an idea. In the same way that Lloyd Grossman has tailored a sauce to suit his own requirements, I'd like to offer my services to Jag to design a special Lloyd Grossman version of the XKR. Only we couldn't call it the Lloyd Grossman because that would be stupid. And we couldn't call it the Jeremy Clarkson, either, because Jeremy is the stupidest name in the world. And Clarkson is a bit dreary. In fact, I haven't thought of a name yet.

But I have thought of everything else. First of all, the seats. They are extremely comfortable and the range of adjustments guarantees everyone can find a driving position to suit. But they are ugly. The squab is too long. And the backrest too short. In my edition, they would be replaced with Recaros.

In the back, there would be some changes as well. I know that Jag couldn't sell the old XK in America when it was a two-seater and that when they squeezed a bench in there, success followed. But this is because Americans are stupid and couldn't see that the bench was not big enough to seat any life form apart, perhaps, from amoeba.

In my Lloyd Grossman version, the seat would be replaced by a lighter, carpeted bench. It would have chromed rails on it, too, so that luggage didn't make scuff marks.

Colour? It would be the metallic olive green that you used

to be able to specify on a Range Rover until they unwisely removed it from the spec sheets. You want blue? Tough. Black? Nope. Brown? Have you thought about a Peugeot?

Other things? I'd fit the new dials that don't exist except in cyberspace from the Range Rover, and all the bongs telling me to shut the door or stop reversing or put my seat belt on would be removed and inserted in Gordon Brown's bottom.

Then there's the exhaust. I know that the sound made by all modern sports cars is fake. Acoustic tuning is now very much part of a car's design process. There are valves and chambers and God knows what else to ensure that after 3,000rpm, when the EU's noise abatement people have packed up their microphones and gone home, the quiet hum becomes a gigantic bellow.

The trouble is that in the Jag the noise that results really does sound fake. It's a lovely crackle, but what I'm looking for on my special edition is an elephantine bellow, with a mournful howl at the top and, on the overrun, a derisory Lambo-style snort. It's as though the whole car is saying, 'Pah. What have you lifted off for?'

You may be thinking then, that with body-hugging seats, a louder exhaust and the smaller Alcantara steering wheel, I've forgotten to mention till now that I'm looking for more sportiness. Not so. The new 5.0-litre supercharged V8 is perfect. I'd leave it alone. Same with the automatic gearbox. But I would address the ride comfort.

Jag has proved it knows what it's doing on this score. The XFR manages to handle like a greased supermodel, but feel as soft as a prolapsed stomach on even the most Belgian cobble. The XKR does not. It's too firm and that's wrong for someone who's forty-nine and three-quarters.

I want my car to look sporty, feel sporty and sound sporty. I want to know it can slide, but most of all I want it to glide.

None of the changes I've talked about here require much effort on Jag's part. The architecture and major components would be unchanged, but the result would be a car designed for me. And, strangely, I bet you'd like it more than the one they've designed for you.

October 2009

Hybrids

Back in the late Seventies and early Eighties, the world's fresh-air fanatics decided the exhaust gases coming out of the world's cars were causing children in Birmingham to grow two heads. And all of science was in agreement that Something Must Be Done.

At the time, I suggested moving Birmingham away from the M6 and the M5, possibly to the Falklands, but this was deemed 'a bit stupid'.

The obvious solution was the catalytic converter. Designed in 1950 by a Frenchman and made to work in 1973 by an American, it was quite expensive, but it did the job. Nitrogen oxides were converted to nitrogen and oxygen. Carbon monoxide was converted to carbon dioxide and hydrocarbons were executed. Lovely.

The only people who opposed the introduction of catalytic converters were 1) old men with chunky jumpers and classic cars, who thought that because cat-equipped cars could only run on unleaded petrol, pretty soon they wouldn't be able to buy the leaded fuel their TR3s needed to operate. And 2) the Prime Minister, Mrs Thatcher.

The Maggon did a lot of jumping up and down and waving her handbag in the air about cats. She thought they were the work of the devil and kept banging on about their one big drawback. They dramatically increase the amount of CO_2 coming out of the tail pipe. Carbon dioxide, according to the Maggon, was a bad thing, but no one else could see what she was on about and dismissed her objections as the rantings of a mad woman.

Certainly, they had no idea why she was so keen on the only real alternative to the catalytic converter – lean-burn technology. 'You are not only a mad woman,' they said, 'you are also a grocer's daughter with bouffant hair, so how can you possibly know anything about engines.'

Lean burn is extremely boring. But, in essence, the petrol engine in your car currently runs on one part of fuel to fourteen or so parts of air. In a lean-burn engine, that can be raised to one part of fuel to twenty-five or even thirty parts of air. The result is much better economy and fewer nasty gases coming out of the back. Including CO_2.

'Oh do stop going on about CO_2, you demented bat,' said the world's fresh-air fanatics.

But still she wouldn't shut up. In 1988, she addressed the Royal Society on the need for science to find alternatives to fossil fuels: 'Even though this kind of action may cost a lot, I believe it to be money well and necessarily spent, because the health of the economy and the health of our environment are totally dependent on each other.'

Then, two years later at a science conference, she was at it again, worrying – long before anyone else in politics – that carbon dioxide was going to be a problem: 'The need for more research should not be an excuse for delaying much-needed action now. There is already a clear case for precautionary action at an international level.'

At the time, most people thought she was simply trying to kill off the mining industry and its one-man carbon fountain, Arthur Scargill. But the fact is this: Mrs Thatcher had seen the evidence back in the late Seventies when she came to power, and she had a degree in chemistry, so she knew what it all meant. Mrs Thatcher, then, was Britain's first eco-mentalist. The first person to recognize the concept of climate change. The first to try to do something about it.

Of course, no one listened. America liked catalytic converters because they were a quick fix. But they weren't alone. Everyone liked cats. So that's what we got and, as a result, the amount of carbon dioxide being produced by the world's car pool shot up. And now, of course, the world is busy trying to get rid of it.

Hybrids are seen as the solution, because hybrids are a quick fix too. Everyone likes hybrids. And as a result – trust me on this – history is poised to repeat itself, because soon everyone will realize we went down the wrong road. Again.

Hybrids need oil to work. And if you burn oil, you will create problems, chief among which, I believe, is this: the oil will run out.

We keep being told that BP has found three billion barrels in the Gulf of Mexico and that underneath Canada's prairies there is enough oil mixed with sand to keep us all going. But for how long? Some say it'll start to run out in twenty-five years. But even if it's 100, we cannot relax because a hundred years is a bit like a nanosecond.

What happened, for instance, in the seventeenth century? Well, British troops captured New Amsterdam and renamed it New York, a man called Rembrandt painted himself, London had a bit of a fire and a King of England's head came off. So you see what I mean – 100 years is a blink. In a school history lesson, they get through 100 years in forty-five minutes.

It is therefore imperative that the world turns its attention to an alternative for oil. Now. That – and there's no argument on this – means hydrogen. And it is equally important that the car makers drop their headlong rush for hybrids because if they don't, not one of them will still be around to capitalize on the bright new dawn when it comes.

I see this month that the company which makes Ladas has laid off 30,000 employees, and that the remaining 72,000 spend most of their time at work playing dominoes and organizing Herculean drinking competitions. We know that Vauxhall's future is not secure, that Saab is clinging to life by its fingernails and that Aston Martin's financial backers in Kuwait 'are doing well'. Which is finance speak for 'are in shit up to their foreheads'.

Some car companies are managing, just, to keep their heads above water in these difficult times, but all of them are putting all of their eggs in one basket . . . bloody hybrids.

You have BMW saying that current supercars are too militaristic and that people want a softer, more caring car these days. What people? Not me, that's for sure. And not you either. And not the hoards of *Top Gear* fans I met in Romania this month who, so far as I can tell, would sleep with a fat middle-aged man just for the chance to sit in an Aston Martin. One man, in a thin white nylon trouser suit, got within six feet of the DBS and, I'm not kidding, started to become erect. In the presence of a Prius, he'd have been Mr Floppy.

Then you have Rolls and Porsche, and Volvo and Saab and Toyota and Mahindra, and Kia and Hyundai and Peugeot and Fiat and Ford and GM and Honda all spending fortunes on the next generation of petrol hybrids and diesel hybrids and plug-in hybrids, all of which meet a fleeting need now, in the same way that cats met a fleeting need thirty years ago. But they aren't the answer.

Yes, hydrogen is difficult and expensive to produce. But it

was difficult and expensive for Ellen MacArthur to sail round the world. It was difficult and expensive to go to the Moon. It would also have been difficult and expensive to make lean-burn engines work. But if someone had done that, the oil we have left would last longer. And the eco-mentalists would be focusing on cows not cars.

The trouble is, of course, human beings never learn from their mistakes of the past. We're like insects, endlessly banging our heads on the window in the hope that this time the glass will have gone. Remember that if you feel tempted to buy a Prius. What you're being, is a moth.

December 2009

Quad's own country

I have bought a farm. There are many sensible reasons for this. Land is a better investment than any bank can offer. The government doesn't get any of my money when I die. And the price of the food that I grow can only go up. But there is another, much more important reason: I can now have a quad bike.

I have always loved the idea of such things. They are like motorbikes but they don't fall over when you leave them alone, they look great and they bring a bit of civilization to Britain's rather dreary green and brown bits.

I am aware, of course, that quad bikes have killed more people than all war and famine combined, and even those who survive a brief ride usually emerge from the experience with no functioning limbs and a distressing habit of dribbling.

Ozzy Osbourne led a wild and reckless life, eating bats and generally pretending to be the king of darkness. But despite this, he remained in good health until one day he thought, I know, I'll go for a ride on a quad bike. Moments later, he had eight shattered ribs, a broken collar bone, bleeding lungs and no blood supply going to his right arm.

Then you have Rik Mayall. In the Eighties, he was on every single television show in the world. But then he climbed onto a quad bike, banged his head and hasn't been seen since.

In 1998, 1,200 people were admitted to British hospitals after accidents on their quad bikes. By 2002, it was 4,200. No figures have been released since, but if that rate of growth has continued, we can say that in 2008, everyone in Britain was killed by an ATV.

If I were in charge, I would make these figures known to the public and allow everyone to make up their own minds about a sensible course of action. But I am not in charge. Mr Brown is. Which is why quad bikes are now covered by all sorts of legislation.

No child may ride a quad bike of any kind, even in their own garden, until they are thirteen. Afterwards, they may ride a quad, but only after they have received instruction from one of Mr Brown's safety agents. You may drive a quad on the road, providing it is classified as a tractor, when you are sixteen. But not if you are Nicholas Soames. And so on and so on and so on.

Meanwhile the Health and Safety Executive has all sorts of guidelines about helmets and carrying passengers and generally sucking the fun out of life. In short, they say you may only drive a quad bike so long as you are always solo, you are dressed up like an ice-hockey goalkeeper and you are at least eighty-five years old.

Sadly, I really don't like people in cheap suits telling me what to do in my own garden, which is why, when I bought the farm, I decided immediately that, despite the certain death, I should have a quad bike.

Where do you get one from? No, really. Just stop for a moment, and think. I bet you can buy all sorts of things in your local town: fridge-freezers, colanders, garden sheds, pornography. But can you buy a quad? No.

Naturally, I went on the Internet, where there are many sites advertising snazzy wheels for your ATV and various power-ranger outfits that can be worn while aboard. But as for a site where ordinary quads may be bought. No, again.

I am aware that many different companies make such things but since most of them also make motorcycles, I don't know anything about any of them. Is a Suzuki better than a Yamaha? No idea. It'd be like asking whether I prefer Tampax or Lil-Lets.

In the same way, then, that I always buy Sony televisions, I decided to stick with a brand I understand and called Honda. A man I know there said they did make quads and that I could borrow a couple to see which one I liked most.

One had racks on the front and the back and a semi-automatic gearbox, which sounded just the job. But in order to change the gears, I had to lift up a lever with my right foot. This made my toe hurt.

The other was quite the most stupid thing I've ever seen in my life. Its wheel arches were about six feet above its wheels, hinting at suspension travel that simply wasn't there. And it had a clutch on the handlebars which is about the most stupid thing I've ever heard of.

It remained the most stupid thing I'd ever heard of until I climbed aboard and went for a ride. This wasn't just fast. It was idiotic. I have no idea how quickly it could get from 0–60, but I would hazard a guess at about no time at all.

As you may know, I like a fast car. I love the surge of acceleration as it pushes you back into your seat, and therein lies the problem with the quad. The acceleration doesn't push you back into your seat because there isn't one. So every time you go near the throttle, you fall off the back.

Once, I opened it up in the Big Field in third gear, imagining that all would be well. But no. I didn't have a stopwatch, but at a rough guess I would imagine it did 60–100 in about no time at all as well.

And so, since I need the quad bikes to plant buddleia, kill trees and dig boreholes, I decided to buy a brace of the plodders; one for me and one for my children, who will be riding around on the farm, despite what Mr Brown says, because when it's three in the morning and a sheep has got its head stuck in a fence up on Partridge Covert, I'm buggered if I'm getting out of bed to go and rescue the damn thing.

Honda did some checking and found that Chipping Norton does have a quad-bike shop. It's called P.A. Turney and it lives, like a sex shop, far from passing trade in a brown paper bag on a little-used and less-well-known industrial estate.

And so now I have my quads, and I'm simply amazed at what damage they can do to a man's bottom as they move about. Fields are not flat; they are ripply, and these ripples are transferred directly into your buttocks, so that after a surprisingly short amount of time, you are in agony. I know that motorcyclists, such as James May, enjoy this sort of thing, but I don't. So now I have taken to riding while standing up.

This looks very cool, but it does mean that very often, especially in the woods, I hit my head on branches that I haven't seen coming because I'm too busy looking over my shoulder to make sure my gun or my daughter hasn't fallen off the back.

Couple this to the pain in my toe every time I want another gear and there is much discomfort, but having talked to other farmers round these parts, this is what life's going to be like from now on. Early starts, massive disappointments, financial ruin and then, when you are loading something with spikes onto the back of a tractor, an unforeseen amputation of your arm.

Then, of course, while hurrying home on my quad with my severed arm on the rack on the back, I will ride too quickly up a hill, the damn thing will roll and I shall become another statistic. I have bought a farm. And soon, it seems, I will buy the farm.

Awards 2009

CAR OF THE YEAR: VOLKSWAGEN POLO

TOP 5 BESTSELLING SINGLES
SONG TITLE – ARTIST

1 Love The Way You Lie – Eminem
  featuring Rihanna
2 When We Collide – Matt Cardle
3 Just The Way You Are – Bruno Mars
4 Only Girl (In The World) – Rihanna
5 OMG – Usher feat Will I Am

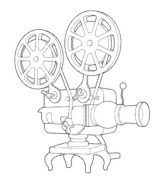

TOP 5 BOX OFFICE MOVIES

1 Toy Story 3
2 Alice In Wonderland (2010)
3 Iron Man 2
4 The Twilight Saga: Eclipse
5 Harry Potter and the Deathly
  Hallows: Part 1

Taste

Every November, I am bundled into the back of a Mercedes and driven around London so that I can spend a day plugging my Christmas DVD.

In some ways, it's quite good fun because all day you bump into lots of famous people running around London in other big Mercs plugging their DVDs, fitness videos, films, books or comedy tours.

Last year, I trailed around in the wake of Ian Hislop as he desperately tried to flog the *Private Eye* annual. This year, I met John Barrowman coming out of Steve Wright's studio, and when I'd finished, Lord Linley was queuing to go in. It was like a dentist's waiting room for the desperate.

On *Jonathan Ross*, I met the charming boys from Muse, who were flogging their new record (or whatever you call it these days) and Laurence Fishburne who was flogging *CSI*, and who speaks much faster in real life than he did in *The Matrix*. Last year, on *Jonathan Ross*, I met Patrick Swayze. Who is now dead.

Whom you meet may vary from year to year but the day itself never does. You start with Chris Moyles in the morning. You chat for a bit about this and that. Then you chat about your DVD. Then you chat a bit more to make it look like you weren't only there to sell your soul. And then you get back in the Merc for a trip to see Phillip Schofield, where you chat for a bit. Then you chat about your DVD. Then you chat about something else and then it's back in the car for your appointment with Nick Ferrari on LBC, where you have to remember what you said in the previous chats so, while chatting, you don't repeat yourself. There's a lot of chatting and a lot of remembering.

Then you have lunch with the PR for the DVD/book/ fitness video and then, in the afternoon, there's more chatting. Until eventually you wind up at Five Live for a chat with Simon Mayo.

Simon, by the time you read this, will have emigrated from Five Live to the afternoon show on Radio Two, which is great for him but a disaster for me, and Ian Hislop and David Linley. Because Simon was usually the last port of call and it was always a bit different to the other chats.

Mostly, this is because Simon had usually bothered to watch/read the DVD/fitness video/book and therefore had slightly more relevant questions. This year was no exception. What he asked is this: 'Would you not be friends with someone if they drove a car you didn't like?'

Well, I had a quick scan through my address book and, with the exception of James May, who drives a Porsche Boxster, all my friends do drive cars that I like. Mainly, though, this has something to do with the fact that just about all my friends shoot and therefore drive Range Rovers.

Would I ditch them as friends if they bought a Vauxhall or a Proton? Of course not. Over the years, various friends have done some unspeakable things, but I try to be loyal – I try to remember that the bond of friendship is an important thing. So the idea that I would Tippex someone from my address book because they bought a car I don't like is absurd.

And yet . . . since the interview, I keep asking myself why is it that none of my friends drives a Peugeot? Or a Rover? Or a Kia? And don't think this is a wealth thing. I don't know anyone with a Porsche Cayenne or a Bentley Continental either.

Could it be, then, that we do, subconsciously, hook up with people that have similar motoring tastes to our own?

The best way to answer this is to not talk about cars. As I said to Simon Mayo, I could not be friends with someone who doesn't like the film *Local Hero*. Not liking this completely faultless movie shows that you are a bore with no heart, and if you are a bore with no heart, we could not possibly be friends.

It's the same story with Monty Python. I don't mind if you don't find it funny now, but if you never found it funny then I'm sorry, you almost certainly live in a house where visitors are asked to remove their shoes when entering. Surrey Rules, I call it. And I've no time for people like that either.

You can be friends with someone who thinks differently, but it usually goes wrong in the end. That's why most of my friends have no time for global warming and think Gordon Brown is an idiot. It should also be noted that the vast majority smoke.

Conversely, none of my friends have children called Chardonnay. None live in Cheshire. And few go on holiday to Florida.

That said, many don't drink, but this is almost always because they did far too much of that when they were younger and have livers like pebbles as a result.

It's often said that people who live in the countryside are forced to get on with their neighbours because the choice is so limited. But this isn't necessarily so. The reason I get on with my neighbours is that, like me, at some point they moved to this neck of the woods. That means we must have something in common.

And that gets us back to cars. If someone has a Range Rover, they must have turned their noses up at the BMW X5 and the Audi Q7 and that gormless-looking Porsche, which means their brains are wired up the same way as mine.

If someone has a BMW, the chances are they work in IT, and this is not something I find interesting. Likewise, because I don't work in construction, few of my friends drive Audis. Jags, yes. But Audis? No. Jags are for people who like and live off the land.

We needed an Aston Martin DBS for filming the other day, and because Aston couldn't help – all their demonstrators were out – we had to rent one from a supercar drivers' club. And I couldn't help noticing its metal gearknob was scratched to hell. This is because people who join supercar clubs wear jewellery. And that's why none of my friends is a member of any such thing.

I shall go on. Because none of my friends is in their eighties, I don't know anyone with a Peugeot. Because none is an idiot, they don't have Renaults. Because they don't like murdering, they don't have Land Rover Discoverys and because they aren't geography teachers or football referees, they don't have Hyundais.

Again, with the exception of May and Hammond, very few of my friends have a motorbike. Although this might have something to do with the fact that most of my friends are pushing fifty as well, which means they've either grown out of bikes, or been killed by one long ago.

Two of my friends do have Mitsubishi Evos, and both of them are very pretty girls, which says something.

And what it says is this. It's very hard to make proper friends as you become older. There's a lot of bottom-sniffing and going round to one another's houses for fact-finding get-to-know-you suppers. It's all very time-consuming and quite dangerous.

Because often you find out that you don't like them at precisely the same moment they decide to be your best buddy. It's hard to shake someone off at this stage and remain tactful.

So I have a plan. If you are looking for new friends, or even a new spouse, save yourself a lot of time and effort. Simply look at what they drive. If you like their wheels, there's a good chance you'll like the driver too. If you don't, you almost certainly won't.

January 2010

Terror

When you read this, I hope to be performing the *Top Gear Live* stage show in either Australia or New Zealand. But in all probability, I'll actually be at Heathrow Airport, standing in a body scanner, while a bunch of security guards snigger at the smallness of my gentleman sausage.

Doubtless, I will have no shoes, no belt, no laptop, no toothpaste, no underarm deodorant and, now that a Nigerian boy has demonstrated it's possible to store explosives in the cleft of your buttocks, no underpants either. And for the privilege of this humiliation, I will have had to stand in a queue that stretched back to Macclesfield.

If I could have driven to Australia – and James considered this before I pointed to the blue bits on his special globe – I would have done. Because a car sets off when you want to set off, doesn't give you deep vein thrombosis and you don't have to sit next to someone who's fat. Unless I've given you a lift.

What's more, it doesn't take three hours to load your luggage into the boot – unless you are Coleen Rooney and you have a Hillman Imp – and you are not invited to buy a watch or a currency converter or a crap book while you wait for someone else to do it either.

Things that I allow in my car include darts, guns, baseball bats, mace, camping stoves and musical instruments. None of this is allowed in a plane. And if you make a joke about terrorism while I'm driving you along, I will laugh. Not put you in prison.

I hate airports.

I wish someone would start an airline called 'I'll Take My Chances Air'. It would work on this principle: you drive up to the door of the plane, you get on immediately with no checks whatsoever, and then it takes off. If it blows up, it blows up and it will have been a small price to pay.

Sadly, however, no one has started such a business, which means we are forced to endure stupid – and pointless – searches before we may board. And don't argue. They are pointless.

In the olden days, you were scanned to make sure you didn't have a gun or a sword with which you might hijack the plane, but those measures did nothing to stop those who think that by committing suicide, they're in for a life of milk and honey and a million vestal virgins. In other words, a metal detector does nothing to stop Johnny Suicide Bomber.

So after September 11, 2001, we were no longer allowed to board the plane if we had a rounders bat or a pair of scissors. And then along came Richard Reid with his amazing exploding shoes, which meant we had to take off our flip-flops and put our toiletries in a clear plastic bag.

And then we had the Nigerian with his undercracker bomb, so now we have to show the security guards our penises. And it'll go on like this for ever. The Americans have a clampdown. The terrorists find a way round it. So the Americans have another clampdown and the terrorists find a way round that.

Meanwhile, you and I are being asked to check in sixteen days before the scheduled departure time, so that a billion people in high-visibility jackets can ask a lot of damn fool questions and examine every one of our follicles. It's all just too stupid for words.

I estimate that in the next ten years, I will spend 1,800 hours queuing at airports. That's seventy-five days of my life stolen by this idiotic idea that suicide bombers can be kept off planes. They can't. The end.

Except it's not the end, because consider this. You don't have security when you get on a train, and if you think about it, why not?

A well-placed bomb on an Intercity Express would not just cause carnage in the carriage itself, but cause many deaths in the subsequent derailment. And unlike a plane, which tends to crash out of sight, into the sea, a train wreck can be seen. It can be filmed. It will be on the news. In terms of casualties and PR, a bomb on a train would be far more effective for the bombers than a bomb in a plane. You know that. I know that. Governments know that. But still we all merrily catch the overnight express to Edinburgh without a care in the world.

And actually, for maximum effect, the terrorists could cause even more mayhem if they forgot public transport and went after the roads.

I know the BBC, which publishes *Top Gear* magazine, is supposed to be regional in its thinking these days and that, for an example, I should choose somewhere like Barnsley or Bombay. But I'm afraid I don't know Barnsley or Bombay very well, so let's stick with London.

Let us imagine, just for a moment, that a security scare shut the Hammersmith flyover where it crosses the Broadway. That would sever London from the M4. Now let's have a similar problem a mile to the north, on the elevated section of the A40. One more incident at Brent Cross, which is London's tummy button with the umbilical cord that is the M1, and that's pretty much it. No one could get into or out of the most important capital city in Europe.

Unless they wanted to go to Essex. Or Kent. And no one wants to do that.

Can you even begin to imagine the mayhem if London were cut off from its main airport and a million or more workers couldn't get to work in a morning? This would be one of the biggest coups in the history of terrorism, and I am not the only person in the world who's thought of it . . .

But do your knees shake when you drive over those flyovers on the way into London? Do you wish for a security gate and a body scanner? No. You trundle along, gently moaning about the bus lanes and listening to Chris Evans to take your mind off the traffic.

And I'm only talking about security scares here. Imagine if there were real bombs. Imagine if those flyovers were brought down. In an ordinary country, they'd have them up again in weeks, but here there'd have to be inquiries. Wildlife bodies would insist that indigenous beetles would have to be removed before repair work could begin. Budgets would spiral out of control. Billions would be spent. More would be wasted. Years would pass. And London would be finished. Finished, because of three small bombs that, if they went off in the middle of the night, might not injure a single person.

I presume the security services are aware of the implications of such an attack. I presume, too, that they have dreamed up more scientific pinch-points than I have, places where even bigger problems would be caused. And what do they do about it?

Well, I drive down the M1, the M40 and the M4 into

London a lot and, apart from a few wonky CCTV cameras, which are mostly designed to catch people making illegal right turns, there's no evidence of any security at all.

It doesn't worry me. I don't want more security on the roads. And nor am I calling here for more security on trains. No. I'm simply drawing your attention to other targets to show that the situation at airports is absurd and ridiculous.

It's counter-productive as well. The only way you can defeat terrorism, ultimately, is by ignoring it. If you react to every tiny thing by running around, waving your arms in the air and screaming, the idiots will know they're getting to you.

And if you paralyse the world's airports, then they know they're not just getting to you; they're winning.

April 2010

Special effects

The other day, for reasons that are not entirely clear, I decided to sit down and re-watch *Armageddon*, an extravagant Hollywood blockbuster in which some Americans have eighteen days' notice to try to stop a rock the size of Texas from crashing into the Earth at 22,000mph.

It's all very exciting. Paris gets wasted. So does Owen Wilson. And so, in a rather harrowing scene, do the Twin Towers. Bruce Willis, meanwhile, pulls a lot of serious faces, and then he gets wasted too. But not before he's saved everyone on the planet from what Billy Bob Thornton calls, 'All the worst bits of the Bible.'

The funny thing, though, is that when you actually pay attention, this is one of the stupidest films ever made. Radios work then don't work. Gravity comes and goes. Oil companies are set up in a day. Ear plugs appear then disappear.

The plot is more riddled with holes than a termite mound.

And then there's the script. Sweet Mary, mother of Jesus. Who thought it was a good idea to ask Bruce Willis to say, 'I don't keep any secrets from my daughter Grace.' It's either 'my daughter' or 'Grace'. Or 'her'. Saying 'my daughter Grace' is ridiculous. Nobody does that.

There's another scene on the oil rig in which Bruce, again, is asked to deliver a monologue of such mind-bending ineptitude that he simply gives up halfway through.

I don't understand how this happens. Why does a director not simply look at the lines Bruce is being asked to say and point out to the chap who wrote them that they don't make any sense? They go to all the trouble of staging incredibly realistic demolition jobs on New York, and the Far East, and the Russian Space Station, but in between the explosions, the cast may as well sit there saying, 'Wibble wibble wibble.'

Inglourious Basterds is a bit different, because the opening scene is almost perfect cinema. No Russian explodes. There is no lesbianism. It's just two men in a room, talking. Mostly about milk. And yet it's so captivating I can pretty much guarantee that if you take a piece of popcorn from the box when it begins, it still won't have reached your mouth when it ends, ten minutes later.

I suppose I should say at this point that I'm a Tarantino fan. And the reason I'm a Tarantino fan is that he pays attention to everything; what people say, how they look and why they're doing what they're doing. Watch *Kill Bill 2* and look at the sofa in Bill's hacienda towards the end. It's perfect.

Then there are the cars. Bill drives a De Tomaso Mangusta. (Italian for Mongoose. The only animal feared by a Cobra.) He would. It's the only car he could have driven: American, and yet not.

Daryl Hannah uses a Trans Am with an eagle on the bonnet. Whereas Uma Thurman, who has two eyes, has a Karmann Ghia. You just know that His Quentin-ness spent hours, maybe even days, agonizing over these tiny details, but it's precisely that which makes (most of) his films so much more watchable than the when-in-doubt-blow-it-up blockbusters.

Now. At this point you are probably wondering how on earth I can possibly land this month's column on the deck of a car mag, without crashing into the model railway magazines and *Horse and Hound* just along the shelf.

Simple. I wish car companies would behave a bit more like

Quentin Tarantino and a bit less like Michael Bay, the slap-happy madman who foisted *Armageddon* on the cinema-going public.

The trouble is that, like Bay, car companies are obsessed with the big-money special effects. They think that what we want are automatic windscreen wipers and what Michael McIntyre called the 'little people' in the bumpers who shriek and wail when we reverse too close to a wall.

They think we want 600 horsepower because their big rivals can only offer us 570, and that we want chilled cubby holes in the boot where we can store the lemonade they think we drink on the picnics we don't have.

All of these things, though, are superficial. They're perfectly good at entertaining us for a short while, but in the long-term, I'd much rather have a sense the dashboard is screwed in place; not clipped. And that the brake hoses are made from titanium, not rubber.

Sometimes I look down into the passenger footwell of my Mercedes and it fills me with a terrible sense of dread that the speaker grille has half come off. It annoys me too that the sound that comes from the stereo would have been unacceptable on a 1974 transistor radio. And that the seat-belt anchor points are inside the side squabs where you cannot get at them if you have a bottom.

Likewise, I was annoyed when I drove a new S-Class last month to find that no cupholder is provided in the front. There can only be one reason for this. Since the man in charge of this car's development could not possibly have said, 'Let's not bother', because that would have been a stupid thing to say, the concept must have slipped his mind. It's therefore a mistake. Like putting *Kill Bill?*'s Bill in a Nissan Micra.

I look, too, at the new AMG SLS, and in some ways it appears to have been designed by someone who was paying attention. The engine is big and simple and loud. The interior is trimmed like an expensive suitcase. And believe me, in the flesh it looks a million times better than it does in pictures. It looks completely fabulous.

But I cannot get those doors out of my head. Yes, they hark back to the SLs of old and, yes, I'm sure the explosive bolts that blow the hinges in the event of a rollover are very clever. But doors like this make getting in and out difficult. They mean you can't park in a low garage. They make you look like a frightful show-off. And if you're less than five foot, Hammond, you won't be able to reach the handles to pull them shut once you're inside. In other words, they've created an amazing special effect, but while they were doing so, they can't have been fully concentrating on the script, and the plot and the things that actually matter most of all.

I've singled out Mercedes in the examples I've chosen, mainly because it's Mercedes who used to get the Tarantino approach so right. Look at the W123 models. There were no aliens. The White House didn't explode, Will Smith wasn't in the glovebox with a wise crack. They were just well-made cars.

I think this is an approach that should be favoured by the people behind Spyker as they wrestle with the next Saab. Since it will be bought, mainly, by architects, and since architects favour a minimalist, crisp, no-nonsense approach, why not give them a modern-day incarnation of that old W123. No bells. No whistles. And please, no idiotic claims that it's a jet fighter with an ashtray.

I want to finish, though, with Jaguar. The engineers there may think they need the bipolar satnav screen and a gear lever that rises from the centre console. They may think they cannot compete in the big and boisterous world of multi-nationalism without such things.

Well, I urge them all to sit down one afternoon and watch *The Hurt Locker*. Made for a pound. Won six Oscars. Everyone loves it to bits.

May 2010

The 911

As you may know, I have always loved the Porsche 911, in much the same way that I have always loved Peter Mandelson, mouth ulcers, Greece, marzipan, caravanning holidays, the smoking laws, British Telecom, pointlessly complicated gadgets, tea before four, Piers Morgan, sweet white wine, ramblers, liberal democrats, beards, the Boeing 777, global warming scientists, average speed cameras and, I don't think I've ever mentioned this before, the feel of a cow.

In other words, I have always rather disliked the 911. Jokingly, and mainly to make them go away, I always tell fans of the breed that my dislike is based principally on the fact that James May and Richard Hammond both have one. But this isn't true. James and Richard both have trousers, but I have no problem with those.

I've also argued that my dislike stems from the fact that it's really a squashed Beetle and, as a result, was designed by Hitler. But this isn't really true either, if I'm honest.

So is it the styling then; the look of the thing? No actually. If you look at Porsche's recent efforts with the Coxster, the push-me-pull-you Boxster – which should really be called the Palindrome – the woeful Cayenne and that wheeled gargoyle known as the Panamera, we have to be grateful they don't ever change the basic shape. And anyway, I rather like the sit-up-and beg windscreen and those eager West Highland terrier headlights.

Most of all, though, I've come to like the size. As other cars have swollen and become fat, the 911 has remained fairly small. That's a good thing.

No, the problem is the location of that engine. Putting it behind the rear wheels is as wrong as trying to invade Russia when you haven't closed down the Western Front. It can't work and it looks like belligerence to endlessly try to overcome the inherent problem rather than simply giving up and starting again.

Yes, putting the engine at the rear means you have more weight over the back wheels, so off the line; when the tail of a car squats, that means more grip, less wheelspin and quicker acceleration. Lovely. You will arrive at the corner in front of your adversary . . . but then what? You will turn the wheel, there will be no weight over the front wheels, you will understeer, and if you lift off to correct that, the nose will pitch down, the rear tyres will lose grip, and any attempt to correct the resultant slide will be pointless because the engine's in the back acting like a giant pendulum.

If you see a corner coming up in an early 911, the best thing you can do is follow these two steps:

1) Undo your seat belt
2) Get in the back

I don't remember what sort of 911 I drove first, but I'd heard so many horror stories about the wayward handling that I didn't dare go more than 4mph. Which meant I had more time to examine the ridiculously basic dashboard and the heater controls, which appeared to be connected to nothing at all.

The first time I drove a 911 on a race track was extraordinary.

Because I was a new boy back then and had no idea how to hold a slide in a Cortina, I was petrified. I felt it would be safer to try to set a lap time on a bear.

As the years wore on, I drove many different 911s and never had a single moment to worry about in any of them. But that's because I knew what would happen if I went near the limit and consequently stayed very far away from it. In much the same way that your mother always stays very far away from the edge of a cliff.

There was, however, another drawback to driving a 911 at this time. You would arrive at your destination covered in a thick film of other people's goz. It was the Eighties. Mrs Thatcher was busy, factories were shutting, the City boys had spent all the BT profits on a 911 and everyone assumed that if you had one, you personally had shut down their dad's mine. So they hawked up a docker's oyster and spat it at you. And usually they hit me because I was going so slowly.

Eventually, and thanks to Tiff Needell's kindly encouragement, I did learn how to make a car slide and hold it there. But even when I'd been doing it week in and week out for years, I still never dared try it in a 911. I'd hit a cameraman. Or a tree. Better to say I didn't like them and drive something else.

But then the day came . . . and it was easy.

It was brilliant. Because I no longer felt intimidated by 911s, I could start to drive them quickly, which meant I was less likely to be hit by the blizzard of spittle. But despite this advantage, I still didn't like the interior, the heater still didn't work, and the cars that worked well on the track really didn't work at all on the road.

Plus, by this stage, Porsche had started making an almost unbelievable number of variations. You had the Carrera, and the Carrera S, and the Carrera with four-wheel drive, or no roof, or fat wheel arch extensions, or a combination of all three. It was all designed, I thought, to make Porsche owners even more dull.

As the beginning of this year dawned then, I admired the way the cars looked, and the size they'd become. I admired, too, the way many of them drove, but like them? No. My prejudice was too entrenched for that.

But then along came the new GT3 and I won't dwell on the whys and the wherefores, but I loved it. Not liked it. Loved it. It had a stupid front splitter that was so low it could give a spider a haircut, scaffolding instead of rear seats and an idiotic rear spoiler that could very obviously be adjusted. No. No. No. Having a rear spoiler that can very obviously be adjusted means that someone, one day is going to ask why. And then you'll have to tell them. And they'll think you are mad.

However, despite the aesthetic shortfalls, and the fact that it's a 911, this is a great car. It goes round roundabouts like nothing I've ever driven. In a test of pure handling and grip, it would be a match for anything. And it only costs £86,000. That's just shy of half what you'd pay for a Ferrari 458. Half.

I was so enamoured of the GT3, I thought I'd try some more 911s, so I started with the GT3RS. With different inlet and exhaust manifolds, this develops 15 more horsepower, the wheels are wider, so's the track, and it weighs 55lb less too. You can cut another 22lb if you specify a £1,268 lithium-ion battery instead of the standard lead-acid item but I wouldn't do that because a) you won't notice the difference and b) again, someone, one day will ask why.

I didn't like the RS at all. The GT3 rides properly. This doesn't. The GT3 has a radio and a brilliant satnav. This doesn't. The GT3 has doorhandles. This doesn't. And, worst of all, the GT3 can be used in Britain, and this cannot.

No really. It's fitted with tyres that don't work below 10 degrees centigrade. Which means, now that we know global warming is nonsense, they don't work here at all, ever. I took it for a spin in the rain in early May, and on several occasions it was very nearly just that. A horrid car. Made for track-day enthusiasts. Or as we know them: bores.

I then tried a 911 Turbo convertible. And this was fairly nasty as well, for reasons Richard Hammond explained. The 911 is supposed to be a sports car. Fitting a turbo tries to turn it into something it is not – a supercar. It felt loose and wobbly.

So it seems, then, that the GT3 is not an indication that, after all these years, Porsche has got it right. It's just proof that if you keep on churning out endless variations of the same thing, one day, you'll get one of them right. In short. The million monkeys have finally come up with *The Merchant of Venice*.

July 2010

Broken Britain

Today, if something is made to perform a function, it will perform that function for a short while, and then it will stop, and you will throw it away.

This applies to everything, except fondue sets. Actually, it might apply to fondue sets as well, but no one can be sure because everyone's fondue set is at the back of a kitchen cupboard, where it's been since the fateful night thirty years ago when it tipped up, spilling hot fat all over your uncle, killing him.

The other exception to this is the tube of 'easy-wipe' oven cleaner that you saw being advertised on the television. Oven cleaners don't stop working after a short while. They never work in the first place.

Anyway, it applies to everything else. Examine, if you will, exhibit A: your mobile telephone. How long have you had it? I'm willing to bet the answer to that is 'less than two years'. Good. So what happened to the one you had previously? It's in a drawer somewhere, isn't it? And it's broken. It might not have been broken when you put it there. But it is now.

That's the miraculous thing about items that are built to perform a function in the twenty-first century. They certainly break when you drop them on the floor or they fall down a lavatory or off a boat. And they break for no reason one Tuesday. But they also break when you leave them alone.

Exhibit B? Well, that can be any electrical item bought for you (or your parents) as a wedding present. Does your old toaster work? What about the Magimix? The microwave? Nope. You threw it out years ago because it suddenly decided one day to die, along with the portable DVD player you bought when they first came out. Still got your first iPod? Of course you haven't. It froze back in 2005.

Let me give you a list of things that I currently have, and which aren't working. The lights on my porch. The lights in my garden. The Internet in my flat. The phone in my flat. My freezer. My Sonos music system. My laptop. The padlock to the paddock gate. Even the left-hand gatepost at the top of my drive.

This was built just ten years ago, but in the winter frosts water, which seeped into the stone, froze, thawed and blew the top piece to smithereens. Yes, that's right. These days, we can't even build a gatepost that lasts. They could build a sodding cathedral in the dark ages, using mud and coal. But we can't build a gatepost now.

And here's the really big nuisance. In the brief period when something does work, it becomes invaluable. You wonder how you ever managed without it. So when it stops, your life is ruined.

Imagine trying to work today without a mobile phone. Unless you are a deep-sea diver, or a miner, it would be impossible. We used to manage, but now it would be like trying to work without a head. Or lungs.

Sky+ is another fine example. We used to watch a TV show when it was on. And then we spent a few years on our knees, with our arses in the air, setting the timer on our video recorders for Tuesday to record a programme that was on on Sunday. And then along came Sky+. When that doesn't work, and it doesn't quite often, it's as though your face has been amputated.

All of this is making life extremely expensive, because when something goes wrong, you cannot repair it. No one can mend Sky+ or an iPhone. You have to get a new one. And you have to get a new one immediately because life is impossible without it.

Part of the problem is the designer. If an item were built solely to perform a function, then it might stand a chance of not breaking. But because everything these days is 'designed', form is allowed to kick function out of the back seat and into the boot. This applies, especially, to shoes.

The idea is, of course, that if you have a 'designer' product, it won't matter when it goes wrong because, by then, it will be unfashionable and time for a new one anyway. This month, for instance, I'm supposed to hope that my iPhone suddenly explodes because then I have an excuse to buy the new version with the HD video facility.

I have decided that if I were to live my life again, I would build a house with no gadgets in it whatsoever. And when I say no gadgets, I mean nothing from the twenty-first century. There would be no insulation in the walls. The windows would be in wooden frames. The lights would be 40-watt bulbs the shape of cul-de-sacs. Low energy, one touch, enjoy-your-food pinging dishwashers? Nope. And I'd have a typewriter.

Strangely, however, I'm not sure that I would apply this logic – and it is logic – to cars.

I have spent a great deal of time in the last few weeks driving around in cars from the Eighties which, when you're my age, was yesterday. But despite this recent-ness, none of them had air bags, or satnav, or anti-lock brakes, or iPod con-nectivity, or valves in the exhaust to produce nice noises at high revs, or adjustable side bolsters on the seats, or automatic wipers or indeed any of the things you find these days on even a Kia Cee'd.

Of course, all of the aforementioned things became invaluable the moment they were first invented. Would I buy a car these days that could not play the songs from my iPod? Not on your nelly. And it's the same story with satnav.

However, what makes these products different from the products in your home is that they are still working.

You bounce through pot holes at 70mph. You leave them outside when it's snowing and when it's 90 degrees. You let your dog play with the buttons. And still they continue to play the Doobie Brothers and find the quickest route to Bishop's Stortford.

It's the same story with the rest of the car. When was the last time you broke down? Unless you have a Peugeot, the answer is 'I can't remember'. When was the last time you had a puncture? Not that long ago, a tyre would burst because it was bored with being a tyre. Now you could drive through a nail factory and emerge on the other side still with 30psi at each corner.

Part of the reason for this is that despite strenuous and understandable efforts from the car makers to turn their products into disposable designer items to be bought and discarded like handbags, they remain a 'big buy'.

There's more, though. BMW knows that if you buy a Z4 and it goes wrong after six minutes, you will replace it when the time comes with a Mercedes. No big deal. It's effectively the same thing. Both have steering wheels, pedals, speedo, wheels and so on.

This is the problem we have with iPods and Sky+ and Gaggia coffee machines and British Telecom's Internet services. If you do decide to switch horses, you end up with more instruction books, more buttons you don't understand and, realistically, just as much of a chance of complete failure within a few days. So when my iPhone goes wrong, I buy another. I don't even consider a Raspberry.

I therefore have a suggestion. To make the world a better and easier place, car firms should be allowed to run it. At the moment they are all running around swallowing one another up. This needs to stop. Instead, they must run about swallowing everything else up. I want Ford to run Apple. I want Mercedes to buy Gaggia. I want BMW to sell me a freezer that works. And I want a chap from Nissan to repair my bloody gatepost.

August 2010

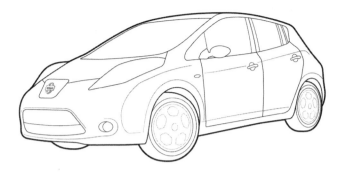

CAR OF THE YEAR: NISSAN LEAF

2011

TOP 5 BESTSELLING SINGLES
SONG TITLE – ARTIST

1 Someone like you – Adele
2 Moves Like Jagger – Maroon 5 featuring Christina Aguilera
3 Party Rock Anthem – LMFAO featuring Lauren Bennett and Goonrock
4 Price Tag – Jessie J featuring BOB
5 We Found Love – Rihanna featuring Calvin Harris

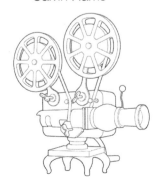

TOP 5 BOX OFFICE MOVIES

1 Harry Potter and the Deathly Hallows: Part 2
2 Transformers: Dark of the Moon
3 The Twilight Saga: Breaking Dawn
4 The Hangover: Part II
5 Pirates of the Caribbean: On Stranger Tides

Fragile supercars

At the end of every *Top Gear* summer series, most of the team heads off to the beach for a spot of rest and relaxation. Not me, though. With the final bombshell still echoing in my ears, I have to start work on my annual Christmas DVD.

This year, you join me at the Paul Ricard track, an hour north of Marseilles. It is a kaleidoscope of colour and noise, a Technicolor blaze in the parched beige and sage hinterland. It's excellent. The sky is an uninterrupted blue dome, away off to the south I can see the Mediterranean twinkling and shimmering, and the on-site hotel has a two-Michelin-star restaurant and an extremely pretty receptionist.

To make everything even more perfect, I'm over here with the *Top Gear* film crew, who are a good laugh in the evening. Last night – after a lot of wine, I admit – we decided that for our Christmas special, James, Richard and I should once again become the Interceptors and go in search of the world's biggest comb-over. This morning, I could see some flaws in that idea, chiefly that I don't want to wear a moustache for two weeks.

But no matter. All is well in my world. Except for one thing. We are filming cars, and cars are a bloody nuisance.

We don't ask much of them. They have to drive round so cameras at the side of the track can record the slides and the smoke and the noise. Then we attach a camera to the chase car and get some tracking shots. And then we fit on-board cameras, and I record the things I want to say from behind the wheel. Simple. Except it never is.

We began with the Ferrari FF, which, as I'm sure you know, is the first Ferrari ever to have a hatchback and the first to come with four-wheel drive. It's a fantastically complicated system that uses a small two-speed gearbox and two clutches mounted to the front of the engine and powered directly from the crank. The idea is that when the rear wheels lose traction, electronics prod the system up front, and drive is despatched to whichever front wheel is best placed to help out.

The trouble is that the car appears to have such a good chassis, the front gearbox seems to sit there most of the time doing nothing. I became convinced that it wasn't actually there at all. Until halfway through the day when I noticed the front tyres were completely shot to pieces. Half a day, and they were gone. Useless.

So we switched to the McLaren MP4-12C, which would be used in a drag race against various rivals. It's easy to film a drag race. You put the cameras on the start line to record the beginning. Then you stop, put the cameras halfway down the straight to record the middle and then you put them at the end to record the finish. That means three standing starts. Three goes with the launch control. Easy peasy.

But unfortunately, after two goes, the McLaren decided it was too hot and needed a rest. So we broke out the Nissan GT-R. 'There's no way this will go wrong,' I said as I climbed aboard.

Two minutes later, I was buried in the handbook, trying to find out what the meaningless warning light on the dash was indicating. And why its launch control had also given up the ghost.

So we wheeled the GT-R into its hospital and began work with the BMW 1M. Ten minutes later, long before we'd had a chance to record any tracking shots or on-board pieces to camera, one of the producers was on the phone to the nearest tyre depot, asking if they did home deliveries.

The track at Paul Ricard is not especially abrasive, and the temperature was a pleasant 31 degrees. And yet none of the cars we'd brought along were lasting more than half a day before needing medical attention.

And that's before we got to the new BAC Mono. It's a fabulous-looking little car. And if you peer beyond the body-work – which was inspired by the F-22 Raptor – you notice the beauty is more than skin-deep. All the hoses and bolts appear to have been installed by a team of people that really care.

So off I went, and immediately I knew that the short item we'd planned for this car wouldn't be enough. I loved it. Unlike a V8-powered Ariel Atom it does not have a determination to understeer into a tree at every opportunity. There's a whiff, just to let you know that you're cracking on a bit, but then it grips and goes. There's no discernible roll, no pitch under braking. It's properly sorted. No question.

But what I loved most of all was the lack of speed. The figures suggest it will do 0–60 in 2.8 seconds and that flat-out it'll do 168mph, which sounds terrifying. But it isn't, and that means I could concentrate on braking to get the fastest possible lap time. Not braking to stay alive.

Part of the reason for this is that although the engine says Cosworth down the side, it's actually the same basic block they use in a Ford Galaxy. And although the gearbox is an F3-inspired unit from Hewland, it changes just like the 'box in a Golf GTi. It's the same story with the steering wheel.

There were all sort of buttons and read-outs, but mostly they were disconnected. In short, then, it felt like a car.

I was comfortable too. I couldn't have done star jumps in the cockpit, or touched my toes. In fact, I couldn't move anything apart from the front of my arms and my feet. But that was all I needed.

Then there was a small fire. No biggie. It was just that a bit of carbon-fibre trim around the exhaust had got a bit hot. Then the gearbox stopped working. And then the engine decided it didn't like low revs very much.

This is in no way meant as a criticism. I was in a pre-production prototype, so I'm not suggesting the cars you buy will behave this way. But I am suggesting that it would be easier to film a DVD about gardening. Soil doesn't wear out. Daffodils don't overheat. Lawns don't have gearboxes.

It is hugely exciting to power-slide a Ferrari 458 around a corner. Much more exciting than deadheading a rose, for example. But you need to remember that after you've laid down some smoke, the tyres will be shot and the diff will be overheating. You can take any car to the limits of its abilities. But only once or twice. And when it comes to making a television programme, that's never enough.

There is, however, an exception to this rule. There is one car that never gets hot, or throws a hissy fit. It's even kind to its tyres. Weirdly, it's the Lamborghini Gallardo.

October 2011

Executive saloons

I can't imagine for the life of me why anyone would want an executive saloon car, but if you decide that you do, you have a choice of four. The new Audi A6, the Jaguar XF, the BMW 5 Series and the Mercedes E-Class. These are motoring's poached eggs on toast and all of them are excellent. So how do you choose between them?

If you are a taxi driver in Geneva, you will take the Merc, obviously. But if you are not, what do you do? The motor industry has had more than 100 years to get the saloon car right, and it has. So each of the four is reliable, economical, reasonably comfortable, well-equipped and fitted with the same-sized engines, the same sort of suspension and the same basic price tags.

Choosing between them, then, is like choosing a location for your honeymoon. Now that the Seychelles is only of any use to those who want to know what it would be like to be eaten by a shark, you have a choice of four island paradises: the Caribbean, Mauritius, the Maldives or Tahiti. And how do you choose between that lot?

There's no use looking in the brochures, as I wouldn't be surprised if all tour operators use the same photograph of the same palm tree to illustrate each one. It's the same story with the models. They're always dressed in linen, and they are much thinner than the actual people you encounter in the traditional honeymoon resort.

The brochures all paint the same picture too, of romantic

evenings at a table for two set up, especially for you, on the beach. Let me tell you something about eating on a beach at night. It's not romantic. It's windy. And there is nothing on God's green earth that kills the testosteronic urges quite so dramatically as a Force Four. This is because your new wife looks like Worzel Gummidge, and everything you put in your mouth is full of sand. Including your new wife.

Then there's the sea. It always looks amazing in the pictures. Turquoise and inviting and calm and lovely. But I have never been on a tropical holiday when someone in the party hasn't emerged from the oggin at some point in considerable pain.

Usually, they've trodden on a stone fish, which will cause some know-all on the beach to whip out his gentleman sausage and offer to urinate on the wound. Again, this is quite bad on a honeymoon. Especially as urine doesn't help. You need vinegar, which will make your bride smell like a fish and chip shop.

Sea lice are bad, too. They are quite invisible, but you know when you've swum through a swarm because, all of a sudden, it feels like you are on fire. And that's before we get to the rays that like to stab you in the heart, and the jellyfish. Get stung by one of those, and on the beach there'll be so many people offering to wee on you, it'll feel like you've woken up in a German porn film.

The worst thing in the sea, though, is the coral reef. It looks so beautiful in the pictures, and you can imagine spending many hours snorkelling around, looking at all the fishes and the pretty colours. I like to do this, too. Which is why I know that at some point, you will accidentally brush against something that's apparently harmless, and it will damn nearly kill you.

Even normal dead coral is lethal, because if a piece punctures your skin, it will never ever heal. Very slowly, you will bleed to death. I'm still bleeding now from a small cut I sustained in 1984.

To take your mind off the many perils and the great discomfort to be found in the environs of the shoreline, many honeymoon hotels like to offer idiotic luxury features, which sound great in print, but don't work in practice.

For example, in Tahiti recently, I stayed in one of those thatched cottages that are built on stilts over the lagoon. And I was offered a choice in the manner my breakfast was delivered: either it could come on foot down the walkways or it could be brought by a man in a canoe.

I chose the canoe, and I'm really not sure why, because if you actually stop and think, it's impossible to deliver a breakfast this way. Especially if the waves are more than two inches tall. Which they were. The poor man did his best to try to keep the sea water out of the scrambled eggs, and the rose petals in place, but since he had to paddle as well, really, he would have needed the anatomical properties of Kali if he were to stand even half a chance.

I'm in the fortunate position of having stayed at all the four major honeymoon locations, and I can tell you that while each resort may offer a slightly different set of options – swimming with dolphins, having your breakfast delivered by hovercraft and so on – they all basically offer the same thing. Too many petals, too many candles, too much sunburn and nowhere near enough vegetables.

Which brings us back to the Audi, BMW, Mercedes and Jag. To try to win you over, the Audi is available with a device that nudges the steering slightly if it detects you are straying out of your lane on the motorway. Is that what's been missing from your life? Well, since it only works below 40mph, I don't think it is.

The BMW, meanwhile, comes with a satnav system that gives you a Google Earth-style view of the area. Is this enough to win you over? I'm not sure, since it would only be of any use if it worked when the scale is down to 200 yards, or so. But it doesn't. As you zoom in to get a closer look on the screen of what you can see out the window, it reverts to a standard map. What's the point of that?

The Mercedes, of course, has one very good feature. You will be able to sell it to a man whose job is taking Dale Winton to the airport. But is that enough of a reason to buy a car?

The Jag? Well, hell. This now comes with a knob instead of a gear lever. And isn't that where your life has been leading? How many times have you climbed into your car and thought, Tsk. I hate this gear lever. It's so awkward? No, me neither.

I'm afraid that you will choose between these cars in the same way that I choose my holiday location. It's the Caribbean. Why? Because I like it.

And with the car? I'd have the BMW, because the bonnet's a nice shape.

Except I wouldn't. Because while the executive four-door saloon is now, after 100 years of solid development, about as perfect as it can be, it's dull and predictable. Much better to buy a hot hatch or an SUV or something a bit more adventurous. In the same way that if you are choosing a honeymoon location, it's much better to go to Capri.

Why? Because no one else does.

November 2011

Car adverts

Despite the best efforts of *Top Gear* to portray the motor car as exciting, and the road network as a spidery web of freedom and speed, nobody is really listening.

A recent survey in my house found that football is more interesting, by miles, than even the most exotic Lewis Hamilton overtaking move, while a rather more wide-ranging questionnaire revealed that, today, most teenagers aspire to own the latest smartphone rather than a car.

Who can blame them? In football, when a player makes a slight mistake, he is given a yellow card and the game soldiers on. When an F1 driver makes a slight mistake, he's forced into the pits and the game is all but finished. You may as well turn over and watch inter-county basket-weaving.

It's the same story with advertising. Not that long ago, car adverts looked pretty much like *Top Gear* does today. Car makers sold the dream. Empty roads. Pretty girls. Men with stubble. Not any more. Now, it's all 0 per cent finance and safety and stuff, which is of no interest at all to people with spots.

In the news, cars are now seen as a nuisance. They clog up the streets, run people over and kill polar bears. So, even if someone does harbour the faint notion that one day it'd be nice to have a Ferrari, the noise coming out of the radio and the view out of the window serves as a constant reminder that, actually, you'd just be sitting in a jam with everyone else, getting unpleasant looks for being successful and selfish.

That's the other problem. Humankind used to celebrate the wise and the rich. Now, we look up to the stupid and the fat. We tune into *The X Factor* to watch people exhibiting their uselessness, and we like *The Only Way is Essex* because everyone's daft. Clever people are mocked. Rich people are hated. And cars, as the most outward signs of someone's wealth, are bound to suffer as a result.

Until very recently, you would have expected the Prime Minister to be seen in the back of a Daimler or a Bentley. Now, you expect to see him on a bicycle or the Tube.

The conclusion is inescapable: soon people are going to stop buying cars in anything like the numbers we've seen in recent decades. We'll stop asking what people drive and ask instead if they do.

And, plainly, I'm not alone in this way of thinking, because not that long ago Peugeot came up with a scheme called Mu, which is like a car club. Though quite why they named it after the measurement for the coefficient of friction I don't know . . .

The idea is that you don't own a Peugeot as such, but you do have access to every single thing it makes. So, you can use a bicycle or a scooter for commuting, then a people carrier should you wish to take the family away for a weekend, then a convertible when the sun shines.

They even say they can offer roof boxes and satnav systems and have a team of people on standby to book you a table at a restaurant. Though I bet if you wanted a convertible on a sunny day, and a table for four at Scott's in Mayfair, you may find they struggle a bit.

This, though, is the least of the scheme's problems. The biggest is this: isn't Peugeot just doing what Hertz and Europcar have done for years? It's just a car-hire business, the only difference being that you end up with a Peugeot. And most of its products, if we're honest, are 14-foot billboards for the joys of public transport.

Honda might be able to pull it off because one week you could rent a quad bike, then a generator, then a hot air balloon and then a speedboat. But, surely, isn't it better to make stuff that people want to buy . . . ?

This brings me back to the world of advertising. It's all gone wrong. There was a time when British agencies such as Goodyear, Stickleback and Bunsen Burner ruled the world with their cleverness and their ability to get the message across, simply by showing a girl hanging her fur coat on a parking meter. They could take even the most dreary product and, using subtle wit, convince us that it would make us attractive. Carling Black Label springs to mind at this point.

Back then, you'd go round the world and laugh at other country's stupid, primary-coloured attempts to make people buy stuff, and you'd long to come home where the ads were by far and away the best thing on ITV.

Not any more. At this year's advertising Oscar ceremony, our agencies came home almost completely empty-handed. We received fewer nominations overall than the Romanians and were beaten in the press advertising category by the Americans, the Spanish and even the Brazilians.

Now, obviously, a lot of the problem lies with the bloody silly rules governing what can and cannot be said by the men in polo necks. When James May and I made our television advert for the Scirocco diesel, both of us were left staggered by the sheer volume of red tape through which a creative mind has to wade. In short, you cannot portray a car as fast, glamorous, exciting, sexy, fun or any of the things it's designed to be. So, obviously, our ad men were going in to bat at the

Oscars with their hands and their feet tied to the nearest radiator, while Borat & Co. had rocked up with a series of ads that said fast cars were more likely to result in a leg-over.

But there's another problem, too. Clients – the people who pay for the ads – are less and less willing to take risks. They don't want to spend half a million quid on a campaign that might offend two people in Nottinghamshire. So they opt for the bland, the safe, the 0-per-cent-finance, bank-holiday-savings, offer-must-end crap, which is even worse than the programming it funds.

And then there's the problem of globalization. In the past, the ads you saw on television here were made here. Now you have Mazdas with reversible number plates whizzing about idiotically to a multilingual zoom-zoom soundtrack that might work in the Europop belt, but is just ridiculous here. The last truly great car campaign was Honda's 'wouldn't it be great if everything just worked' series. But they seem to have given up with that now.

Well, it's got to stop. Car bosses need to remind their marketing managers that unless they pull their fingers out, and allow the creative minds to roam free, they will end up running a scheme like Peugeot's. Renting bicycles out to fools. Mind you, I have thought of a campaign for that. 'Anything for the weekend, sir?'

December 2011